Teaching English as a Foreign Language

FOR

DUMMIES®

Teaching English as a Foreign Language

FOR DUMMIES®

by Michelle Maxom

A John Wiley and Sons, Ltd, Publication

Dedication

This book is dedicated to Mrs Keturah Samuels, her children past and present and all my family members who approach life with such faith, courage and grace.

Author's Acknowledgements

I would like to thank my colleagues and students who responded to this project with such enthusiasm. You truly inspired me.

During my career there have been certain TEFL people who have given me special support. These are the folks at Salisbury School of English, Oxford School Mantova, Avalon School of English and TEFL Training. Thank you for giving me one stepping stone after another while allowing me to be myself inside and outside the classroom.

The input from Wejdan Ismail, Simon Bell and Kathleen Dobie at John Wiley has been invaluable. I certainly could not have written this book without you.

Last but not least, thanks to Mum, Monique and all my dear brothers and sisters for constantly egging me on and for putting up with me.

Publisher's Acknowledgements

We're proud of this book; please send us your comments through our Dummies online registration form located at www.dummies.com/register/.

Some of the people who helped bring this book to market include the following:

Acquisitions, Editorial, and Media Development

Project Editor: Simon Bell

Content Editor: Jo Theedom

Acquisitions Editor: Wejdan Ismail

Publishing Assistant: Jennifer Prytherch

Copy Editor: Sally Lansdell

Technical Editor: Chris Groves

Production Manager: Daniel Mersey

Cover Photos: © avatra images / Alamy

Cartoons: Rich Tennant (www.the5thwave.com)

Composition Services

Project Coordinator: Lynsey Stanford

Layout and Graphics: Reuben W. Davis, Christin Swinford

Proofreader: Susan Moritz

Indexer: Cheryl Duksta

Contents at a Glance

Table of Contents

Introduction

●●●

*T*he English language is officially big business. There could be as many as a billion students learning English around the world at this time and that is reason enough to consider moving into Teaching English as a Foreign Language (TEFL). However, when you combine this with the freedom the job gives you to move around the world and earn your keep, the case for TEFL gets even stronger. While English speakers move out to different lands, students of English migrate to other parts of the globe in search of a better life and new horizons.

Teaching English is something people do when they are ready to change their lives and this book gives you some of the basic tools you need to make that happen.

Most people who speak the language well can teach others to some degree. We do it all the time with children and with foreign friends. We explain words and concepts to each other on a daily basis. TEFL is an extension of what we do naturally and this book helps you zoom in on your language skills and structure them. People often surprise themselves by discovering that even without attending months and years of language study, they can teach. You are probably no different.

About This Book

I have been teaching English for many years now and I have found it an entirely rewarding experience. I have met the most fascinating people and had a hand in helping others reach their goals. My goal in this book is to help you enjoy TEFL too by giving you the confidence and know-how to get a job and deliver effective, engaging lessons.

You could read the book from cover to cover before deciding whether TEFL is for you. If you do, you will have a solid overview of the skills involved in teaching English well. On the other hand, you could use it as a resource that you dip into whenever you need some input because your lessons are falling a bit flat or you are short of ideas. The table of contents will point you to specific areas of concern or maybe even areas you have never thought about but should have.

A book of this size can't cover all the different ways of planning and delivering a lesson. There are probably as many teaching techniques as there are

TEFL teachers, so I have chosen to present the tried and tested path to solid courses. If you do come across other effective ways to help students don't discard them because they are not included here. Use *TEFL for Dummies* as a starting point. Hopefully it will inspire some great ideas of your own.

I should also mention that this is not a photocopiable resource book with ready made lesson plans. The aim is to show the kinds of activities and techniques you can use with your classes, adapting them to your own situation.

This book is not strictly applicable to teaching in language schools which have their own trademark methodology and materials. In such cases the schools will expect you to teach in very defined ways with little room for other techniques.

Conventions Used in This Book

Throughout this book I use a few conventions which you need to know about up front:

- ✔ I use the words *student* and *learner* interchangeably.

- ✔ Presentation, Practice and Production written with capital Ps refer to specific stages of a lesson, not general concepts.

- ✔ *English* refers to whatever is normal in most English speaking countries not just England. There are so many countries where English is an official language that I have chosen to keep it simple in this way.

- ✔ Web addresses appear in the book in `monofont` type, so they stand out.

- ✔ Sidebars – boxed text on a grey background – are chunks of material which you might find useful as background knowledge, or as enhancements to the techniques you read about in the main text. Fun and helpful, but not essential reading: skip them if you want.

Foolish Assumptions

I wrote this book with the intention of helping people who want to teach English for the first time, or who are inexperienced at the job and need some tips to improve their teaching.

I assume these things about you:

- ✔ You are a native speaker or proficient in speaking English.

- ✔ You are not a fully qualified TEFL teacher although you may have an initial qualification.

✔ You want to do a responsible job in the classroom and give students value for money.

✔ You are more interested in the mechanics of teaching than the methodology behind language learning.

✔ You are not enrolled on a full TEFL course leading to a diploma or MA.

Please note that this book is not for you if you just want to improve your own English. The focus is on how to explain language points to students not simply to you, the reader.

How This Book Is Organised

This book is organised into six main parts, and two Appendixes. The parts cover the TEFL industry, putting together lessons and their content, and then to the courses as a whole.

Part 1: Getting Started In TEFL

In this first section of the book I cover the information you need to know about the kind of people who go into TEFL and what the job can do for them. I help you to decide whether to only teach for a couple of summers or as a career, by explaining what the job entails. I tell you what the students expect from you too. You find out about the qualifications and training you need, if any, as there are different kinds of courses you can enrol on. As well as this, I include the points you need to keep in mind if you are moving abroad to teach. This is an introduction to the industry as a whole.

Part 11: Putting Your Lesson Together

For most people who are new to teaching or have never done it before, the task of finding a point to teach and then working out how to package the information into an effective lesson is rather overwhelming. In these chapters I break the lesson down into different stages, known as Presentation, Practice and Production so that there is a clear structure for learning. There is also advice on how long the stages should last and who should be doing the talking. I include lots of examples and suggestions for classroom activities, whether you use a course book or design your own materials. You find out when and how to correct the students' errors and keep them in check during the lesson through good classroom management.

Part III: How to Teach Skills Classes

In language courses there are four main skills which need to be included to make students truly proficient. These are listening, speaking, reading and writing. In this part of the book I take a look at each skill in isolation, showing you how to put a lesson together which is dedicated to one skill. These lessons have a slightly different structure from grammar and vocabulary ones. There is also a chapter on pronunciation which is so vital to good communication that there are phonetic symbols and particular techniques for assisting students to speak clearly.

Part IV: The Grammar You Need to Know – and How to Teach It

Grammar for foreign students is the topic of this section. It is the area which so many native speakers dread teaching, not having done much of this at school themselves. Although this book is not an exhaustive reference on the English grammar, here I cover most of the questions you need answered in order to hold your own in the classroom. You can you use this part of *TEFL for Dummies* along with your dictionary and reference works if you want to go deeper. So, you review the way sentences are put together with subjects, verbs and objects. Then you find out how to improve your students' sentences with adjectives, adverbs and conjunctions. I present each tense explaining what it does and what it looks like. Finally there is a chapter covering modal verbs, phrasal verbs and conditional structures. There are lots of suggestions on practising grammar too.

Part V: What Kind of Class Will I Have?

First in this section I provide advice on using tests to get students in the right class and how to use testing progressively during the course. Following this there are sections on different kinds of courses and advice on handling them. You learn about one to ones classes, business English, teaching young people from small children to adolescents and exam classes. Finally, I compare two kinds of classroom situations. The first is the class with students who all speak the same language and the second is the class with students from all around the world. I take a look at one nationalities of students in detail. As a TEFL teacher you need to be ready for anything!

Part VI: The Part of Tens

Part VI is the part of tens which gives you ten tips each on a couple of TEFL issues. The first offers suggestions on making your lessons more lively and the second one looks at resources you can use to improve your teaching skills.

There are two appendixes offering you extra information. Appendix A gives you templates which help you plan, observe and assess lessons. Appendix B takes a brief look at popular locations around the world for TEFL teachers and gives you an idea of what to expect from the country and the job.

Icons Used in This Book

When you see this icon, you know you'll be getting a real-world illustration of a language teaching idea or situation to help you grasp what's going on.

This icon draws attention to points you should try to lodge in your memory.

This icon highlights helpful ideas for making your lessons run more smoothly.

If you want practical suggestions for how to go about teaching a particular point, look out for this icon.

This icon alerts you to common mistakes among newer teachers and suggests pointers to help you avoid problems.

Where to Go from Here

If you have never taught English before but are considering it as a source of income, the best place to start is probably Part I. That way you'll know what the job is before you start digging deeper. For example Chapter 3 tells you about who is eligible to teach.

If you are living abroad and have already examined the local demand for English lessons you probably know who your prospective students will be. In that case, take a look at Part VI as you can start finding out about specific teaching situations. You could browse Chapter 19 on business English, for example.

Existing teachers should already know something about their shortcomings, be it explaining grammar (Part IV) or correcting students (Chapter 7), so you can find individual chapters which deal with your weak points. Perhaps your boss has just given you a new kind of course which is making you nervous and you want to know the best approach: Try Part VI.

Be confident as you proceed. There are many things in your favour:

- ✔ You already know English. You have probably been learning it since infancy.

- ✔ You have probably taught someone something before and seen them apply what they have learned.

- ✔ Most people who start out in TEFL are not academics. They just enjoy travelling and like people but they manage to pull off great courses. You can too.

- ✔ If you gradually go through this book you will have all the information you need to get started.

Part I

Getting Started in TEFL

The 5th Wave   By Rich Tennant

©RICHTENNANT

"Of course I've had experience teaching English as a foreign language. My corgi understands over 20 commands."

Looking at the TEFL Marketplace

For most would-be TEFL teachers, the draw of the job is the ability to travel and work. Even if your responsibilities don't allow you to leave your own shores, at least working in TEFL brings other travellers to you.

Considering countries – both home and abroad

Before entering TEFL, give some consideration to where you want to teach and who your ideal students would be. Subtle differences exist between the criteria for teachers in English speaking countries and elsewhere. The training you need for particular student groups also varies. In addition, unlike a career change at home, teaching abroad presents challenges you may not have considered.

Staying in the home market

Finding work in TEFL in an English-speaking country can be more difficult than doing so abroad. The problem is that, unlike being a foreigner overseas, you have no novelty value when you're at home. As many English-speaking nations are economic powerhouses, they tend to have various regulatory bodies governing the employment of teachers and trying to ensure high standards in education. In other words you need to jump through more hoops to get a decent job.

Very often TEFL jobs are advertised as *ESOL (English for Speakers of Other Languages)* or *ESL (English as a Second Language).* Teaching English as a Foreign Language, English as a Second Language and English for Speakers of Other Languages are all the same kind of work depending on which country you're in and who your students are. There's a slight difference between learning a language to survive in the English-speaking country you now live in and learning English while you're in a non-English speaking country.

ESOL students may be refugees or economic migrants who need help with day-to-day situations such as seeing the doctor or understanding letters from their child's school.

Many students are entitled to attend government funded courses or free classes run by charitable organisations. In addition, private language schools offer courses from two weeks up to two years. In the latter case, students pay for their lessons and often have other activities to make the experience more fun, including a social programme that teachers generally get involved with too.

Although the basic skills of the job are the same in each sector, you may not be eligible to apply for all of these jobs. The first thing you need is to be able to speak English well (whether you're a native speaker or not). Most employers require teachers to have a first degree and a TEFL qualification (certificate, diploma or Master of Arts) although in the public sector you usually need a qualification specifically for teaching adults in further education. Non-graduates can often get onto a training course but fewer job opportunities are available to them.

Amongst countries in the European Union things have been changing. Citizens of the EU have rights in the UK, including the right to enrol on courses offered by the state. This means that instead of learning English in their home country and then moving to the UK to look for work or higher education opportunities, it's quite feasible to move over and then learn the language through the state system and full immersion. There have been quite a few changes in the number of jobs offered in countries like Poland for these reasons. Unfortunately the British economy is not what it was, and as the world struggles with the recent banking crises, people are thinking twice about their prospects abroad anyway.

Working abroad

You can find far more opportunities for TEFL abroad than on home soil. The world is a big place, after all! However, despite the thrill of setting off on a new adventure overseas, you need to approach a TEFL work with a balanced outlook that considers both the advantages and the disadvantages.

The advantages are that:

- ✔ You get to experience another culture and broaden your horizons.
- ✔ You're involved in a rewarding occupation through which you can help others to change their lives.
- ✔ You get paid as you slowly travel around the world.
- ✔ If you already live abroad, you can find a job before you have mastered the local language.
- ✔ You work with a skill you already have, speaking English.

But the disadvantages are that:

- ✔ It's difficult to know what kind of employer you're getting involved with until you arrive in the country.
- ✔ Once you've given up your home and job it isn't quite as easy to turn back.

✔ You may feel thrown in at the deep end. Even if you get extensive training first, when you actually have your own class, most of the time it's just them and you.

✔ You're unlikely to get rich. The best most EFL teachers abroad can hope for is a decent standard of living by local standards (which may be different from what you're used to) and enough money saved to get back home again.

✔ You're out of the loop as far as your home country is concerned, both socially and professionally (if you already have another line of work).

So many TEFL operators in the world – almost anyone who speaks the language well can find work somewhere but, as with jobs on home soil, the best opportunities go to graduates with a recognised TEFL qualification.

Ask a school abroad if you can contact one of the current foreign teachers to get some insight into local living. Even if the school declines, you can still put out some feelers among friends and Internet forums such as on www. eslcafe.com. You can ask just about anything and you'll find someone out there who can help you find the answer.

Changing with the seasons

More often than not, TEFL jobs abroad follow the academic calendar. So in most countries jobs start in September or October and run for nine months to a year. Start looking for a good contract in the summer if you want to fly off in the autumn. Some positions begin in January, so December isn't a bad time to look for a position either.

Considering China

These days many TEFL teachers are heading to China. It has become one of the biggest economies in the world and is a huge market for the TEFL industry. It's estimated that less than 1 per cent of Chinese people in China currently speak English and with a population of over a billion, the potential is huge.

That being said, there isn't as much regulation of language schools as you find in other countries, so you need to be very cautious about visas, work permits and contracts and make sure that they're genuine.

With such a large country, you should also give some thought to where you want to teach. Some like to be around other Westerners so they don't feel lonely, whereas others want to immerse themselves entirely in the new culture. Apparently the weather varies greatly too, inside and outside the classroom, so check that you're going to be working in a climate you can manage and that the school has appropriate facilities – like air-conditioning.

When the academic year finishes, students visit English speaking countries so they can practise their language skills. That's why TEFL job opportunities in the UK and other similar places mushroom for the summer. You can often find short contracts from two to twelve weeks long at summer schools. Advertisements for these jobs start appearing in spring, typically in March and April.

So if you want to work all year round, check whether your school closes for long periods and if so, make sure that you can save enough to tide you over or find a temporary position for the 'holidays'.

Teaching trends

English language teaching has become more tailored to the varying needs of students. ESP (English for Specific Purposes) is big news, so instead of studying general English for years, more students are opting for business English, EAP (English for Academic Purposes) or similar courses that address their needs more directly.

Another trend is towards online learning and training for students and teachers. Many resources are available on the Internet so students feel less inclined to ask a teacher for help in person these days. And with fewer students around, employers are looking for a higher standard from their teachers.

Getting Out There

There's a lot to think about when you shut up shop and re-establish yourself in a new location. You need to prepare your mind in advance, not just your suitcase.

Preparing to leave town

If you already know where in the world you want to teach, find out as much as you can about what you're likely to meet in terms of bureaucracy and daily life.

Find the answers to these questions:

- ✔ Do I need a working visa?
- ✔ Do I need any jabs?
- ✔ Will I be eligible for medical treatment and if not what kind of insurance covers me in case of emergencies?
- ✔ Which home comforts may I need to take with me?

> ✔ What are the implications for my tax and pension contributions back home?
>
> ✔ Have I set up a forwarding address for my post?
>
> ✔ What do I know about the currency and economy? How much money do I need to take and in what form?

Don't close your home bank account if you can help it. It's really tricky to start all over again when you return because you often have to provide proof of address and accounts for three months just to rent a flat. Have your paperwork sent abroad or to a safe place back home.

Setting up elsewhere

Arriving in another country is a very exciting and frightening experience. When everything is new, you can find yourself feeling a bit isolated and homesick at first, especially if you don't speak the language, but if you're open minded things usually get better.

Use these tips to help start feeling at home:

> ✔ Learn the language to a reasonable extent.
>
> ✔ Be curious. Find out all you can about your new environment.
>
> ✔ Listen to advice. Local people try to advise you about all kinds of things. You don't have to follow it all but if you pay attention you'll probably avoid some pitfalls.
>
> ✔ Accept invitations. If your students are going for a drink, go along from time to time (as long as your employer approves).

The lifestyle of an EFL teacher is usually a pleasant one. Jobs are most often three to five hours a day plus the time you spend preparing. So you can usually find time to explore your surroundings. Take some of your lesson planning out and about with you as you try out local cafés and beauty spots. You may find that if you look different from local people, they start conversations with you out of curiosity or on the other hand they may just stare. Either way, be friendly. When people get used to seeing you around, they're more likely to accept you being there.

A small piece of advice is to judge accommodation by local standards. If you must complain, save it for your friends back home. It does annoy people when they hear 'In my country . . . ' too often.

Use the Internet to keep in touch with your friends and family. Even though you may be too excited to keep in touch when you first arrive, you'll miss your mates a bit when things settle down, so don't lose touch.

Thinking About a Stint or a Life in TEFL

Some spend a few months in TEFL, others a couple of years and still others a lifetime. Believe it or not, TEFL work can meet all of those needs if you're brave enough to set your reservations aside and go for it.

Taking someone from the basics of the language to independence is continually rewarding. There's something very special about hearing or seeing the penny drop in a lesson.

Filling gap years and career breaks

TEFL is the perfect antidote to a life chained to a desk. You may be one of those professionals who find that you just can't bear the rat race unless you take some time out. Sales targets can really lose their appeal when you can't see what's really being accomplished by your work. For students, gap years in TEFL can give you the kind of life skills and experience that lectures just can't match.

Real benefits can be gained from taking a year out; they include:

- **Refocusing:** You may have thought you had it all worked out but suddenly you wonder whether your chosen path is really what you want. Giving yourself time to think and look at other possibilities should set you straight.

- **Recharging your batteries:** Perhaps you've made the right career choices but you're a little burnt out. A short diversion into TEFL can energise you again.

- **Appreciating what you have:** Seeing how others live can really help you see the good in your own lifestyle when you return home.

- **Giving something back:** You can use TEFL to help people who don't have the same advantages as you.

✔ **Broadening your skill base:** You can gain by:

- Finding out how to be independent

- Leading a team

- Taking responsibility for yourself and others too

- Building rapport and communicating with others

- Solving problems

- Improving your planning and organisation skills

Planning a new life

On a personal level, TEFL can take you around the world, which is a goal in itself for many people. But even if you don't cover the whole globe, it's fascinating finding out new things about yourself or rediscovering them. Being in a new environment helps you to sort out the things you want to do from the things you previously just went along with and being exposed to other cultures truly inspires the imagination.

If you do happen to take to the job like a duck to water, you can work up the career ladder too. Once you've been teaching for a couple of years and you have a TEFL certificate (representing at least 100 hours of tuition) you can then become a senior teacher, which introduces you to teacher training roles and added responsibilities such as controlling learning resources. There may be extra money in that but by this time you'll be ready to take your skills outside the classroom sometimes anyway. The next steps are ADoS (assistant director of studies) and DoS (director of studies), which are positions offering a higher salary but which generally require additional qualifications – namely a diploma or master's degree. The problem with managerial roles though, is that they tend to take you away from teaching and into the office. So you may want to embark on more of a sideways move:

✔ As an official examiner for the exams students of English as a Foreign Language sit.

✔ As a teacher trainer.

✔ As a materials writer.

✔ As a home-stay course provider, who accommodates and teaches students in their own home.

✔ As a marker for distance learning courses.

✔ As an agent connecting students with schools and colleges in different countries.

Addressing some qualms

Do you still need a final push to get out there? When you speak to people who have taught EFL, you usually find that there's no need to hold back if this is what you want.

Some common fears include:

- **Money:** You don't need to have huge amounts of money put by. Save enough to pay for some TEFL training, a return flight, and enough to set you up in the local currency (which may be comparatively little).

- **Commitments at home:** Although you have commitments, if you think positively you may be able to get nine months abroad without changing your whole life. Have you asked your boss about taking an unpaid sabbatical? You never know, he may be keen on the idea. You can also speak to an estate agent about letting your home for a year and even your loved ones may be happy for you to take a break (in my experience, they love to have a place to visit for a free holiday).

- **Age:** Don't start thinking that only youngsters get TEFL jobs. Students love to a see a mature face in the classroom. Most employers expect older teachers to be more dedicated and have a better work ethic, so there's no need to write yourself off.

You may just have the time of your life working in TEFL, so go ahead and take the plunge.

Chapter 2

Looking at What TEFL Teachers Actually Do

1n this chapter you get an insight into the world of teaching English as a foreign language. You find out what the job entails from the teacher's point of view and the student's too.

Answering Common Questions

Many would-be teachers are plagued with fears and insecurities about what TEFL is really like and whether they're up to the challenge. In this section I give you some of the most common – and commonly troubling – questions and their answers.

Can I teach English without knowing the students' language?

In a word, yes! The only language you really need to know well is English. Some schools use the students' language in the classroom but this is by no means typical of the TEFL industry as a whole, and it's positively discouraged in most cases.

With so many different kinds of teaching situations and places to teach in, you'd have to know the language of everyone you may meet in the classroom at any point in your career, so neither you nor any other teacher would ever get started.

Do I have to translate?

Even though your students inevitably speak to you in their mother tongue from time to time, you can respond in simple English, with gestures or pictures. Of course, you may not understand what they're saying anyway and this just gives them real motivation for learning your language. In a way, it makes the whole situation more authentic.

If you do translate in the classroom, you have to be absolutely certain that what you're saying corresponds exactly to the students' language. Students sometimes expect one language to translate word for word into another, but it just doesn't work like that. For example, you can't translate 'bon voyage' into 'good journey' if you want to get the sense of the expression.

Will the students be children?

Youngsters in many countries need English lessons, but the state takes care of this by using primary and secondary school teachers. TEFL teachers sometimes give support to the state education system but do most of their work in the private sector. Parents often pay for extra English lessons, especially during the summer months.

However, many adults and teenagers preparing for work abroad or in an international environment have a great desire to learn English. These students are highly motivated and usually well behaved.

Do I have to know all the grammar in the English language?

You don't need to know every last bit of English grammar, but you should aim to have a good working knowledge of all the tenses and be able to identify and explain all the parts of speech (nouns, verbs, adjectives and so on). Check the chapters in Part 4 for some help with grammar issues.

The aim of TEFL is to produce students who can speak the language almost as well as you can, at the most. In reality, very few students have the time and resources to stay in the classroom setting beyond upper-intermediate or advanced level (proficiency is the highest level). As soon as students feel confident that they can use English for whatever purposes they need, they often get on with their lives. This is why you don't need to know every last predicate and gerund.

Can I teach without a degree and formal qualifications?

Yes you can, but finding work is easier if you have them. Most schools advertise vacancies for graduates in any discipline who have a TEFL certificate comprising about 100 hours of training.

However, if you actually live overseas and are prepared to trawl around the local language schools, you may find that these schools welcome native speakers with open arms, without or without the typical entry requirements.

Get some training if you can as this gives you better opportunities.

I hated language lessons at school. Will the job be like that?

I remember some of the phrases I learnt in my O-level French lessons. Most of them are pretty irrelevant to my life now and even to my life back then. Fortunately, language teaching has moved on rather a lot in the last thirty years. So these days there's less emphasis on grammar drills and more emphasis on practical role-playing and creating a relaxed learning environment.

Even if education in general in your chosen destination is still rather dry, you can expect to teach according to the livelier techniques of the modern TEFL industry.

Are there lots of books and exercises for students to work through?

You can make use of the stacks of course books, work books and resource books on the market but most schools encourage teachers to use their own ideas too. Depending on the country and the employer, you probably have a book and syllabus but a fair amount of latitude as well.

Most large bookshops have a section on English as a foreign language, so have a browse through some popular course books to get an idea of the kind of material teachers use. Some examples of course books that are popular in many countries are titles such as *Innovations*, *Cutting Edge* and *English File*, which are available for each level of English students and cover elementary, pre-intermediate and so on.

What kind of person makes an ideal TEFL teacher?

A good EFL teacher enjoys meeting people and is interested in other languages and cultures. The most successful teachers are often the ones who can put the students at ease and who have a sense of humour.

On the other hand, it's not all about personality. You have greater insight into the students' learning issues if you speak another language yourself, but this is not a must.

You definitely need to have a methodical approach, which usually includes taking the time to do your research and preparation before you enter the classroom. So, in a way, good teachers of English are also good students of their subject.

Does it matter that I'm not a native speaker?

The answer to this depends on your level of English, who you're teaching and in what situation. Most employers expect you to be proficient in English and have excellent, native pronunciation. You may get away with fewer skills if you're teaching young children or if you're teaching in your own country where native English speakers are in short supply.

You're far less likely to find work in the private sector in an English-speaking country because students who pay to travel to and study in the UK, for example, quite reasonably expect their teachers to represent the vocabulary, grammar and pronunciation of that land fully. However, in the public and voluntary sectors this may be different, as the students are usually immigrants who may relate well to a fellow immigrant who has found her feet in the English-speaking community.

How many students will I have?

Most classes have 10 to 20 students in them, but I have heard of 'classes' with more than 40 students, which are actually more like lectures. It depends on the country, the economy and the integrity of your employer.

Is it okay if 1 don't 'talk posh'?

Yes, but you need to have good grammar and a clear speaking voice, with or without a regional accent. If native speakers have trouble following you, you need to make some changes. However, there's no point trying to sound aristocratic because the vast majority of students are unlikely to mix with the upper-class set in real life anyway.

Will the students like me?

Although you should aim to put your students at ease so that they're more receptive to learning, you're not there to be their best mate. Students should like your lessons and respect you as their teacher. If they happen to like you personally, it's a bonus, not a prerequisite for a good course. In general, you can be a likeable teacher by being fair, considerate, responsible and well prepared.

How will 1 know what to do?

If at all possible, get yourself some training and observe some lessons before you start teaching. Once you've done that, speak to your colleagues for tips and guidance.

Use up-to-date course books to help you. Most course books have a teachers' book too that gives you a complete lesson plan and some even include online training so you can see model lessons.

Talking to Students and So Much More – Teaching Basics

The human brain is a marvellous instrument with the built-in capacity to decipher language. If you hear the same words in the same context enough, you start to work out what they mean – it's like cracking a code. You discovered this as a baby. Mum said the word 'teddy' every time she waved that cuddly little chap in front of your face and pretty soon you made the connection. Perhaps your Indian neighbour says 'Namaste!' every time he sees you. Pretty soon you understand that this means 'Hello!'

Picking up language this way is almost effortless. However, busy people wanting to learn a new language can't go back to the restful days of babyhood, or take a couple of weeks to pick up a simple greeting. So, when students attend language classes, they need a system or methodology so that they can measure their progress and balance this against the money they pay. The next sections give the basics on teaching methods.

In the classroom, students learn actively through direct instruction from the teacher and pick up the language incidentally at the same time. It's surprising how many of your favourite phrases your students imitate just because you drop them into your lessons. A couple of mine are 'Okie dokie' and 'Here we go'.

Teaching the easier words first

When you pick up a language by hearing it spoken, everything is thrown at you at the same time and you have to wade through a lot of 'noise' before you hear something you recognise. However, when you teach systematically you generally start with easy words and phrases and then add a bit more each time. You save the most difficult words for the end.

In TEFL you *grade* whatever you say so that your speech matches the students' level of English. When you start a beginners' course, for example, you use a lot of pictures, gestures and repetition to put across the meaning of basic words like 'car' and 'bus'.

Figure 2-1 uses an imaginary language – we can call it Dummese – to illustrate a dialogue typical of a Dummese beginner-level lesson.

The teacher in Figure 2-1 uses only four words to teach 'car' and 'bus' – 'deeba' and 'dooba' respectively. How about 'Dum dim'? They must be equivalent to 'this is a . . .' in English. With only four words to decipher, the visual aid of the pictures, along with the reassuring smiles of the teacher, it's quite easy for students to crack the code.

The lesson would logically continue with another few words connected with vehicles and transport as you use easy words in a clear context and build up from there. If you had to pick out words like these by listening to a complicated traffic report in Dummese, you would have a much more difficult, if not impossible, task.

Dum dim 'deeba'.

Deeba! Deeba!

Deeba!

Dum dim deeba

Dum dim 'dooba'

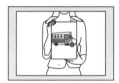

Dooba!

Dum dim deeba

Figure 2-1:
Starting off
simply with
props.

Dum dim dooba

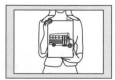

Focusing on the most useful words

In theory you can spend your whole life learning a new language, especially a global language such as English to which new words are added or borrowed from other languages all the time.

Most people, however, make do with a few thousand words and leave the rest to those who particularly need them. So the question is, if English has around half a million words in its vocabulary, which ones do you teach? Obviously, you can't teach them all.

The idea is to focus on teaching the words that allow the students to function competently in the language.

You only have 90 minutes or so per lesson, and perhaps 60 hours or so to complete a course, whether it's a beginner, elementary or intermediate course. With that in mind, you can't afford to be sidetracked by talking about words that particularly interest you but are seldom used.

Your students need to know all the words typically associated with a given level of English so that they can measure their progress and move on. The best way to become familiar with what students need to learn within each level is to refer to the syllabus at the beginning of an EFL course book. Usually the syllabus sets out the vocabulary areas and grammar chapter by chapter. In most cases the language school has approved a course book or set of materials, which you should use as your guide.

Giving students room to talk

Learning a new language is a great deal harder if you feel stressed. You're likely to feel embarrassed about pronouncing the words and discouraged by grammar rules and differences from your mother tongue. This is why an important aspect of TEFL work is to present lessons in an enjoyable and engaging way.

In the TEFL industry, you challenge the stereotype of teachers as boring, sour-faced characters who spend most of their time writing on the board with their backs to the students. Neither do you lecture the students, forcing them to simply listen and take notes.

Actually, the students should be doing the talking for most of the lesson. They need to try out what they've learned, get to know their classmates better so they work as a team, and feel relaxed enough to laugh at their own mistakes. Speaking to a classmate in small groups or pairs and role playing is one of the more effective ways to learn. In TEFL the aim is to give your students practice and a nice safe environment to try out everything they learn.

People really need to be able to speak a language to master it, so remember that in your lessons.

Keeping things relevant

Whatever you teach the students should be realistic and have some relevance to their lives. Depending on the situation, students sometimes come to you with their own goals. If the class is a general English course, the onus is on you to select the words and phrases most used in the situations your particular students are likely to meet. For example, youngsters often compare their ages as soon as they meet, but adults rarely do (it's actually quite rude to ask someone's age in many cultures) so teaching the 'How old are you?' question is far more relevant to a class of children than to a class of adults.

Likewise, students who are living in an English-speaking country need some colloquial expressions to survive. For example, in London you teach students that the underground transport system is called 'the tube' within the first week, whereas a class of students in Costa Rica may never need to know that.

Some students have very specific goals such as passing exams or getting a job. Once you know what these are you can more easily tailor your classes to fit their needs. This is especially true if all the students are working towards the same goal.

TEFL does comprise some very focused areas, such as business English, EAP (English for academic purposes), and even courses adapted for particular jobs like football coaching and hairdressing.

Recognising What Your Students Want from You

You may wonder what students expect from an EFL teacher when they enrol on a course and gingerly enter the classroom. To be honest, students don't always have their list of wants and needs crystallised from the outset, but as they go along they certainly pick up when things aren't right. Then, they start complaining or stop attending.

From the moment a student turns up at the reception area of your school or makes contact with you directly, she expects you to understand that she has a lack in her ability and that communicating in English is beyond her level and presents a problem. Students want help. They don't want to feel embarrassed or stupid.

You first need to determine your students' level of English by some form of testing. In a country where English is not the first language, students tend to make contact with a school or teacher in their own language. However, a form of speaking test happens quite quickly when (in the case of a language school) a student is introduced to a teacher or teaching manager who begins a conversation in English. You can buy written placement tests from EFL publishers such as Oxford University Press or you can put one together using questions that move progressively through the grammar and vocabulary typical of each class level. It depends on the school and a student's needs whether to test speaking, grammar writing skills or all three. At the appropriate level, students stretch themselves but won't struggle too much.

Students need to make measurable progress from their starting level. Proof of this may be completing a syllabus, gaining confidence or passing a test. However, by the end of your course your students want to feel that it was all worthwhile because they've bettered themselves.

Encouragement goes hand in hand with improving English skills. Your class wants to know that you're on its side by the praise you give the students when they do well.

From the students' perspective, it's reassuring when the teacher seems to know her stuff. You don't have to be a professor of the language but you do need to inspire confidence overall. Students want to know that you as the teacher are an expert (and as a native or proficient speaker of English you are) and that you know the process involved in making their English better.

Nobody wants to have a boring experience, so students rely on you to make their lessons as lively and memorable as possible. They don't want a stand-up comedian or anything too eccentric, but there should be smiling, laughing and interesting contexts. In this way your students won't just remember that they had a lesson about words for sports, for example, but they'll remember the story of a great athlete that you gave as the backdrop to the vocabulary. Remembering is also a big deal for people learning a language, because they need enough repetition to drive the point home but not so much that it becomes tedious.

In most cases you use books and handouts to help you present your lessons. Students want nicely presented, informative documents that they can still understand when they look back at them a year later. Conscientious students always turn up with a pen and notebook because they want to make their own notes on the course, but they expect any materials you provide to be concise and effective.

Unless you're teaching a dedicated speaking class or writing class, most students want some kind of coverage of the four main skills in language – reading, writing, speaking and listening – so that they can function fully in English. They don't usually want to cover all four to the same degree but they expect to work in each area.

Because TEFL doesn't require the same degree of training as some other educational roles, teachers sometimes forget the importance of professionalism. Even though your students may be of the same age group as you, and some may encourage you to socialise with them at the local pizzeria or wine bar, as a class they expect you to work professionally and conduct yourself in a dignified way. This includes the overall management of your classroom – what it looks like, what time your lessons start and finish and your supervision of the students.

Some people enrol on language courses because they want to make new friends but you can still help them to focus on the course aims so that they take learning seriously.

Students want you to be both fair and flexible. They become irritated if you seem to favour one student over another. Equally, they expect you to understand the real world involves many pressures so it's not always possible to do homework to perfection or arrive early every single time. When something of particular interest happens in the world, they want you to depart from your lesson plan so that they can talk to you about it (hopefully in English). The USA and UK are major players in world politics so some students want to discuss current affairs with their new tool, the language of those nations.

Culture is very important in a language lesson; it's almost impossible to teach one thing without the other. So students want a role model who can give them a window into the English-speaking culture while showing due respect to their own. They definitely don't want a hint of superiority from their teacher but instead they want to know about any pitfalls in terms of appropriate behaviour and expressions.

Students want you to point out the customs of English speakers in certain situations but they don't want to be forced to accept these as good or right.

Believe it or not, students love it when their teachers correct them. I mention this because new teachers are sometimes too polite about this as they think that students may be offended. In my experience, students want to know where their errors lie and what to do about them.

Chapter 3

Examining Courses, Qualifications and Jobs

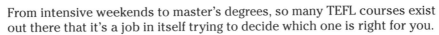

In This Chapter

▶ Deciding on your level of teaching

▶ Signing up to the right courses and training

▶ Gearing your work to the salaries available

▶ Finding work

Gone are the days when a native English speaker could set off with a rucksack, arrive anywhere in the world and expect to be greeted with open arms by eager language school owners. Such scenarios are still possible, but the TEFL (Teaching English as a Foreign Language) industry has moved on, so you need to put a little more thought into it before you start packing. In this chapter I show you how to take your first steps in TEFL by deciding whether you need training, what kind to choose and how to go about finding a job.

Teaching the Teacher

From intensive weekends to master's degrees, so many TEFL courses exist out there that it's a job in itself trying to decide which one is right for you.

Before you set out to teach, get a decent dictionary and the best grammar book you can fit in your case (see Chapter 24 for some suggestions).

Finding your level

In the world of TEFL there are four or five levels of 'teacher'. Deciding whether you want to earn enough to keep you in beer money whilst on your travels or whether you're looking for a long-term career helps you decide what kind of training is appropriate.

The various types of native and proficient speakers of English working fit into these categories:

- ✔ The opportunist who has no training in EFL or any other teaching qualifications but needs to find work.
- ✔ The teacher who has a basic level of training amounting to 20 hours or fewer. He's been introduced to the overall principles of TEFL.
- ✔ The TEFL initiated teacher who has completed a certificate level TEFL course of about 100 hours.
- ✔ The teacher qualified in another subject who needs to learn the principles of teaching EFL. At this same level are people who have studied the English language extensively, perhaps having a degree in English literature or linguistics, but who have no experience of teaching.
- ✔ The TEFL qualified teacher who has a diploma or master's-level qualification in EFL.

Don't underestimate the responsibility teachers have. Once you're facing 20 eager students who've parted with their hard-earned cash hoping that you can change their lives, it's a little late for regrets.

Get some training or do your own research but never walk into a classroom completely unprepared. A little training is better than none at all.

Being an unqualified teacher

Most language schools belong to professional bodies, which set criteria for teaching staff so that there's a level of quality control. This means that usually you can't find paid work in an English-speaking country without a well-recognised teaching qualification. However, there are exceptions to this if the school runs its own training programmes for would-be teachers. Charitable and state-run organisations with volunteer programmes sometimes welcome people willing to share their knowledge with others and you get some teaching experience in return.

If a school trains staff to use its own teaching methods, you've a better chance of finding work with them without a teaching qualification. Big chains like Callan and Berlitz employ staff in this way, depending on the location.

On the other hand, if you're travelling to a part of the world where there are few native English speakers in residence, but the locals have some disposable income, you're more likely to be viewed as a great catch by schools and individual students looking for a tutor, despite your lack of qualifications and experience. Being a native speaker can be your USP (unique selling point), but try not to be complacent.

Many EFL teachers have no training whatsoever but still manage to find work and develop their skills while in the job. If you won't be relying on an income from teaching and are unlikely to spend more than a few months in one place, a short taster course is probably all you need. Various organisations offer weekend and short courses in TEFL that give you a taste of what is involved in the job and help you decide whether teaching is for you on a long-term basis.

In the UK, for example, Berlitz (www.berlitz.com) won't employ a teacher who doesn't have a degree and teaching certificate. However, if you apply to one of their schools abroad, you may have the chance to prove yourself on their unpaid training course which lasts one to two weeks.

Unfortunately, employers don't view all native speakers as equal. UK, Australian and other accents from economically strong nations are viewed as high status and are more sought after. Students tend to mimic the pronunciation of their teachers and many have distinct preferences about the accent they want to acquire. Countries that use English as just one of their national languages often bring influences from the other language (or languages) into the pronunciation, grammar and vocabulary of their particular variety of English. Some students find Asian and African varieties of English, for example, less desirable than those of the single-language nations. Whatever your accent, practise speaking clearly and accurately.

When you start approaching schools, project a professional attitude, a sense of humour and an interest in meeting and helping people.

Once you find work, you need more than a great accent to get through the lessons. If a choice of work comes your way, teaching conversation lessons is your best bet for easing yourself into TEFL. Teaching conversation is a little easier because you can concentrate on teaching less technical areas like fluency, vocabulary and pronunciation and avoid tricky grammar questions until you build up your experience. It's inadvisable to advertise yourself as merely a teacher of conversation lessons though, as this can limit your chances of finding work and you may find yourself feeling pigeonholed even after you've expanded your skills. It pays to brush up on your own grammar anyway and take an interest in how the English language works. (Look at Chapter 15 for info on grammar.) Think about when and why you say the things you do.

Getting initiated

If you intend to teach for more than a few months, make a reasonable living at TEFL, and give your students value for money, you really should invest in a TEFL certificate course of 100 hours or more. Teachers at this level are officially called *TEFL initiated*. Most EFL teachers remain at this level as this is what the majority of employers require from job applicants.

Before enrolling on a certificate course, consider who you want to teach and where. Each country has its own standards and preferences, so failing to meet the criteria for visa applications and the standards set by local employers hampers your chances of finding work.

The UK TEFL market is a prime example. The two strands of English course providers are the private sector and the public sector:

- **Private sector:** The more established private language schools tend to be accredited by the British Council who expect EFL teachers to be graduates (in any field) and to hold the CELTA (Certificate in English Language Teaching to Adults) or Trinity CertTESOL (Certificate in Teaching English to Speakers of Other Languages) qualifications. Other qualifications are technically acceptable but school managers have to jump through hoops to convince inspectors that their teachers are worthy if they don't meet the British Council's standard for EFL teaching qualifications or if their qualifications are not so well known. As a result they usually avoid hiring anyone who doesn't fit the profile or may cause them extra work.

- **Public sector:** On the other hand, in the public sector, schools and colleges have to meet ever changing government standards. So these days, all new teachers have to take a 'Preparing to Teach in the Lifelong Learning Sector' qualification.

Unfortunately, one certificate alone won't easily grant you entry into both sectors. The point being that, if you know where, who and how you want to teach, you can do your research and select the right course.

Look at TEFL job ads specific to the country you intend to work in and even call or email a few employers to find what exactly they are looking for. If you need a work permit before you can work as a teacher in your chosen destination, check whether you qualify for one. If not, you may have to put in a bit more planning, otherwise you'll find yourself dependent on dodgy operators who run courses with poor facilities and ridiculously low pay. Find out too if the schools there have a strong preference for one qualification over another.

Becoming a qualified teacher

A *fully qualified EFL teacher* is someone who has a diploma in TEFL and has at least two years' full-time experience in teaching EFL.

The best-known diplomas are the Cambridge DELTA (Diploma in English Language Teaching to Adults) and Trinity DipTESOL (Diploma in Teaching English to Speakers of Other Languages). You may also have a master's degree in ELT or a similar field (such as Applied Linguistics) in addition to teaching experience.

These qualifications are for people who want to make progress in their career and apply for managerial positions such as Director of Studies. You need a qualification like this if you're interested in training roles too. The good news is that all these positions attract higher pay and even if you're teaching the same courses as your less qualified colleagues, you're likely to have a better hourly rate than them.

Diploma and master's-level courses are not for the faint hearted. You need to get thorough experience in TEFL before considering a qualification at this level.

Getting on Course

After you decide that some form of training is in order, you need to find the right course.

Doing a training course abroad may be cheaper than doing one at home.

Entering introductory courses

Various organisations offer weekend courses of about 20 hours that introduce you to TEFL. Courses aren't accredited by any of the best-known bodies, so word of mouth is an important indicator of quality.

Even though the certificate may have an accreditation stamp, it may be from an organisation most employers haven't heard of. So it's worth finding out about the tutors' qualifications and experience and of what the course consists before parting with your cash.

In most cases, courses have a minimum age requirement of 17 or 18. To be honest, you need to have an A-level standard education or similar to get your head around it all, but more importantly, you should have the confidence to manage people, which is something teenagers may struggle with unless they restrict themselves to teaching small children.

There's no upper age limit, but once again, the pace is rather hectic on these courses. Be honest with yourself as you need to be the kind of person who can absorb knowledge quickly and put it into practice to get the most benefit out of these TEFL weekend programmes. Trainees sometimes underestimate what is required of them and end up a little discouraged. So be warned. Weekend courses are fast and furious!

If you're not a native speaker, you usually need to show that you've achieved an advanced level of English by passing an exam such as IELTS (International English Language Testing System) with a minimum band score of 7. However, even if you're a native speaker, your grammar should be of a reasonably high standard or else you can find yourself doubting your English and losing the confidence of your students. You should know that your English is correct even if you cannot explain why yet.

What you can do with this certificate

A certificate from a weekend course tells employers that you're responsible enough to undergo basic training before applying for a job. It doesn't mean that you're now a qualified EFL teacher, regardless of what the advertisement says.

In fact, after a training weekend, you're likely to feel a lot more enthusiastic and aware of what the job entails. You won't feel ready to go anywhere and teach anyone but at least you know a bit more about how to put a lesson together and the kind of the information students need. View the course as a taster and tell employers that you're keen to develop your skills on the job.

What the course covers

A weekend TEFL course follows similar lines as a full TEFL certificate because it touches on most of the same course components but in a very brief way.

A weekend course should include:

- **Basic grammar:** There's far too much grammar in the English language to teach everything in such a short time, but the course should make you aware of different tenses (you may think that there's a past, present and future tense and that's it, but believe me, the truth is a little more complicated). You usually touch on the different kinds of words you use in a sentence too – nouns, verbs, adverbs and adjectives.

- ✔ **Classroom techniques and activities:** Very often the tutor treats you as though you're a foreign student and shows you how to handle warm-up activities and pair or group work in the classroom.

- ✔ **Lesson planning:** You should learn one of the different formats for planning a lesson so that you know in which order to do things and how to make your lessons fun and effective.

- ✔ **An opportunity to practise teaching:** You teach a mini lesson or part of a lesson to volunteer students or to your fellow trainees.

The maximum class size should be about 20; a tutor can't effectively teach more than that.

How much it costs

A weekend course should be a lot cheaper (about 25 per cent of the cost) of a full certificate in a school, but don't forget to factor in the cost of accommodation and travel too. In the UK courses cost approximately £200 for 20 hours training.

i-to-i (www.i-to-i.com) has been offering weekend TEFL courses in the UK, USA, Ireland, Canada and Australia for several years.

Signing up for a certificate course

TEFL certificate courses come in a variety of packages these days. You can do intensive or part-time courses or complete a distance course online or by post.

You have to be at least 18 years old to do a TEFL certificate in most cases, which is practical as you'll be managing people in your classroom. There's no upper age limit.

Course providers generally prefer to take students with degrees or a good standard of education (good enough to go to university). Don't despair if you don't have any formal qualifications though. It's worth speaking to the school or college in person. If it's satisfied that you have a good head on your shoulders and a respectable level of English, it may well accept you.

Applicants with teaching experience are also favoured. Most schools ask you to take a test to prove how good your English is, so inform the school beforehand if you have a learning difficulty that affects your writing. If you're a non-native speaker, schools expect you to have an exam pass at advanced level in English as well.

Intensive TEFL courses last four or five weeks. Don't try to keep up your part-time job or even your favourite TV show because every waking moment is filled with lesson plans and projects. However, this type of course is a great way to jump in and get started.

If that sounds a bit too much for you, plenty of courses are spread over three months or even a year, enabling you to attend sessions in the evenings and at weekends, so you can fit it in around your job.

In any case, you need over 100 hours of tuition, plus feedback and homework time to gain your certificate.

What you can do with this certificate

With a bachelor or master's degree in any field and an EFL teaching certificate you're eligible to apply for the majority of vacancies.

To be honest, many university graduates have no idea what to do in a classroom so some employers bypass your level of education if you've managed to prove yourself and passed a certificate course.

What the course covers

The overall aim of certificate courses is to provide initial training for people who want to teach English to speakers of other languages and to make sure that they meet the criteria for teaching by demonstrating English usage accurately, by giving well balanced lessons and by evaluating their lessons.

Objectives for the course usually include familiarising trainees with all those areas that go into English language teaching – methodology, classroom procedures, techniques and aids, language awareness and testing. You have the opportunity to teach and to find out how to prepare and evaluate lessons too.

Other objectives for taught certificate courses are:

- To help trainees learn about the main pronunciation, vocabulary and structural features of current English.
- To raise awareness of the learning needs of individuals or groups of learners and of the motivation they have in a variety of circumstances and environments.
- To make sure that trainees can work cooperatively as members of a teaching team or group.
- To help trainees develop the ability to create and maintain the learners' interest and establish rapport.

✔ To make sure that trainees can plan lessons with clear and achievable aims using methods appropriate to the learners' levels of achievement and age.

✔ To give trainees basic classroom management skills and the ability to provide relevant activities.

✔ To make sure that trainees are able to use and adapt published teaching material and create their own basic teaching material.

✔ To highlight the main advantages and disadvantages of various language teaching approaches.

✔ To ensure that trainees can continue their development in TEFL after completing the course.

Before you start, the course provider sends you an EFL reading list and often asks you to complete a work book that provides an introduction to three important areas of the course. One is the unknown language section, the second is a grammar section and the third section is about how to teach.

Some courses include lessons in a foreign language so that you understand how the students in your class feel. Through these lessons you can gain the dual perspective of both a teacher and a student and experience various teaching techniques. You produce a project based on these lessons near the end of the course.

Teaching practice is an essential part of the course so expect real live students to volunteer to take part in your lesson. You also have the opportunity to see various other experienced teachers at work and your tutor gives you continual advice, feedback and support.

Courses with a _learner profile project_ give you the opportunity to get to know one EFL student a bit better and analyse their language skills in depth. For the project, you usually conduct an interview with the student and record it. In addition you set them a written task so that you can write about their strengths and weaknesses and discuss ways in which you would help them through EFL lessons. You may teach one lesson with the student in which you address one of that student's weak points.

A _materials project_ is designed to help you use and adapt basic materials, such as a photograph, in the classroom. You're asked to show how to use the same set of materials with students of different levels and abilities.

At the end of the course there's often a test on grammar and phonology (pronunciation).

Speak to local schools and colleges about their teacher training programmes. CELTA and Trinity CertTESOL are the most widely accepted certificates for the private sector and employers worldwide recognise them. If you're currently studying for a degree, check whether your university runs TEFL courses in the summer.

How much it costs

The average cost of the CELTA and the Trinity CertTESOL is £1,000. You may need to consider accommodation and travel costs too if no course provider exists where you live.

Keeping your distance

Distance learning courses never share the same high profile as taught courses because they don't let you experience teaching practice, but they have their own advantages.

Many people find it easier to fit the course into their normal lives by studying in this way. You can go at your own pace – and distance courses are a lot cheaper. On the other hand, you may never meet a student until you're teaching a class yourself and your tutor can only offer feedback on your written work not your actual performance. So distance learning has a few disadvantages too.

Many people who already have a suitable teaching qualification, such as a PGCE (Postgraduate Certificate in Education), but have no experience in EFL choose to take a distance course because the certificate itself is not as important for them. The skills to do with presentation, classroom management and lesson planning are transferable, so with this kind of course it's easier for the teacher to choose which areas to spend more time on.

What you can do with this certificate

Overseas employers appreciate the fact that you've taken the trouble to study and get yourself a certificate, and this tends to carry more weight than the actual certificate itself. This is because the organisations offering distance courses aren't as well known as CELTA or Trinity, which provide taught courses.

This area of the market has far less quality control than taught courses. However, the College of Teachers is one body which accredits distance TESOL (Teaching English to Speakers of Other Languages) courses as does ACTDEC, which is specifically for distance courses in TESOL. Courses accredited by these bodies offer a reasonable standard of professionalism and someone to talk to if the course or course provider falls seriously below your expectations.

What the course covers

Most distance certificate courses run along the same lines as taught courses (see information in the preceding 'Signing up for a certificate course'). You usually have assignments or work books to complete and get feedback from a designated tutor.

Some course providers work in collaboration with a school so that trainees can get practical experience in the classroom, at least through observing others if not through teaching lessons themselves.

How much it costs

Prices vary widely depending on what the course has to offer. However, you can expect to pay up to £400 for a course with about 100 hours tuition.

Contact TEFL Training (www.tefltraining.co.uk) for introductory weekends in the UK and mainland Europe and distance courses. This is a well-established organisation with very professional tutors.

Going for a diploma course

After you've been teaching English for a couple of years and have decided to make TEFL your career for some time to come, you can consider doing a diploma course. This means demonstrating deeper theoretical knowledge and more practical ability than holders of a TEFL certificate.

If you're going to invest your time and money in a diploma course, stick to the most well-known courses for the country you live in. In the UK these are the Cambridge DELTA and Trinity DipTESOL.

What you can do with this certificate

With a diploma, you can now call yourself a fully qualified EFL teacher. You're in a position to apply for most DoS jobs (Director of Studies) and ADoS (Assistant to the DoS) roles too. Employers usually require officially recognised teacher trainers to have this qualification and schools accredited by more prestigious bodies such as the British Council need to have a certain ratio of diploma qualified teachers on staff, so this makes you more desirable to employers. You can legitimately ask for a pay rise once you have your 'dip' so that you're set apart from the initiated teachers.

You can study a diploma intensively over about three months or by distance learning over a year or two. However, with both the Trinity diploma and the DELTA you need to sit an exam and have your teaching assessed internally by your course provider and externally by the awarding body.

Although you're expected to have a degree before applying, if you speak to the course provider and demonstrate how competent you are, there's a chance that the provider may accept you on the course without one. You can't get away with a lack of experience though. So, make sure that you've been teaching for two years, and mostly to adult classes.

Some universities give you credit points towards a degree if you have a recognised diploma, which means that you may not have to study as many modules, and this is particularly helpful for mature students returning to full-time education.

What the course covers

This course goes into far more depth than the TEFL certificate.

You teach and you're sometimes observed while you teach. You also observe other experienced teachers and submit coursework.

The DELTA is a modular course, which sometimes offers you more flexibility about what you study and when. The three modules you need to study are:

- ✔ Understanding language, methodology and resources leading to a three-hour written exam.

- ✔ Developing professional practice leading to course work, written assignments and a lesson that is observed by a moderator.

- ✔ Extending practice and an ELT specialism (such as teaching business English, younger learners or one to one lessons) leading to a research project.

On a Trinity diploma course, even distance learning trainees have to undertake a practical block where you teach lessons in preparation for the classroom teaching part of the exam. You're regularly observed by a tutor who gives you detailed feedback and helps you analyse your own lessons. The exam is actually a lesson in which you teach while being observed by the Trinity moderator, so you need to prepare meticulously.

You also sit for a 30-minute interview with the moderator during which you show your understanding of pronunciation (phonology) and the theory behind what you do in the classroom.

Most course providers give you work books that follow the Trinity stipulated syllabus along with extensive reading tasks.

How much it costs

A diploma course usually costs about £1,500 for the course and exam fees. Don't forget to factor in accommodation and travel costs if your course provider is another city and you need to commute or stay over for a week of teaching practice. In addition, the reading list includes some essential books, so get yourself a library card or be ready to cough up. You can probably recoup your money within 18 months as your salary increases.

Schools often need diploma qualified teachers to meet their quotas and raise their prestige. So, before you get out your cheque book, speak to your director of studies about funding for your diploma course. You may have to sign a special contract agreeing to stay at the school for a specific period of time after you pass, but you can save yourself hundreds of pounds if your employer pays some or all the costs.

Another point to keep in mind is that the reading lists for diploma courses are rather long and expensive. Who really wants to keep all those books after the course is finished anyway? So ask the school to buy them and then they can keep them in the teachers' room for the next diploma candidate who comes along.

Staying in for in-house training

Schools that have their own unique methodology often offer in-house training in their method. These programmes offer several advantages:

- ✔ You know that the training course exists because there's a need for teachers. So, providing that you impress the trainers, you usually have a job waiting for you.

- ✔ The school probably has its own materials and course books so you don't have to use too much imagination to come up with lesson plans. It's all done for you.

- ✔ Schools like these are also more likely to take a chance on someone who has no formal qualifications; 'the proof of the pudding is in the eating' as they say.

- ✔ Some of these schools are also part of an international chain so you can transfer from one place to another using internally advertised vacancies and contacts.

It's not all good news though. Some people find schools with a strict methodology a bit stifling to their creativity. Teachers sometimes get bored and want to move away from the prescribed material, which may not be allowed.

Professional development programmes are one of the hallmarks of responsible, caring TEFL employers. So there should be opportunities to improve while on the job. Hopefully the director of studies has a budget for seminars and conferences for teachers and even if money is tight, it's usually possible to set up peer observations where teachers watch each other teach and offer constructive feedback.

Ask about ongoing professional development at the initial interview if you're applying to a larger school.

Banking on Salaries

So the question is: can you get rich in TEFL? To be honest, it's unlikely. However, it's not all bad news. What TEFL jobs lack in riches, they certainly make up for in charm and interest. So this job is for people who like people, who like travelling, or at least meeting travellers, and like sharing knowledge.

Due to nature of the job, it's pretty difficult to give you an hourly rate that translates to all the places in the world where TEFL teachers work. Let me put it like this: the average full-time job should pay enough for you to share a decent flat, eat out once a week and take the odd day trip. Now, by a full-time job I mean 25 to 35 hours a week depending on the teaching method.

Consider the amount of time you spend preparing when you're deciding whether an hourly rate is appropriate. Some teaching methods require no preparation at all whereas others require about 20 minutes preparation per hour of teaching for an experienced teacher. Your timetable may also include teaching the same lesson to more than one class and this reduces preparation time as well.

As a measure of comparison, in central London where language schools are plentiful and range from shady visa factories to prestigious colleges, the hourly rate for teachers ranges from an appalling £8 per hour right up to around £25 per hour, depending on the job. The average is £10 to £15 per hour. Business English and one-to-one-tuition organisations often pay more but fewer teaching hours are available.

Teaching is a very full on job, so don't be tempted to adopt the same hours as an office worker. You're better teaching one or two private lessons a week on the side than having an extended timetable every day.

Before accepting a job, find out whether you have to pay your own local taxes and whether the salary advertised is gross or net. Ask about the location of your classes too. If you have to travel around town to teach your clients, you need to agree on travel expenses. You can also expect an employer to pay for your flight if you're applying for a job abroad from your home country.

By the way, you should ask about holidays and seasonal closures because in some countries the schools close for three months a year during the summer in which case you'll need to save up or find another form of income.

Finding Work

The most common way to find a TEFL job in any country is by using www.tefl.com. This excellent website has various search options and a facility for entering an online CV so that you can respond to jobs adverts in an instant.

TEFL.com advertises dozens of summer school jobs from March onwards. This is a good way to get your first teaching job in EFL. Summer schools employ teachers with a range of experience and qualifications for a few weeks or even three months at a time. You may have to move away for a while but most offer subsidised accommodation.

Even if you haven't got your teaching qualification yet, you can apply for a job as an activity leader or a similar non-teaching role. This gives you experience in being around groups of foreign language students and puts you in contact with people in the industry.

Another option is to use the contacts of your TEFL course provider. Employers very often have close links with schools and colleges in the UK or other English speaking countries. Ask your tutor about job vacancies early on in your course and you may just get a head start on your classmates.

Two newspapers in the UK advertise TEFL positions regularly: one is *The Times Educational Supplement* which comes out on Fridays and the other is *The Guardian*, which publishes an extensive Education section on Tuesdays.

Some larger chains of language schools have job opportunities worldwide. Keep in mind that the academic year starts in September, so start sending these organisations your CV in the summer. Apply in March and April for summer jobs. In most cases you write to the director of studies and include a brief covering letter.

I have seen too many CVs wind up in the bin because of poor grammar and spelling. So check and double check before you send yours off because if your English is poor, you don't stand a chance of getting a job teaching English. And try to make your CV as relevant as possible by emphasising experiences where you travelled, learned a foreign language, taught someone or managed people.

Potential employers you can try include:

- ✔ English First, known as EF advertises scores of vacancies worldwide. Take a look at their website www.ef.com.

- ✔ Language Link has vacancies in Europe and Asia. Its website is www.languagelink.co.uk.

- ✔ Wall Street Institute International employs graduate teachers without a TEFL certificate in their schools around the world. See www.wsi.com for worldwide vacancies.

- ✔ Avalon School have a network of affiliated schools throughout Europe, Brazil, Poland, China and France, and its main branch in central London. Email dos@avalonschool.co.uk with your CV. You must have a degree and TEFL certificate to apply.

- ✔ VSO – short for Voluntary Service Overseas – offers placements in Africa and Asia, preferably to graduates. Salaries are modest but VSO provides accommodation and you can apply for various grants. See www.vso.org.uk. You need to be under 68 years of age to apply.

- ✔ International House has an excellent reputation for teaching worldwide and operates in about 30 countries. Contact hr@ihlondon.co.uk for vacancies if you have a recognised TEFL certificate.

- ✔ Bell International operates in 18 countries. It advertises vacancies on its website at www.bell-worldwide.com.

Part II
Putting Your Lesson Together

The 5th Wave   By Rich Tennant

ENGLISH AS A FOREIGN LANGUAGE
LESSON 1:
PRO WRESTLING – REAL OR FAKE?

"Let's move on to the second part of the lesson which is 'How To Counter A Reverse Arm Bar.'"

In this part . . .

*B*eing able to structure and deliver a lesson effectively and engagingly is what TEFL is all about. This part gives you the inside track on how to do just that.

In the chapters in this part, I break the lesson down into different stages (Presentation, Practice and Production), so that you can see how to deliver a clear structure for learning. I also provide advice on how long the stages should last and who should be doing the talking, and how to engage your students in learning.

This part teems with examples and suggestions for classroom activities, whether you use a course book or design your own materials. You can find out when and how to correct the students' mistakes and keep them in check – and interested – during the lesson.

Chapter 4

Starting from the Beginning: Planning the Lesson

So you get the job and the students enrol on your course, ready to get started. But what on earth are you going to teach them and how are you going to put it together into a lesson? In this chapter, I tell you about the content and structure of an EFL (English as a Foreign Language) lesson.

Deciding What to Teach

When you select information to teach in your lessons, you need to think about what level the students are at and how well your lesson fits into what they already know and what they need to know.

Most courses have a basic syllabus that acts as a road map. An EFL *syllabus* lists the major areas of grammar, vocabulary and functions (what you can do with particular expressions) a course covers. Most EFL course books have a list within the first few pages. Even if you're working from your own materials, it makes sense to set specific course goals including which words and grammar you definitely want to cover.

However, when you begin teaching it can be quite difficult to know what students are likely to comprehend at each level and few EFL teachers follow the same students from beginner to advanced level.

So to give you a guide, the next sections offer a basic run down of what you may expect to teach students at the different levels. I include a list of grammar and vocabulary students should cover during the course, along with examples.

Unlike many other courses people enrol on, EFL courses can be for adults or children and include students with an incredibly wide range of interests and goals. However, their basic needs in learning are similar. For example, all students want to learn how to speak about the past, present and future in English.

Beginner

Beginner-level students aren't necessarily children. Many people discover a need or desire to study English later in life. Students at beginner level can't speak or write accurately in the present simple and present continuous tenses. Those who know some words in English but aren't ready to join elementary level are called False Beginners. When there's no distinct beginner's class, beginner level is absorbed within the first 15–20 hours of an elementary course. This is a difficult level to teach as you have so few words to work with when explaining things but it's also very rewarding because every new word marks significant progress for the class.

Grammar to cover includes:

- The subject pronouns: I, you, he, she and so on.
- Demonstrative pronouns: this, that, these, those.
- Question words: what, who, where and how.
- Possessive adjectives: my, your, his and hers.
- Singular and plural nouns.
- Expletives (not the naughty ones): there is, there are.
- The verb *to be* in positive, negative and question form: I am, I am not, am I?

Vocabulary to cover includes:

- The alphabet.
- Numbers 1 to 100.
- Jobs: doctor, teacher, taxi driver.

- ✔ Countries and nationalities: 'He is from the UK. He's British.'
- ✔ Basic food: fruit, vegetables, meat.
- ✔ Days of the week.
- ✔ Everyday objects: bag, pen, telephone.
- ✔ Immediate family: mother, son, husband.
- ✔ Rooms in the house: living room, bathroom, kitchen.

Elementary

At elementary level, students learn to use many more verbs instead of only *to be* (I am, you are, it is). This is because with other verbs you have to use '*to do*' as an auxiliary verb, which is rather strange for them and quite different from other languages (Do you like apples? No, I don't). At this level students learn to talk and ask about matters related to daily routines. They also begin to refer to past and future time.

Grammar to cover includes:

- ✔ Basic verbs in the present simple positive, negative and question forms: I live, I don't live, do I live?
- ✔ Simple adverbs of frequency: usually, sometimes.
- ✔ Quantities: How much, how many? Some, any.
- ✔ Showing ability: using can/can't.
- ✔ The past simple tense with *to be*: was/were.
- ✔ Future simple tense: I will go.
- ✔ Past simple tense with regular verbs: I looked, I listened.

Vocabulary to cover includes:

- ✔ Simple adjectives: opposites, colours.
- ✔ Language for telling the time: hat time is it? It's half past three.
- ✔ Language for shopping: types of shops, asking for what you want.
- ✔ Asking for directions: straight ahead, turn left/right.
- ✔ Months and years.
- ✔ Weather: What's the weather like? It's raining.
- ✔ Comparative adjectives: bigger, nicer, and so on (superlatives wait until the next level).

Pre-intermediate

At pre-intermediate level students learn to discuss their experiences and future plans. They learn vocabulary related to travelling. In addition they're able to discuss leisure activities and explain their preferences.

Grammar to cover includes:

- Modal verbs: These give more meaning to the main verb in a sentence. Two examples are: can/can't and must/mustn't. *I can't wait any more because I must get to the shops.*

- Possessive pronouns: mine, yours and so on.

- To be going to: This isn't a tense but you use this structure to talk about plans. *I am going to study medicine at university.*

- Present perfect tense: I've eaten.

- Past simple tense with irregular verbs: I ate, I thought.

- Past continuous tense: I was eating.

- Adverbs: slowly, well.

Vocabulary to cover includes:

- Types of films: comedy, western, thriller.

- Clothes: trousers, shirt, coat.

- Hobbies and interests: jogging, eating out, reading.

- Language for booking hotels and restaurants: Can I book a single room please?

- Landscape words: mountain, river, field.

- Parts of the body: shoulder, knee.

- Superlatives: the best, the most wonderful.

Intermediate

At this level students tend to lose their initial enthusiasm for learning English. They already know how to make sentences that refer to the past, present and future and they have a basic vocabulary for everyday situations. However, at this level the language you teach adds sophistication and fluency, instead of basic communication. It becomes harder for students to measure their progress so you need to work hard at maintaining interest by using topics they really enjoy.

Grammar to cover includes:

- More modal verbs: (should, may, might). Too many modal verbs exist to teach at once so you teach a few at a time.
- Zero conditional: If it rains, I use my umbrella.
- First conditional: If it rains, I'll use my umbrella.
- Second conditional: If it rained, I'd use my umbrella.
- Non-defining relative clauses: The man, *who I thought looked great,* was at the office.
- Gerunds and infinitives: *going* and *to go.*
- The verb *will* for spontaneous decisions: I'll pay!
- Present perfect continuous tense: I have been singing, he has been dancing.
- Past perfect tense: They had seen it, you had not watched it.

Vocabulary to cover includes:

- Comparing and contrasting: both, neither, whereas.
- Polite forms: Would you mind? I'm afraid I can't.
- Expressions for generalising: On the whole, in general.
- Stages of life: infancy, childhood.
- Reviewing films, books and so on: describing the plot, characters, strengths and weaknesses.

Upper-intermediate

At this level students can speak and write with reasonable fluency using a range of tenses and expressions for linking ideas. They can use appropriate language in a variety of situations demonstrating an understanding of formal and informal language.

Grammar to cover includes:

- To have something done: students are used to speaking about actions they do themselves. With this grammatical structure they can express the idea of paying or instructing other people to do things. For example, *I had my house painted.*
- Third conditional: If I had known, I wouldn't have done it.
- Reported speech: She said that she . . .
- Defining relative clauses: The man *who is standing over there* is nervous.

✔ Modal verbs in the past: I could have come.

✔ Passive verb forms: The room was cleaned.

✔ The verb *to wish*: I wish I could go, you wish you were me (after *wish* you use a verb in one of the past tenses, so students have to learn this verb separately)

✔ To be used to/ to get used to: *I'm used to London now but I'm still getting used to my new job.* Students easily confuse these two grammatical structures for familiar activities and activities that are becoming familiar .

✔ Past perfect continuous tense: I had been working.

✔ Future perfect: I will have written it.

Vocabulary to cover includes:

✔ Adjectives of personality: generous, manipulative.

✔ Medical problems: ache, bruise, sprain.

✔ Crime words: to arrest, fraud, mugging.

✔ Feelings: hurt, fascinated, relieved.

✔ Science and technology words: software, appliance.

✔ Media and communications words: broadcasting, the press.

Advanced

Students at this level are able to communicate with native speakers without much difficulty. They get the gist of most texts and conversations and have sufficient vocabulary to express themselves on a wide variety of topics. The grammar and vocabulary they use is similar to that of native speakers even when it's not strictly necessary to be understood. Question tags, which I show in the following grammar list, provide a good example of this.

Grammar to cover includes:

✔ Prefixes and suffixes: **un**like, like**able.**

✔ Compound nouns: tooth + paste = toothpaste.

✔ Ellipsis and substitutions (words you can leave out or replace with something else): *This one is bigger. One* represents another noun so it's a substitution. Sometimes you leave words out completely because the meaning is clear. For example: *This one is bigger (than the other thing).* When I leave out the words in brackets it's an example of ellipsis.

✔ Question tags: You like that, *don't you*?

✔ Active and stative verbs (actions and conditions): She bought (active) a motorbike and also owns (stative) a car.

✔ Future perfect continuous tense: I will have been working.

✔ Detailed rules on phrasal verbs: Phrasal verbs consist of a verb and a preposition or two that together make a new meaning. For example: *to get on with someone, to put up with something.*

Vocabulary to cover includes:

✔ General idioms. An idiom is a phrase that has a meaning quite different from the individual words within it. For example, students may understand all the words: it + is + a + pain + in + the + neck. However they won't get the point unless you explain what the whole expression means.

✔ Newspaper headlines. There are a number of words that are favourites for newspapers but hardly used elsewhere, for example, *Minister Rapped After Expenses Probe.* Journalists also like to be very playful with the language. They use nicknames, rhymes, and slang and students want to be in on the joke so that they can understand the press for themselves. However, it sometimes takes a great deal of explaining and a detailed analysis of the language for students to get the point.

✔ Words with different connotations. *Old* and *elderly* have basically the same meaning. However, *elderly* is more polite than *old* when referring to people, so the connotation (attitude behind the word) is different. When students understand that words have similar meanings they also need to know the subtle but important differences between them.

✔ Metaphors and similes. You use metaphors when you say that one thing is another because they're somehow similar. *There was a storm of protest. Storm is a word that describes violent weather conditions but here it means a violent outburst.

Proficiency

It's pretty difficult to come up with a syllabus for proficiency level as many of the questions are more like A-level English for native speakers. Proficiency has more exercises based on inference (reading between the lines).

Keeping Things Relevant

Not only do you teach according to the students' level – a concept called *grading* – you also teach what is relevant and useful to them.

So if the syllabus for beginners doesn't include detailed descriptions of furniture but your student works in the sofa shop, you can adapt the syllabus to fit in relevant vocabulary. On the other hand, if your class is made up of children, they may not recognise half of the professions on your list of job titles, in which case you can drop the professions list and substitute names of games or sports equipment.

A good syllabus covers not what people *can* say in English but what they actually need to say or usually say.

For example, it's grammatically correct to say, 'I shall depart forthwith', but when was the last time you heard someone come out with that?

TEFL is not about language as beauty; it's about language as communication. So, select the practical bits and keep anything else to a minimum.

For example, the occasional poem is a great demonstration of culture and rhythm in English, but don't handle poetry as though you're teaching a literature course, going into all the artistic features. Just find aspects related to the syllabus and everyday life.

Getting into Grading

In TEFL you *grade* what you say so that things become progressively more difficult step by step. It's a bit like climbing a hill with a gradual incline. If the hill is too steep, your students get exhausted before they near the top; too flat and they become bored with the familiar and inattentive. Figure 4-1 shows a good learning slope.

Figure 4-1:
A good
grading
system
gets more
difficult
gradually.

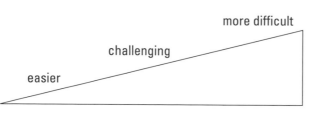

more difficult

challenging

easier

You start by teaching your students the word *bathroom*. It's not a difficult word, and it's one used every day, more or less. But a student at a low level doesn't know the word, and you explain it this way:

It's the room where you have a sink, and a mirror and a bath.

It's the place where you brush your teeth.

This explanation is an example of poor grading. Logically, if your student knew both the words 'bath' and 'room' they would understand 'bathroom' without too much trouble, so using these in the explanation doesn't help them. The other words like 'sink' and 'mirror' are even more difficult.

A better approach at the right level for your student is to approach bathroom by starting with 'house'. Make sure that everyone knows the word by drawing or showing a picture and saying 'What is it?' Then divide the picture into separate areas and teach 'rooms'. Show a picture of a bathroom or do a mime of someone taking a shower to teach 'bathroom'.

Good grading influences many things you do in the classroom. You need to keep grading in mind on a couple of levels:

- ✔ **Grading a lesson.** To grade a lesson well you need to select new language that builds on what students already know. Students should have sufficient knowledge to grasp the concept. During the lesson too, you grade by explaining to students how to complete a task using rules, reminders and examples before actually setting the task. Each task in the lesson should also be more challenging than the one before it.

- ✔ **Grading the course.** You want a logical order within the course syllabus too. This means that the grammar and vocabulary should get more difficult as you go along and the skills tasks (reading, writing, listening and speaking) should only include language that has already been taught or is under consideration in that lesson. So you can't really teach the names of ailments before you've done the parts of the body. Or, it doesn't make sense to teach the past continuous tense before you've done the past simple.

A well graded lesson starts simply and builds.

Within a lesson, it helps to have particular activities for your students to work on.

Say you want your students to write a letter telling their friends back home about tourist sights in the UK. List what your students need to know in order to complete the task:

- ✔ Present simple tense
- ✔ There is/there are
- ✔ The layout of a letter in English
- ✔ Expressions such as 'Dear . . . ' and 'Best wishes'
- ✔ How to spell the names of the sights
- ✔ Adjectives for describing places

If your students don't know any of these things, you may want to reconsider whether they're ready for the task. It's really discouraging for your students when you set the activity and then start back pedalling because the class can't cope.

A letter writing session with students who know the grammar can have a running order like this:

1. Students read a letter from one friend to another and analyse the layout and typical expressions.

2. You explain that the class is going to write letters about the UK and have them brainstorm their favourite sights.

3. Find out why students like the sights and put the adjectives they use on the board.

4. Put a plan of the letter on the board showing how many paragraphs to write and what kind of information should go in each one.

5. Have them write.

Setting Aims and Objectives

At the planning stage of your lesson, you need to think about your aims and objectives:

✔ **Aims** are the overall points you want students to understand as a result of the lesson.

Sample aims may be:

- To provide revision and practice of the present perfect.

- To increase rapport amongst the students.

- To teach vocabulary for hobbies and interests.

- To teach students to express likes and dislikes using the structure I (don't) like + a *gerund* (a verb with 'ing' added).

✔ **Objectives** are the skills you want students to be able to demonstrate by the end of the lesson or their accomplishments during the lesson. Objectives relate to specific activities.

Sample objectives may include specific goals, for instance that students should:

- Be able to compare their travel experiences with other people by saying 'Have you ever . . . ?'

- Write a questionnaire using verbs associated with travel in the present perfect, and try it out on at least three other students.

- Learn the vocabulary for their hobbies and interests, including pronunciation.

- Know when to use the gerund and when to use the noun.

- Know how to write sentences requiring the gerund.

- Discuss their likes and interests together in groups

Even in a conversation class you ought to have a clear idea of what you intend the lesson to accomplish.

Both you and your students benefit when you write down your aims and objectives:

✔ You consider the lesson from the students' perspective as well as your own.

✔ There's less likelihood that you'll go off on a tangent during the lesson.

✔ You can assess the relevance and effectiveness of activities you intend to use more easily by seeing whether they're closely linked to the aims and objectives of the lesson.

Getting Your Timing Down and Planning for Interaction

A very important factor to consider when putting your lesson together is the amount of time available to you and how you want to spend it. English lessons can vary from 45 minutes to 3 hours but there is a basic format for dividing the time: an initial stage in which you teach new information; another in which you practise what you've just presented in a controlled way and a final stage that involves students expressing themselves with less guidance from you. These stages are called Presentation, Practice and Production respectively. Each stage is longer than the one before it so that the students end up doing most of the talking.

So if the triangle in Figure 4-2 represents a one-hour lesson, P1 (Presentation) would be about 15 minutes, then P2 (Practice) about 20 minutes and finally P3 (Production) about 25 minutes.

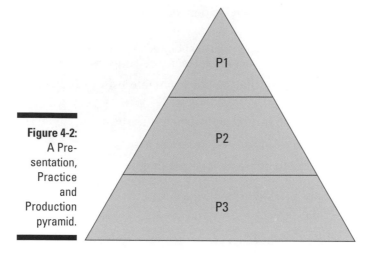

Figure 4-2:
A Presentation, Practice and Production pyramid.

Within each stage and throughout the lesson, think about who should be talking to whom – the *interaction patterns*. You want to plan it so that you don't end up speaking for too long and the students keep busy. The traditional way of doing this is by using abbreviations like these in the margin of your lesson plan:

- ✔ **T-ST:** The teacher talks to the students
- ✔ **ST-T:** The students give feedback to the teacher
- ✔ **ST-ST**: The students talk to each other
- ✔ **Pr:** Students work in pairs
- ✔ **Gr:** Students work in groups

Figure 4-3 shows an example from a lesson plan.

Figure 4-3:
A sample lesson plan sets out time and interaction patterns.

Presentation

Tell ST an anecdote about last weekend using

| watched | listened | enjoyed | **2mins** | *T-ST* |

Ask ST to tell me what I did while I write it up on the board · **2mins** · *ST-T*

Underline the regular past simple verbs and point out ...ed ending · **2mins** · *T-ST*

Assembling Presentation, Practice and Production

After you decide what you want to teach, you need to have a explain matters to the class thoroughly and efficiently.

Introducing the point

If you chose language at the right level for your students, there's a good chance that they've heard it before. Or it may be that some students recognise it, although you can't rely on that fact. So first of all you need to find an interesting way to bring this new language to their attention.

Usually EFL teachers prefer to make their students curious rather than to simply state: 'Today's lesson is all about . . . ' In the real world, people learn language in context rather than through direct statements or recited rules. As a child, your family probably never mentioned grammar, they just spoke. By the same token, introducing language within a story of some kind, a conversation or with the aid of a picture or object is very effective.

Analysing the point

After introducing the new language, perhaps by means of a story or picture that creates a realistic context in an interesting way you analyse it. You explain whatever rules, patterns or information the students need to make the language their own in this stage. For example, for a vocabulary lesson teaching several fruits you begin with a picture of a market stall and move on to highlight and name the pears, grapes and so on.

Make a connection between what students already know and the new language – add a new building block to their language tower.

Use the board to set things out clearly so that the class can take notes. Provide examples so that they have a guide as they complete the tasks later in the lesson.

If there are several ways to use the new word or grammar point, don't overload the students by trying to cover everything all at once. You can have a 'Part 2' lesson later on.

Use this analysis stage to explain and check your students' understanding before you move on to practising. Don't take anything for granted. Ask lots of questions so that the students can demonstrate that they get it (rather than just saying they do). As this is the stage where you get to do more of the talking, make the time count.

Trialling the language

Following the presentation stage in which you introduce new language, you need to set up an activity or task that requires the students to focus on it.

A good practice activity is one which:

- **The students can do together without the teacher.** You can step back and make notes on any errors or teaching points that come up during the activity.

- **Makes the new language point vital to completing the task**. This ensures that the students concentrate on using it.

- **Is communicative in whole or in part.** This means that the students should not work individually throughout the lesson. They need to interact with each other. So, for example, even if the students are working on a written exercise, they should be able to compare and discuss the answers with other students in pairs or groups. This may happen while they complete it, or afterwards.

- **Is structured so that students must actually understand the new point in order to use it properly.** If the students are simply following a pattern they may not put much thought into it and end up not being able to use it later. Take a look at two examples in Figure 4-4.

The bad exercise is poor because the students only needs to work out that they need to add 's' to the verb. The next example requires more thought because the learner has to work out which pronoun to use as well as how to change the form of the verb.

Bad exercise

Example: He/like/cats – He likes cats

1) She/drink/coffee – She ....

2) It/eat/fish – It ....

Good exercise

Example: What is Peter's favourite animal? (like)

He likes cats

1) What does Mrs Smith do in the morning? (drink/coffee)

....

2) What does the cat have for dinner? (eat/fish)

....

Figure 4-4:
Bad and
good
exercises.

Giving your students free practice

By the time you reach the production stage of the lesson, the students should be fairly comfortable with the new language point. After all, they've heard what you had to say about it and practised it for themselves. Now, in this stage they get to practise in a freer way. In the production stage the aim is for the students to be fluent and use the language in a natural way rather than just an accurate way.

When students engage in free production activities, they have a chance to express themselves and show off all they know that's relevant to the topic. They have the opportunity to use the new language point but they can decide when to use it and when to opt for something else.

Storytelling is a typical activity for production exercises. There's a theme but not a sentence by sentence structure. Other activities include debates and report writing. In Chapter 6 I talk about ideas for practice and production activities and how to use them.

Stepping Out of the Spotlight to Let Your Students Shine

In the TEFL industry, *TTT*, or Teacher Talking Time, is seen as something to be minimised. Unlike the traditional image most people have of what a teacher does, in TEFL, it isn't a good thing to be standing at the board talking for the majority of the lesson for several reasons:

- ✔ **Students need time to practise speaking in the lesson and if the teacher hogs the limelight this becomes difficult.** Bearing in mind that the lesson is sometimes the only opportunity the student has to speak English, it would be tragic if the only person speaking is the one who already knows the language perfectly.

- ✔ **Students get bored when they have to sit listening**. Much better to have them actively involved in a task or interaction.

- ✔ **Lectures leave no room for progress checks**. Students need to demonstrate understanding throughout the lesson, which means they need to speak and write. Even if they smile and nod while you're speaking, it doesn't guarantee understanding.

You can employ a variety of techniques to avoid talking too much to the detriment of your students:

- ✔ **Encourage students to solve problems.** Whenever possible, get students to work things out for themselves. Eliciting means asking students questions that lead them where you want them to be. So ask focused questions instead of making statements.

- ✔ **Promote learner independence.** Encourage your students to develop strategies that allow them to cope without you. For example, show them how to organise information in their notebooks in a logical fashion so that they end up with a sound reference book, instead of asking you all the time.

- ✔ **Make dictionaries available.** If there's a class set of English-English dictionaries (with the key word and the definition both in English instead of translated from language into another) in the classroom, you won't have to define every difficult word.

Lesson planning checklist

Use this checklist to make sure that you're prepared for each lesson.

❑ I know what level my students are at.

❑ I know who my students are – their nationality, language, background and so on.

❑ I know how long the lesson is.

❑ I set aims and objectives.

❑ What I want to teach fits in with the course syllabus.

❑ I know what my students need to know about this piece of language – its rules, patterns and so on.

❑ I have an appropriate context for this language point.

❑ I anticipated problems and have thought of ways to prevent them from occurring.

❑ I have a planned activity or exercise for providing controlled practice.

❑ I have a planned activity for providing free practice.

❑ I have any materials I need.

❑ My activities are communicative, which means the students spend some time interacting with each other to complete a task.

❑ My teacher talking time is 30 per cent or under.

You can find lesson planning templates in Appendix A.

✔ **Write your interaction patterns into your plans.** On your lesson plan, indicate who is speaking to whom and for how long. Plan TTT (teacher talking time) for no more than 30 per cent of the lesson time. This helps maintain a good balance.

✔ **Simplify your classroom language.** Avoid rambling and overly polite language. I'm not suggesting that you be rude but it's far easier for students to cope with 'Open your books to exercise F on page 10 please', than 'If you're all finished then, we'll just take a little look at an exercise; the one on page 10. Yes that's right, it's exercise F I think'.

✔ **Write up instructions.** When you write up instructions on the board (perhaps while the students are busy doing something else) you don't have to repeat yourself later on.

✔ **Drawing and miming.** Use these techniques to get students describing what you're doing so that you don't have to engage in long explanations.

✔ **Wait patiently for the student to answer.** Try not to jump in too soon. Your students may just get there if you allow them a little more time to answer the question.

- ✔ **Avoid echoing.** Over enthusiasm may make you repeat everything the student says as though you're egging them on, but this is unproductive and increases TTT.

- ✔ **Ask open questions.** Open questions start with words like 'why' and 'how' so the student can't just say 'yes' and 'no' in response.

- ✔ **Monitor quietly.** Once you get the students working in pairs and groups, try not to butt in. Just listen and make notes.

Chapter 5

Standing in the Spotlight: Presenting to the Class

. . . .

In This Chapter

▶ Asking for answers

▶ Using visual aids

▶ Making sure that your students understand

▶ Expanding vocabulary

▶ Using proper grammar

. . . .

Y ou generally divide a lesson into three distinct parts – Presentation, Practice and Production. This chapter concentrates on the Presentation stage of the lesson and I show you what to include.

The Presentation stage of the lesson is the shortest stage, and happens right at the beginning. The teacher explains the new words or grammar as thoroughly as possible using examples, definitions, pictures, tables and so on. During this stage the students should get all the information they need to use the new piece of language well and complete the tasks that follow in the Practice and Production stages.

Eliciting Answers – Ask, Don't Tell!

Eliciting means getting your students to tell you what they know by using questions instead of simply giving them the information.

In your mind you need to be several steps ahead of the students throughout the lesson. So the questions you ask should keep them mentally active and move them along to the next step. Elicitation questions are generally short and snappy. For example, ask the class how to spell words, for the meaning, for examples, for similar words and opposites, what they remember about a previously taught point, and so on. You can use props and pictures if they help to clarify the meaning or add interest.

The pros and cons of using this technique are set out in the following list, but most teachers find it very useful.

The pros first:

- ✔ **Eliciting keeps your class on their toes.** They're interested and involved because they have constant opportunities for interaction. Passively listening for extended periods is dull, so in EFL you rarely give lecture-style presentations.

- ✔ **Eliciting gets the students guessing.** When you ask them questions they try to work things out spontaneously. This is a great skill because in the real world your students often have to take a stab at the meaning of words or sentences and may not have anyone there to explain. So, being prepared to have a go and guess is a good habit.

- ✔ **Students really understand what's going on.** When you elicit, you're getting regular feedback from the students so you can gauge whether or not they're with you, so to speak.

- ✔ **You reduce Teacher Talking Time (TTT).** As the students should do most of the talking in a lesson, eliciting allows you to reduce TTT and instead, keep students interacting with you.

Eliciting has a few drawbacks, though:

- ✔ **It can drag on.** If your students don't get the point quickly (possibly because you're asking the wrong questions) this stage of the lesson can be rather long and drawn out. It's definitely quicker to just tell the students what's what.

- ✔ **It encourages dominant students.** Far be it from me to suggest that you may have a teacher's pet in your class but it has been known to happen. Sometimes you have one student who has their hand up permanently, or who you know is pretty smart, so that one student ends up answering all the elicitation questions. This is obviously annoying for everyone else.

- ✔ **Poor or excessive eliciting may put students' backs up.** If your questions are too easy the class may feel that you're somewhat condescending and refuse to answer. The class may also wonder whether you're capable of uttering a simple statement if you seem to turn everything into a question.

With these points in mind, follow a few suggestions when eliciting to make it a positive experience for your students:

- ✔ Make sure that your questions have a definite answer that the class has a good chance of guessing or knowing – no vague questions.

✔ Deal with learners according to their level; don't try to elicit an intermediate level answer from an elementary level student.

✔ Once students are speaking, don't cut them off mid-sentence. Remember that one of the aims of eliciting is to increase student talking time.

Creating Interest with Visual Aids

Visual images and aids add interest and often add meaning in a way that words can't. This is especially true of EFL students who don't have sufficient words to understand detailed spoken explanations.

Showing and telling – pictures and objects

People learn in different ways. For example, some people learn well by listening (*auditory learning*), some by movement and touch (*kinaesthetic learning*) and many people respond well to seeing things (*visual learning*). These are some of the different learning styles. So having variety in your presentations gives attention to these different styles and helps everyone succeed.

Bringing something of interest into the classroom gets students quite excited – there's a certain novelty value involved in pictures and objects you personally have chosen.

Things visual learners love to see in a presentation include:

✔ **Flash cards:** Not just for primary school, flashcards are good fun for adults and children alike. The traditional flashcard has a picture on the front and the equivalent word in writing on the back or below. By holding up one side of the card you can elicit the information on the other side.

You can use flash cards for vocabulary groups such as jobs, food, animals, weather and hobbies. Or how about having the infinitive verb form on the front, and the past simple and past participle on the back? Likewise, try having opposites front and back.

✔ **Drawings:** A simple stick figure drawing is enough to make students smile and give them something to talk about. If you're a bit nervous about your art work, do it before the lesson and then just stick your picture to the board. Use a clipart website if you really can't draw anything recognisable.

✔ **Photos:** Celebrity photos seem to work particularly well in EFL lessons, perhaps because of the glamorous international flavour they give your lesson. Save old magazines, or even catalogues, as photographs are great for explaining the meaning of a word, or setting a context.

✔ **Videos:** Short video clips really grab your students' attention and lend themselves to further activities in the practice and production stages, which I cover in Chapter 6.

✔ **Realia:** The term for real objects you use to help you teach. Students feel involved when they get to touch something or move it around. Realia works to reinforce learning for visual and kinaesthetic learners alike.

In a lesson aimed at teaching 'used to' and 'any more' to contrast the past and present, you can bring in an old childhood photograph. I usually bring in a photograph of myself aged ten, dressed in school uniform and complete with dodgy 70s hairdo. First you find out if the students recognise you. Let them have a giggle and guess how old you are in the picture. Then tell them that you had hobbies at that age and ask students to make suggestions about what they were. Show the clues like stamps or a skipping rope. With each suggestion say 'Yes, I used to . . . ' or 'No, I didn't used to . . . '. When they've guessed one or two hobbies correctly you can switch to the present and ask whether they think that you still do that activity. This leads to the statement, 'I don't do it any more'.

You can sometimes find cheap children's games and activities that you can adapt for the classroom. For example, children's playing cards are often pictorial, showing animals or a variety of jobs. Model cars and trains are useful when you explain transport words or describe directions (left, right, forwards and so on).

Travelling along timelines and tenses

In TEFL and in Western cultures in general, you represent time as a straight horizontal line showing the past on the left and the future to the right. With a timeline, you can show how tenses refer to an aspect of time and compare them. So timelines are most common in a presentation of a new tense.

By using timelines you help students to understand the function of a tense – what it does basically. However, you need to highlight the form of a tense or piece of grammar too. In other words, show exactly what it looks like.

Showing simple tenses

When you want to show that an action is in a simple tense (present simple, past simple, or future simple) you put an individual point on the timeline with an X or a spot and label it, as in Figure 5-1.

Figure 5-1: The spot marks when I went to the cinema.

With a simple label you can elicit a statement in the past simple tense: 'I went to the cinema'.

Likewise, you can demonstrate the simple future tense, as Figure 5-2 does for the statement, 'I will go on holiday'.

Figure 5-2: Showing the simple, but hopefully fun, future.

Carrying through with continuous tenses

An action in a continuous tense (present continuous, past continuous and so on) should occupy more space on the timeline. You can emphasise the duration of time by using continuous X's or a wavy line as in Figure 5-3.

Figure 5-3: Continuous tenses take more room.

You can use a similar method to show an action in the present perfect that started in the past but continues into the present.

From the timeline in Figure 5-4, you can elicit 'I have lived/ have been living in London for a while'.

Figure 5-4:
The present
perfect on a
timeline.

Adapting the timeline

When you use a timeline you can use specific times, days, months or years instead of past, present and future. In addition to that, you don't need to include both ends of the line if one isn't relevant.

In Figure 5-5, the timeline shows two actions in the past so the students can see what happened first and what happened later. For example, 'I was hungry this morning because I hadn't eaten', which illustrates the past simple and past perfect tenses respectively.

Figure 5-5:
Showing the
past simple
and perfect.

Using the board effectively

Whenever you use the board, the first thing you should check is whether you have markers that work – pens or chalk – and then make sure that all the students can see the board. You may need to alter the seating.

Keep your board clutter-free at all costs. Nothing frustrates a student more than looking down at his notebook for a second, then looking up again to see a board so disorganised and busy that he can't find the thing he wanted to copy down. Rub off information you no longer need. Clean the board before and after each lesson.

Whatever you have on the board should be legible and logical. Some good practices for board work are:

- ✔ Writing in a straight line.
- ✔ Using different colours.
- ✔ Dividing the board into sections if you have slightly different fields to consider.
- ✔ Stepping back to check spelling and punctuation.

If you're a bit poor at spelling, have dictionaries in the classroom and encourage students to check words for you as you write.

You can use the board quite a few ways to make meaning clearer through diagrams in the Presentation stage. For example, use diagrams like the one in Figure 5-6 to show clearly the relationship between items of vocabulary, including subordinate groups or categories. You can have students add words to each group to demonstrate that they understand. It's a fairly simple diagram to copy down too.

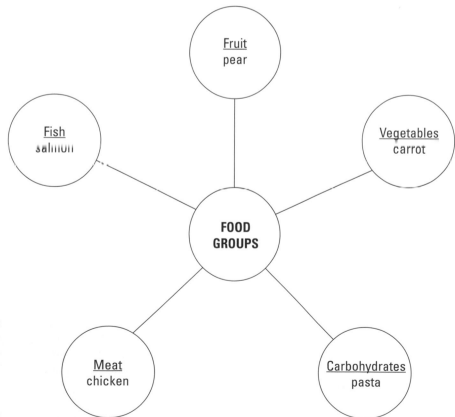

Figure 5-6:
Showing relationships on the board.

Fruit
pear

Fish
salmon

Vegetables
carrot

FOOD
GROUPS

Meat
chicken

Carbohydrates
pasta

In Figure 5-7, I show some words for weather and how they're related. You could elicit from the students a temperature for each box, for example.

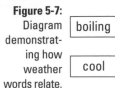

Figure 5-7:
Diagram demonstrating how weather words relate.

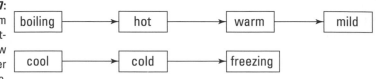

So, the way you organise words on the board can show a hierarchy or a scale from most to least, best to worst and so on.

Depending on the topic, you can draw a chart or label a diagram to give visual input. For grammar presentations, charts and equations are very common.

In a lesson about asking questions, you can lay out the structure on the board this way:

Question word +	Auxiliary verb +	Subject word +	Infinitive verb
How	does	he	travel?
Why	can	Roger	eat?
Where	will	the girls	stay?

Try to keep talking as you write on the board. Otherwise the atmosphere in class goes flat because of the silence and the fact that your back is turned. The students may also get up to mischief if you don't keep them busy so it's a good idea to elicit as you write.

Doing Concept Checks

It's never useful to ask students if they understand. After all, how do they know whether they've misunderstood until they end up getting it wrong? So instead, you need to find out by getting the students to demonstrate understanding, usually through *concept check* questions. Concept check questions are questions that test understanding. For example, a concept check question for the word 'breakfast' is 'What time do people usually eat breakfast?' The student is only likely to get the answer right if he understands that breakfast is a morning meal.

Translation isn't used in most EFL classrooms, but it's an easy way to check that students understand certain words. Sometimes you can do a straight, like-for-like substitution from one language to another. In this case the students translate in their heads by simply changing the label. However, checking a concept can be a challenging exercise when different cultural or religious perceptions are involved. For example, a bed may involve a mattress, headboard and base for some, a mat on the floor for others or a hammock for yet another culture. Is a bed a piece of furniture or just a place where you sleep?

If you don't make clear what the concept behind the English word is, lines can become blurred.

Boundaries also exist between one word and another, and you need to define them. So for example what's the difference between a bench and a sofa in practical and design terms? Clearly you can't just describe them as long chairs.

Concept check questions come in various forms:

- **Yes/no:** It's quick and easy to ask closed questions. So for example, if you're teaching vocabulary for vehicles you can ask:

    - Is a van bigger than a car?

    - Is a car bigger than a lorry?

    Of course to make these questions work, the answer shouldn't always be yes or always be no. If it is, the students can work at your pattern and just bluff.

- **Multiple choice:** Offering students a range of possibilities is another good way to concept check. Multiple choice questions don't require students to come up with the vocabulary for the answer themselves but they do require a little more thought than closed questions if the options are similar. For example, in a lesson on the present perfect, ask students to tell you whether the action in the statement 'I have seen the pyramids'. is in the past, the present or both past and present.

- **Open questions:** When you ask students questions that start with words like 'who', 'how' and 'why', their answers needs to go beyond 'yes' or 'no'. They really have to think about it and use their own words to explain.

- **Physical response:** Another approach is to ask the students to actually do something to show they understand. A phrasal verb is a verb together with a preposition that has a new meaning, often different from the meaning of the verb by itself. 'To pick' means to select whereas the phrasal verb 'to pick up' means to raise it from a surface. You can read more about phrasal verbs in Chapter 17. So for example, during a lesson on phrasal verbs including 'pick up' and 'hold on' you can give commands such as: 'Pick up your purple pen now but hold on until I say "Write this down"'. If they do what you say you can tell that they understand.

Don't spend time on inessentials. A basic object like a bath plug doesn't really warrant having much time spent on it as most people rarely say the word, and a verbal explanation is more complex than the object itself.

Introducing Vocabulary

When it comes to teaching vocabulary, the Presentation stage can include a combination of any of these things:

- ✔ **Meaning:** Sometimes a straightforward definition
- ✔ **Synonyms:** Similar words
- ✔ **Antonyms:** Opposites
- ✔ **Connotation:** The emotion a word conveys
- ✔ **Spelling:** Self, explanatory, hopefully
- ✔ **Collocation:** Words that fit together
- ✔ **Syntax:** An explanation of how a word fits into a sentence grammatically

  'To like' is followed by a noun, an infinitive or a gerund: to like something, to like to do something and to like doing something.

- ✔ **Register:** How (in)formal it is.
- ✔ **Pronunciation:** This can include transcription into phonemes, marking the stressed syllable and drilling (repeating).
- ✔ **Word families:** You can introduce other words that come from the same root. For example:

  - to inherit (verb)
  - inheritance (noun, thing)
  - hereditary (adjective)
  - heir (noun, person)
  - heiress (noun, woman only)

- ✔ **Visuals:** Pictures, mimes, realia, board work and so on.
- ✔ **Part of speech:** A noun, a verb and so on. (I talk about the parts of speech in Chapter 15.)

Aim to teach only about seven new words or phrases per lesson. Students find it extremely difficult to absorb any more than that.

Presentations for vocabulary lesson on bodies of water to meet certain standards:

- **Class profile:** Mixed nationality class of six students studying English for higher education.
- **Level:** Pre-intermediate.
- **Materials:** Photos of bodies of water.
- **Problems:** Difficulty remembering which word is which.
- **Lesson aims:** To teach 'puddle', 'pond', and 'lake' as bodies of water; to continue the theme of the week, 'Water'; to aid project work.

A Presentation procedure that takes 12 minutes follows these steps:

1. **Hold up a bottle of water. Ask students to take out their notebooks and brainstorm adjectives that can describe water, for one minute.**

2. **Give out pens and ask students to write their adjectives in the designated section on the board.**

   Allow students to ask each other about any words they're unfamiliar with.

3. **Draw a puddle shape on the board. Elicit from the students any ideas about what to call water in this shape.**

   Make a tiny puddle of water on the desk to illustrate if possible.

4. **Now indicate the size of the body of water by drawing a child jumping in it, complete with splashes.**

5. **Elicit 'puddle' if possible and drill the word chorally and individually. Write the word, its part of speech and phonetic spelling on the board.**

6. **Highlight syntax.**

   Have students fill in the blank: A puddle of . . .

7. **Draw the same puddle shape again but this time draw a couple of fish in it and a house nearby. Elicit and drill the word 'pond'. Write the word, its part of speech and phonetic spelling on the board.**

8. **Highlight collocates and compound nouns.**

   You can go through fish pond, freshwater pond, muddy pond (make the picture on the board brown if you can).

Follow the same pattern for 'lake' but with a large boat in the water. Include drilling and board work. Show how the name of the lake usually comes second – Lake Erie, for example.

You can use concept check questions such as:

- ✔ Do fish live in puddles? Why not?
- ✔ Give me an example of a famous lake? (For example, Garda, Michigan, Windermere.) Is there one in your country? How big is it?
- ✔ Why are ponds, lakes and puddles similar?
- ✔ If you break a big bottle of wine what do see on the kitchen floor?

Show pertinent pictures and get descriptions from individual students. Encourage them to use the adjectives already on the board.

Sharing function and connotation

When you explain vocabulary or grammar, you generally need to show how people use it. It's easy with some words. For example, *tall* is a word for things or people of great height. However, some phrases and grammar are more open to interpretation. Take the word *cheers*. It has several uses – you say it while clinking glasses before you drink, you use it informally to express gratitude and it's associated with happiness too (cheer, cheerful).

Filling in students on functions

When you teach language according to the situation you need it for, this is called a *functional approach*. If you take a functional approach to teaching, you usually introduce the setting before you introduce the new piece of language. I talk about using a functional/notional syllabus in Chapter 19.

So, if you're teaching *cheers,* you can design a lesson about going to the pub, and teach:

- ✔ What are you having?
- ✔ I'll have a pint/glass of . . .
- ✔ Whose round is it?
- ✔ It's my round
- ✔ Bottoms up!

You focus not on the grammatical structures but simply on what you say in this particular context.

Even if you take a structural approach to the lesson, meaning that you teach particular grammar, you still need to show very clearly how a word or phrase is actually used in realistic situations.

Conveying connotations

Certain words imply emotions or attitudes – they have *connotations*.

Think of one of those famous supermodels. Which of these words would you associate with her?

thin	trim
slim	wiry
skinny	bony
svelte	twig-like

The word(s) you choose reveal whether you view her as truly attractive or not and this is what you teach with connotation.

You need to point out whether a word is positive, negative or neutral, a compliment or an insult. Failure to do this can leave students embarrassed because they may come across as rude or over familiar.

Fish and . . . ? Teaching vocabulary in chunks

In English some words are often grouped together and seem to have an especially close relationship. These are called *collocations*. For instance, even though the words 'constructive' and 'criticism' can be used perfectly well apart from each other, together they form a common phrase. 'Positive criticism' renders the same idea but just doesn't sit right. It doesn't collocate. Equally, it's fine to say 'very serious' but 'deadly serious' is so much better and mirrors what a native speaker is likely to say. It's collocation.

Going for more than one

Look for opportunities to teach chunks of language. Instead of teaching just one word, try teaching two or three all at once. One way of doing this is by highlighting collocations in reading texts. For example, ask students to underline all the occurrences of a particular word in a text and see which other words come before or after it each time.

You can also reinforce collocations through multiple choice whereby you offer the students several logical possibilities to partner a word, but show that only one is the true match.

Give readers choices to finish a sentence:

> I'm going to a pop . . .
>
> a) concert; b) recital; c) performance

The most common collocations are in the form of:

- ✔ **Subject and verb:** The music blared, the engine roared.

- ✔ **Verb and object:** Brush your teeth, scrub the floor.

- ✔ **Adverb and past participle:** Ideally situated, highly strung.

- ✔ **Adjective and noun:** Black tea, heavy make-up.

Teaching certain words together

When you teach a particular word, you need to give students all the tools they need to actually use it. With that in mind, take note of:

- ✔ **Words that can't be used without other words**: Some words are so uncommon that they become almost meaningless without their collocates. Take for example 'beady'. Is anything else 'beady' except eyes?

- ✔ **Expressions set in stone**: Even though it may be true literally you can't say 'black and green' to mean bruised. It's definitely 'black and blue'.

- ✔ **Compound nouns:** These are nouns made up of two words together. So you can teach similar compounds as one vocabulary group. For example, you can teach coffee table, dining table and kitchen table in the same lesson.

- ✔ **Clichés:** Some expressions are tired but common phrases such as 'no stone will be left unturned'. It's worth teaching clichés as one chunk.

- ✔ **English verbs that don't translate:** Some verbs in English have particular collocations which students find tricky because when translated they don't seem to follow a pattern. Foremost are:

    - **Do:** a deal, harm, the shopping, business

    - **Get:** the sack, home, lost, ready

    - **Make:** the bed, a mistake, trouble, amends

    - **Take:** a look, the lead, advantage, a bite

All right mate! Teaching posh words and slang

Because people face such a wide range of situations in life, it makes sense to teach a wide range of language to meet them. So there's good reason to teach formal and informal language as well different styles of communicating according to the students' requirements.

Tabloid and broadsheet newspapers provide great examples of how style can differ even when the subject matter is the same, as the following sample headlines about the same story show:

- ✔ Desperate Danielle Beats Jail Rap!
- ✔ Tragic Mother Acquitted
- ✔ Sad Mum Escapes Prison Sentence

Presentations using such comparisons demonstrate cultural awareness, connotation and synonyms too. (I talk about connotation a few sections earlier and synonyms in the next section.)

Choose the words frequently used in situations the students may encounter, whether slang or posh. It's realistic to expect students to expand their knowledge into new areas sooner or later, so the occasional exposure to new styles helps motivate them. In any case, everyone needs formal and informal language in order to reflect the different relationships in their lives.

In your presentation, you can indicate this kind of information in brackets after the word:

toilet (n)   loo (n) (UK slang)

clothes (n)   gear(n) (informal)

Make students aware of varieties of English from various parts of the globe but focus on the ones to which students are most likely to be exposed.

Talking about words that mean the same and opposites – synonyms and antonyms

Using the *antonym,* or opposite, of a word is a very useful way to explain its meaning. It's as though half the job is already done for you. So you can teach that the opposite of 'cheap' is 'expensive' or that 'increase' and 'decrease' go hand in hand.

Synonyms, words that have exactly the same or similar meaning, are especially useful as students learn to expand their vocabulary. Some examples are:

- ✔ huge/enormous
- ✔ messy/untidy
- ✔ happy/glad

Use a little caution when using synonyms and antonyms because they sometimes fit only in particular circumstances. For example, synonyms of 'buy' are 'get', 'acquire' and 'purchase'. However you can't really 'purchase' time. Only 'buy' fits in that expression.

Presenting Grammar

When you present grammar, usually one of the tenses in English, you include points such as:

- **Form:** Show what the grammar actually looks like even when you manipulate it in different ways. For instance:

  - **Positive:** He had written it.

  - **Negative:** He had not written it.

  - **Question:** Had he written it?

  - **Contraction:** He'd written it.

- **Pronunciation:** Consider any features that you need to highlight and drill.

- **Function:** Demonstrate exactly when you use the grammar by putting it in context. Timelines help to represent this visually.

- **Examples:** Use realia or pictures as well as sentences to explain.

- **Concept check questions.**

- **Comparison with other grammar if necessary.**

A Presentation for a grammar lesson on bodies of water to meet certain criteria might consist of:

- **Class profile:** Mixed nationality class of six students studying English for higher education.

- **Level:** Pre-intermediate.

- **Materials:** Diagrams showing simple processes.

- **Problems:** Remembering the difference between active and passive forms.

- **Lesson aims:** To teach the present simple passive for describing a process; to continue the theme of the week 'Water'; to aid project work.

To teach this lesson, follow these steps:

1. **Have a soft drink on the desk but complain that it's too warm. Ask students what to do. Then find out who likes ice in their drinks.**

2. **Have the students tell you the procedure for making ice and write the stages on the board:**

   1) Put water into container.

   2) Place container into freezer.

   3) Leave for 2 hours.

3. **Lead the students to get to the past participle of each of the verbs – put, placed and left.** I talk about past participles in Chapter 16. It's one form of a verb that you sometimes use when you speak about the past.

4. **Ask students to identify the object of the sentence in step one – water.**

5. **Ask them to identify the verb – put – and highlight that there's no person doing the action.**

6. **Set out the equation for the present simple passive form (the equation shows the necessary parts of the sentence in the right order):** Object + the verb *to be* in the present simple tense (*am*, *is* or *are*) + past participle (+ *by someone* if you want to say who did it). I talk about the present simple tense in Chapter 16.

7. **Complete the examples for each stage by eliciting the words and writing them on the board:**

Object	*+ to be in present simple*	*+ past participle*	*+ where/how long*
The water	is	put	into a container
It	is	placed	into the freezer
It	is	left	for two hours

8. **Demonstrate how to transform one sentence into a negative and one into a question on the board:**

   • Is the container placed in the fridge?

   • It isn't left for two minutes.

Check that your students understand the concept by asking:

✔ Who puts the water into the freezer. Is it important?

✔ Are the sentences in the past or present simple?

✔ What's the difference between the present simple active and passive?

Chapter 6

Holding the Reins and Letting Them Loose – Giving Students Practice

. . . .

In This Chapter

▶ Practising new vocabulary

▶ Introducing production activities

▶ Mastering the art of giving instructions

▶ Grouping students

▶ Organising practice and production activities

. . . .

Most teachers plan EFL lessons in three stages – Presentation, Practice and Production. How to handle the first stage is the focus of Chapter 5. In this chapter, I tell you about the differences between the Practice and Presentation stages and offer suggestions for activities.

Experts generally agree that people learn languages by listening before speaking. In a similar way, the class hears what you have to say and they begin to own the piece of language themselves.

Practising New Words

The second stage of the lesson, called Practice, or more specifically, Controlled Practice, is an important period of transition for the students. During the Presentation stage, students are fairly passive as you explain the form and function of the new piece of language. During the third Production stage students have freer expression. During the practice stage, they repeat what they learned in a controlled situation before moving into the more active Production stage. This means that you set the students an exercise with entirely predictable answers and these answers are rather repetitive because they're designed to practise the new piece of language several times over. So in this part of the lesson you aim to get the students concentrating on the new words or grammar without them showing off everything else they know. The students take their first tentative steps at using the words to test whether they can get it right.

Some of the many benefits of the Practice activities include:

✔ **They help the students to focus on accuracy.** This doesn't mean that the activities should be dry, meaningless exercises like the old days of Latin lessons. It's very important that you challenge students with an activity that can only be completed if they really understand how the piece of language works. You should be able to predict the the students' responses, though. In these exercises the answers are predictable because there's only one correct way to complete the sentences. In the following examples the only possible answers are *have, has* and/or the past participle form of the verb given.

An example of a **bad** practice activity first:

> Complete these sentences in the Present Perfect
>
> Example: I . . . (have) seen that movie.
>
> They . . . visited the zoo.
>
> You . . . read that book.
>
> We . . . eaten there.

Students can simply take a guess and write 'have' in every gap. Here's an improvement:

> Complete these sentences in the Present Perfect, using the verb in parentheses.
>
> Example: I . . . have seen . . . that movie. (to see)
>
> They . . . the zoo. (to visit)
>
> She . . . that book. (to read)
>
> We . . . there. (to eat)

Notice that students have to apply the grammar rule more vigorously to come up with 'has' for the third person *she*.

✔ **These exercises force attention on the new piece of language through frequent repetition.** Students can fix their attention on the new point without being distracted by too many other rules they've learned.

At the same time, by repeating the new language, students form new habits in the brain.

✔ **This type of exercise allows students to come to a gradual recognition of the new language in a safe way.** That is to say, the students feel very supported.

One thing to avoid is letting students make a habit of an error. Once engrained, bad habits are really difficult to root out. For example, students say things like 'Is good!' and 'I gonna do it', even though they know the correct grammar, just because no one forced them to break the habit initially. So while the students are practising, monitor closely.

This practice is called *controlled* because of the limited range of what the students have to do, not because you stand over them commenting on every word. That would be counter-productive. You need to step back and let them get on with it, but make notes.

Use the feedback session immediately after the activity to root out any problems you've picked up on and tackle additional questions from the students. Keep the target language as priority though. After all, if you spend too much time going through errors in other areas, students may forget what the primary aim of the lesson is. You can cover any significant error that's off the point right at the end of the lesson.

Make your Practice activities long enough to allow you to go round and listen to everyone in the class. You're bound to miss some errors, but that's life! And by the way, arrange the room so you can walk around as easily as possible.

Practising with the whole class first

During Presentation you had the attention of the entire class (hopefully). So the transition from Presentation to Practice is seamless if you continue to work with the entire group. This also allows you to offer correction that benefits everyone; after all, the students are likely to make similar errors. You can egg them on, offer reassurance that they're doing well and quickly spot anything you'd forgotten to include, before the students work in small groups out of earshot. Doing practice activities with the whole class gives students tools for doing the activity that follows, because the practice activities serve as examples.

Pairing up with a student

Open pairs is one way of practising while you remain in control. In an *open pairs* exercise, you ask a student questions or role play in full view and hearing of everyone else in the room. The class sees an example of how to use the new piece of language, but because you're one of the partners in the exchange, the level of accuracy is very high. Students also know that you'll point out immediately any mistake made by your partner.

You can continue open pairs with two students as partners, but still in front of everyone else. You have slightly less control but still plenty of opportunity for correction – by you or the classmates.

If you're practising the future perfect tense, you can proceed this way:

> Teacher: Mary Jo, what do you think you'll have done by the time you're 30?
>
> Mary Jo: I think that I'll having a baby by the time I'm 30.
>
> Teacher: Could you repeat your sentence using the correct from of 'have'?
>
> Mary Jo (refers back to the board): Oh yes! <u>I'll have had</u> a baby.
>
> Teacher: Well done! Ask Olivia a question in the future perfect please.
>
> Mary Jo: Olivia what <u>will you have done</u> by the time you're 60?
>
> Olivia: <u>I'll have travelled</u> the world.

Using the board

You can involve the whole class by putting gapped sentences or questions on the board. You can then ask for a volunteer to fill in the correct answer.

Alternatively, if you plan to give the students written exercises you can include a set of questions on the worksheet that the whole class can discuss before individual study.

Practising alone

Controlled Practice activities that students do alone are based on listening, reading or writing.

Even when students work alone, they can still compare their answers in pairs afterwards to add a communicative element to the activity.

Recognising the structure

Activities that help students recognise the new structure or vocabulary may be in the form of a text (listening or reading). Students can assess it and note examples of the new structure.

Read the story and <u>underline</u> all the verbs in the Present Continuous.

Monique is an accountant. She works at home. This morning she<u>'s using </u>her computer in the kitchen. She<u>'s looking </u>at a lot of information but she doesn't think it's difficult. She's very clever with numbers. Monique <u>is wearing</u> her tennis clothes because she wants to play tennis with her friends when she stops working. She isn't thirsty, because she's drinking a cup of coffee too.

Remember that students need a challenge. In this exercise I include another gerund (stops <u>working</u>) to see whether the students can distinguish between this structure and the Present Continuous, which always includes the verb 'to be' plus a gerund.

Finding specific words in a text

You can use other ways to use a text without underlining tenses. When you're doing a vocabulary based lesson, try using identifying and categorising tasks.

This exercise from a more advanced lesson is about descriptions of personality.

> Decide whether the underlined words are positive, negative or neutral and write each under one of the headings after the passage. Cheerful is already slotted for you.
>
> There are five people in my department. Sometimes we get on well but there's also friction when we're under pressure. Bill is the most <u>ambitious</u>. He's pretty <u>frank</u> but on the whole a <u>cheerful</u> chap. Then there's Rick who has more experience than the rest of us so he's a <u>shrewd</u> character. Being more <u>mature</u> he likes to be <u>selective</u> about the projects we take on. Sarah and Beverley are both very <u>cooperative</u> but Sarah is far more <u>assertive</u>.
>
> **Positive**   **Negative**   **Neutral**
>
> cheerful

Mixing up anagrams

You're probably familiar with *anagrams,* which are basically words with the letters jumbled up. By putting the letters in order, the students not only have to remember the words but also make sure of the spelling of the new words.

Put the letters in order to find three sports

> lolyallevb: volleyball
>
> skoorne:
>
> scattehil:

The last two are *snooker* and *athletics* in case you're wondering!

Scrambling sentences

To practise the word order of a particular structure you can design an exercise in which words in a sentence are jumbled.

Put the words in order to make a third conditional sentence.

If Joanne was her boyfriend have known that 60 old years she never would gone had out with him.

If Joanne had . . .

Transforming tenses

This traditional exercise in language courses works best when there's a clear context instead of arbitrary sentences. The idea is to set out one tense (or structure) and have the students accurately exchange it for another.

Make one sentence using the Past Continuous.

She typed the letter from 7.30 to 7.45. At 7.40 the telephone rang.

While she . . .

You can use timelines and pictures to generate sentences too.

Matching exercises

Activities in which students have to match opposites, or words and pictures or make other similar connections are very controlled and also useful for getting students accustomed to new words.

In a lesson on classroom language, you can have students match verbs and activities together:

raise	to your partner
ask	the gaps
compare	your hand
talk	your answers
fill in	a question

Practising in pairs

When students work in pairs they can practise their speaking and get to know each other better. Lessons are livelier than with solo activities and classmates can spur each other on and offer correction.

To encourage communication in pairs, get students to share some materials by handing out one worksheet or text for two students to share. If it's something they each want to keep, you can give out another copy later.

You need to have your wits about you for pair work activities. It isn't quite as easy to control students when they're all speaking at once and the noise level can be pretty high. However the students are generally happier because they're actively involved.

I talk about pair exercise in the next sections.

Ranking

With a list of vocabulary you can have pairs discuss the appropriate rank from best to worst, or most to least useful perhaps. You can have students practise the target vocabulary and the expressions for justifying opinions as well. You need to have taught them expressions of opinion well beforehand, though, and you can use examples by first of all asking a few students, in front of the whole class, for their opinions about the vocabulary.

With your partner, decide on the most important electrical items from the list to have in a kitchen with 1 the most important item and 8 the least important.

> freezer
>
> microwave
>
> dishwasher
>
> kettle
>
> cooker
>
> toaster
>
> fridge
>
> food processor

Filling an information gap

Use activities in which students talk to each other in order to access information. The idea is to give them different information about the same topic. Instead of just looking at the other person's worksheet, they have to ask for what they need to know.

Have students living in the UK practise saying 'What's the weather like in . . . ?' along with weather words and place names, and having given each pair the following worksheets. (The pronunciation of place names is tricky so I regularly find an excuse to slip the ones they know into a lesson.)

Complete your weather report by asking your partner, 'What's the weather like in . . .?'

Weather Report A

Aberdeen: warm and cloudy

Carlisle:

Dundee: hot all day

Edinburgh: rain in the morning

Glasgow:

Ipswich:

Kidderminster: cold and windy

Liverpool: foggy in the morning

Manchester:

Norwich:

Weather Report B

Aberdeen:

Carlisle: warm and sunny

Dundee:

Edinburgh:

Glasgow: mild and grey

Ipswich: rain in the afternoon

Kidderminster :

Liverpool:

Manchester: hot and dry

Norwich: foggy then bright

You can get some more ideas for speaking activities in Chapter 13.

Role playing from a script

If you use a course book in class, it probably has the tape script for recorded dialogues at the back. The way students use intonation when reading out a dialogue is a strong indicator of their comprehension.

Practising in groups

You can use larger groups of students or the whole class again for the Practice stage. Sometimes it's fun to have a competitive element or just the camaraderie of working side by side.

Here are a couple of ideas:

- **Using a blindfold:** One student in a group covers her eyes and then has to listen to the directions of her classmates in order to find a particular location of an object.

- **Running dictations:** Organise two teams and two copies of a written text full of the target language for the lesson. You place the texts at one end of the room while the students remain at the other end. Each team has a blank sheet of paper and a pen. One by one, students come up and look at the text. They each memorise a chunk of the text, as much as they can manage, and reproduce it on the blank sheet. By the end of the activity the teams should have their own handwritten versions of the text. They practise accuracy and remembering chunks of language.

Moving to the Production Stage

In this third stage of the lesson, called Production or Freer Practice, the focus is on fluency. Students have a chance to experiment a bit and add the new language to everything else they know by, for example, having extended discussions, describing things in detail and telling stories. The aim is to set the students a task that gets them speaking, or writing, in their own words but that's a suitable context for including the target language. Having concentrated on being accurate in the Practice stage, students can now try to sound natural when they incorporate the new language.

The Production stage tests the students subtly. They should be able to show off what they can do without you holding their hands or guiding them.

A Production activity involves speaking or writing primarily and encourages creativity.

Writing and speaking

Writing activities are usually solitary affairs. It's pretty straight forward to set students an essay task, for example, and ask them to include particular words or phrases. If you do this, you should have some involvement in planning the written piece with the students so that they have sufficient structure. Use the board to show what kind of information or expressions can be used to go in each paragraph before they start writing by themselves. See Chapter 11 for tips on organising writing lessons.

In the next section I talk about ways to engage students in writing and presenting.

Miming a story

A fun way to set a writing activity is by miming it. Students love to watch you doing all the actions while they make notes and later write the entire story in the tense(s) you set for them. Of course, you need to make it an amusing story full of actions and without too many characters.

Making speeches and presentations

An example of an individual freer practice activity for speaking is to have students do a speech or presentation. This is particularly applicable for business English students who may need to do similar activities at work. However, if there's an election running, students can try delivering a mani-festo speech.

Students need to do this kind of activity from time to time because it allows stronger ones to show off without compromising for the sake of their classmates. It also reveals students' true speaking levels without the support of a group.

Role-playing in pairs

Role-playing is an effective way of speaking freely in pairs. In the Practice stage the students can just act out a role-play from a script. However, in Production you can get them writing the script themselves and then perhaps performing for the rest of the class.

What's the question?

An exercise in using creative language is to give students just the answers to an interview and asking them to come up with the most interesting questions they can think of to match.

Write a question in the Past Simple to match each answer.

Answer: Vanilla ice cream.

Question: What did you want for breakfast when you were a child?

Interviews

Very often students interview each other on particular topics. So in a lesson on vocabulary for clothing try setting tasks like this:

> Ask your partner about the newest item in her wardrobe. Find out why, where and when she bought it. Ask her whether it matches anything else.

Getting dramatic in groups

You can have great fun with freer group activities.

Doing drama and improvisation

I've met many a trained actor working in TEFL as a day job so it's no wonder that drama has established itself as a Production activity. Drama has real advantages in the language classroom:

- ✔ You repeat the same dialogue many times. This is very reassuring for students as they get better each time and this helps them build up their confidence.

- ✔ The context for the language is very strong because a story is involved.

- ✔ You can record and play back the piece for analysis and self correction if you have the equipment.

- ✔ Drama tends to teach language and culture together.

A short extract lasting five or six minutes is sufficient and it's interesting for the students if you can show a film clip of the same scene afterwards.

In real life, language is generally spontaneous so you can mimic this by using improvisation.

Give students a card with a secret role on it. Perhaps it's a hospital situation and each person has a complaint that influences what they say. Or maybe it's a quirky dinner party with a string of guests who need to get their own secret words into the conversation. The students can all work out what the others are up to.

Retelling the story

Paraphrasing, summarising and even embellishing are everyday skills, so asking students to tell each other about something they've read, watched or experienced is a valuable activity. For example, have partners read separate texts, then tell each other about what they read and add any other information they know about the topic.

Integrating different skills into one activity allows for the students' different learning styles and adds variety.

Fostering discussions and debates

Sometimes debates kick off spontaneously and that's great. It's exactly what you want to use language for and you shouldn't feel that your lesson plan is compromised if you occasionally go off the beaten track.

If you want to orchestrate a discussion or debate yourself, you need to teach all the appropriate vocabulary (or at least give students access to a glossary if there's too much or some is less relevant) and occasionally add fuel to the fire.

Giving Instructions

One of the keys to a successful activity in the classroom is the way you give instructions to set up the task. It may seem simple to say 'Talk about X in pairs!' but there's a little more to it than that.

Consider these presentation tips:

- ✔ **Speak well:** Talk slowly even if the students are at a higher level. It encourages them to pay attention. Be clear! Don't mutter or ramble. Use short sentences and imperatives (commands). Grade what you say so it's at the right level.

- ✔ **Use visuals:** Use pictures and diagrams to show what you want the students to do. Give examples of what you want. Use lots of gestures.

- ✔ **Plan your instructions:** Write the instructions for the exercises into your lesson plan. This helps you present them clearly and succinctly. Don't start giving instructions until everyone's listening and be sure to allot enough time for the instructions – give them out step by step and not all at once. Very often students get confused when you tell them too much. Be sure to repeat the instructions and write them on the board, giving students time to write them down if necessary.

Ask open questions to see if the students understand the instructions. You can even get them to repeat the instructions back to you.

Putting Students into Pairs and Groups

When it comes to organising your students for pair and group work, avoid simply telling them to pair up themselves. It's your responsibility to say who works with whom and you ought to have a strategy for doing so.

Why? First, you're likely to have mixed abilities in the class and you definitely don't want two weak students working together. On the other hand, if you have two very strong students it may be motivating for them to be put together sometimes so that they can express themselves to their full potential. Unfortunately you sometimes have an annoying class member too (the joker perhaps) and it would be unfair for the same student to be stuck with that person in every activity. Share the load.

If you can, change the seating order in your classroom regularly. Ask the class to sit in alphabetical order, in order of their front door numbers in their addresses or according to their dates of birth. Use anything that moves them around.

For pairs, use your left hand to point to the first student (an open hand is friendlier than a single finger) and then the right hand for the second student. Show that they're now a pair by bringing your palms together.

Of course, you can just say 'you're A and you're B' if the students understand but you can also inject a bit of fun by using other vocabulary. You'll get a smile with: 'You're an apple and you're a banana!

When you're working with groups, it's great to switch them around after a time so they can pool ideas. First you label each student A, B, C, or D and put them together in a group of four. After they've had time to generate ideas you can now group all the As, all the Bs and so on.

Encourage students to move their chairs so that they face each other if possible. Communication involves body language too.

Trying Out Practice and Production Activities

Practice and Production activities come in many different forms but they should be interesting, varied and challenging according to the level of the students. Here are some examples of activities that carry the same theme throughout each of the three stages of the lesson.

Writing a blurb

The *blurb* is the text at the back of a book or film that tells you why you should buy it. It usually contains a synopsis of the plot and some information about the cast or author. Over the years I've noticed that very often the language used is quite sophisticated even when the entertainment is aimed at children. So rewriting an existing blurb and creating new ones are great ways of exercising language skills with students who are intermediate level and above.

After an initial Presentation stage focusing on vocabulary for describing films, for example, students can tell each other specific details about a recent film they've seen – plot, stars, genre, format and so on.

Next introduce the film(s) using the title and pictures from the cover. You can use different films for different groups or just one for the whole class. The students can use this initial information to make predictions about the film. For this you may decide to use a less well-known movie so that the students really have to discover the information.

Now you can distribute the blurb(s) for students to examine.

Pair students and ask them to skim the blurb for particular details about the new film(s).

Next the students should analyse the language content of the blurb and, using dictionaries and/or a glossary, ask students, in pairs, to simplify the blurb using synonyms for the tricky words.

Form the students into new groups based on a film they've all seen.

Together they must now pool their knowledge to come up with a blurb for that film.

Spin off activities from this include listening to, acting out or narrating clips of the film.

Doing class surveys and reports

Find out from the class about topics they're all interested in. From this starting point you can determine a good topic for a survey and have the students prepare survey questions based on the topic.

The answers to questionnaires like these are usually limited, so they provide excellent controlled practice of the tenses.

A survey on musical tastes may incorporate questions in various tenses:

- ✔ **Past tenses:** What was the first CD you bought? Had you heard all the tracks before you bought it?

- ✔ **Present tenses:** What are you listening to these days? Do you use CDs, MP3 or a different format?

- ✔ **Future tenses:** Will you be going to any concerts this year? In your opinion which artist will be 'the next big thing'?

Students can distribute the questions and mingle to conduct short interviews with each other.

Mingling (as though at a dinner party) is a great way to incorporate group work and create a buzz.

After that they can collate the information and prepare graphs and charts to demonstrate the results. As a freer writing activity the students can now prepare reports on their findings. They could also have a final discussion analysing the reasons for any surprising results.

Playing Mastermind

You've probably seen this game on television. It's the one where a contestant prepares to answer questions on a specialist subject. Well, in the classroom you can organise a similar game that allows groups of students to research a particular topic (maybe an area of vocabulary) and answer questions about it. They can ask each other questions you've prepared and later write questions themselves.

Apart from the revision of particular topics, a sub-aim is to get students using questions with and without auxiliary verbs, as in the following examples:

When **did** this happen?

What happened?

Which film **did** Brando make in 1978?

Who directed *Jurassic Park?*

So that you can reduce TTT (teacher talking time), hand the questions over to another group. For example, if Team A prepared Hobbies as their specialist subject and Team B prepared Occupations, each team can have a quizmaster who asks the other team questions. They can have a spokesperson each to answer. A question and answer session may run something like this:

> Quizmaster A: What is the name of the person who has the job of organising funerals?
>
> Spokesperson B: Undertaker.
>
> Quizmaster A: Correct.
>
> Quizmaster B: Which pub sport has small metal arrows and a target?
>
> Spokesperson A: Darts.

After the specialist knowledge round, which is practice, do another short presentation to remind students of the grammar of questions. Then students can come up with questions for the general knowledge round themselves.

If a piece of language is needed later in the lesson, instead of expecting the students to learn it at the beginning and remember it throughout, you can do another mini presentation when it's needed.

Producing predictions

Several ways can be used to render the future in English so here's a suggestion for using the various future constructions:

> In 1979 Margaret Thatcher famously predicted that there would never be a woman Prime Minister in her lifetime and in 1916 Charlie Chaplin said that cinema was little more than a fad.

1. **In the Presentation stage, analyse the different expressions and tenses used.**

2. **Have students respond to a set of predictions for the year 2050, saying whether they're likely to come true or not and comparing their ideas with a partner.**

3. **Come up with your own or find out what the scientists say.**

4. **Ask the students to make their own predictions on various areas of life.**

Chapter 7

Giving Correction and Feedback

· ·

In This Chapter

▶ Sorting out which errors matter

▶ Using gestures to correct

▶ Having students correct themselves

▶ Using students to correct other students

▶ Giving your class feedback

▶ Correcting written work

▶ Giving tests

· ·

All language learners make mistakes. It's part of the learning process. But what should you do about them? In this chapter I tell you about the different kinds of error students make and various techniques for handling them.

Knowing What to Correct and When

There seems to be little disagreement that students ought to receive correction in the classroom. They expect it, and teachers rightly feel the need to take action when students get it wrong.

Of course, in the real world outside the classroom, people make errors all the time and still communicate effectively. And even though you teach English, you generally don't interrupt them, especially as this may come across as rude and actually put them off speaking. Taking the person to one side afterwards and pointing out an error, is more polite but maybe a little picky. After all, the moment has passed. And in any case, it does no harm to let some things slide – you don't need to be a staunch defender of the Queen's English on all occasions.

But the classroom isn't the real world. It's a safe environment where your students can try language out. And as the teacher, you're no ordinary listener; you're paid to point students in the right direction.

That being said, the issues for TEFL teachers when it comes to correction, boil down to these:

- ✔ Striking the right balance between accuracy and fluency.
- ✔ When to correct: immediately or later?
- ✔ The particular errors to correct.
- ✔ The techniques you use for giving correction.

The guidelines for dealing with the first three points all boil down to a set of definitive rules:

- ✔ **Accuracy and fluency:** These should combine to make for good communication. If lack of accuracy hinders communication, the speaker doesn't achieve anything by carrying on.
- ✔ **Good communication:** When this takes place, correction can usually wait. When communication is poor or non-existent, step in more quickly.
- ✔ **Correcting errors:** Errors related to the topic of the lesson and which stop communication should receive the most attention.

I talk about correction techniques later in the chapter.

Judging accuracy, timing and value

On the subject of accuracy, most students want to get it right. This is one of the key differences between people who just pick up a language as they go along and those who actually study it. The fact that the student is in the classroom at all means that accuracy is important to him to some degree. It should therefore be important to you too.

Even though students may not achieve total accuracy, try for it at least in the language area you're practising in that particular lesson. This gives the student something to aim for. It's a bit like target practice. You need to identify the target and actually aim for it. You hit it sometimes and miss at other times but it's clear to you when you miss and that you need to practise. When the arrow misses the target you can still applaud the effort. Likewise, you need to encourage effort but make sure that the student knows when he has to work harder.

So, suppose that the lesson is about the present simple tense and your student, John, says, 'I am go to the shopping.' You may want to interrupt him to make the error, ' I am go', the focus of attention because it indicates that the he may not have grasped the information you just presented on the present simple tense. However the meaning is fairly clear, especially if it occurs within a more extended dialogue. So if you don't stop him, John continues, '. . . and there I buy vegetables because I don't want meat.' The benefit of allowing him to continue, or to be fluent, is that you discover the extent to which he understands the tense. He may have just slipped up initially because of nerves or distraction. His next two attempts at the present simple, 'I buy' and 'I don't want' are very good. So, by allowing John to continue the conversation, it also becomes clear that he really wants to say the present simple 'I go' – not 'I am going', which was the other likely option. Also, if John continues to use the present simple very well, you can handle his first error very quickly, leaving time for a mention of the second error 'to the shopping'.

To encourage fluency then, you should allow students to keep talking. You can make a note of the errors and deal with them later.

Try not to put words in your student's mouths when you offer correction. Find out what they actually want to say before wading in.

In a lesson about health, Paola makes a different kind of error:

> Tano: Do you have a cough?
>
> Paola: Yes I have one cup in the morning and one with lunch.
>
> Tano: Not cup, cough!
>
> Paola: Yes, every day.

This time communication is actually breaking down and very soon the two students are likely to become exasperated. Knowing her Brazilian Portuguese background, I detect that Paola is talking about coffee, not a cough. This is an occasion when it would be wise to step in immediately as fluency has no benefit without true communication. By the way, inaccurate pronunciation is the usual culprit when this happens.

Exploring the nature of the error

Students get things wrong for different reasons. Sometimes they just slip up although they really know it. Even native speakers do that. At other times they make mistakes because they really are confused or they've missed the point.

If a student just slips up, you can tell because he gets it right most of the time. In that case he only needs a reminder instead of a full explanation. As long as the student is aware that he's got something wrong, he stands a good chance of putting it right. Having said that, students find it most useful if you point out what kind of slip up it is.

If the atmosphere in your classroom is generally relaxed and friendly, students won't feel too self conscious about making mistakes. You can even laugh along with them when the result of a mistake is rather amusing.

If the problem is more than a minor slip, the student needs an explanation that shows that he's made an error and exactly why it's wrong.

Letting Your Fingers Do the Talking

Students have their eyes glued on their teacher quite a lot of the time, so they get to know your gestures and mannerisms quite well. For that reason alone, it makes sense to use your body language effectively instead of just waving your arms around for emphasis.

Don't worry about whether or not the students understand your gestures. Just go ahead and they very quickly get used to them.

Using your hands

You can use your hands to indicate where a student has made errors in a spoken sentence. These ideas may come in handy, if you'll excuse the pun.

✓ **Using fingers as words or syllables:** One way to indicate where the error is in a sentence is by using your fingers to represent words.

A student has come up with this sentence: *She have been to France.*

You can highlight the problem by holding out your left hand (right if you're left handed) and pointing to a finger as you say each word:

- she = the thumb
- have= the index finger
- been = the middle finger
- to = the ring finger
- France = the little finger

When you say 'have' waggle the index finger and use a questioning tone, then carry on to the next finger/word.

✓ **Pointing for time reference:** To remind a student that he should refer to the past, the present or the future, you can point back over your shoulder for the past, to the floor in front of you for the present and straight ahead for the future.

✓ **Extending:** If the student has used only the base of a word ('go' instead of 'going' or 'inform' instead of 'information'), say the word using your thumb and index finger: Start with them pressed together and separate them as you say the word. Draw out the word as you say it too.

If the student needs to extend the whole sentence, you can use both hands, pulling them apart from a 'praying' position. At the same time, draw out the last word of the student's sentence as you say it.

✔ **Reducing a word:** Sometimes students attach endings to words unnecessarily. They say, for example: I might watching a film.

You may not need to speak at all if you can quickly make a gesture like a pair of scissors cutting while the student is saying the word. If you miss your chance, say the word again yourself along with the gesture.

✔ **Re-ordering:** When students get their words in the wrong order, try to get them to do a reshuffle without interrupting by using a quick mime of shuffling little boxes around in a straight line on a table in front of you.

Teaching with body language

You can give a lot away with your body language, but it isn't necessarily just an unconscious form of communication. In the classroom you can use it like this:

✔ **Smiling and frowning:** Your face is a strong indicator of approval, or not, as the case may be. When you smile a lot, students feel encouraged and comfortable. On the other hand, you can use a frown to show that something is not quite right. Hopefully the student then starts to tread more carefully and possibly self-correct.

✔ **Nodding:** When you do this, people want to continue speaking to you. They know that you're listening and interested. In this case of students, they know that they're doing well and that real communication is taking place because you understand. When they make an error, a confused or quizzical expression is less off-putting than shaking your head.

✔ **Hums:** In English *hmmm* can mean yes, no, I'm not sure or scores of other things. It's a good way to show your opinion unobtrusively.

You can take it a step further by humming a whole sentence to demonstrate the right intonation.

✔ **Pointing to clues:** If you have charts and instructional posters up in your classroom, you can point to the one that indicates the nature of the student's problem. For example, if you have a verb table up, point to the past participle column when your student says 'He had often sang'.

Gestures aren't universal so students learn the body language of English speakers by watching you.

Leading to Self Correction

Give a man a fish and you feed him for a day. Teach a man to fish and you feed him for a lifetime.

— Chinese proverb

According to the proverb, there's wisdom in allowing people to fend for themselves once you explain how. This works in TEFL too. Students remember the answers they work out for themselves better than the ones you tell them explicitly. So if you always say 'not *x* but *y*' your students may lack the skills to correct themselves when you aren't there.

After trying to help students correct themselves, and if they still don't get it, tell them the answer and make sure that they understand any principal involved. It becomes exasperating if the correction process is drawn out for too long a time.

Progressing by prompting

Of course you can't always wait for students to fathom things all by themselves, so instead you give them clues and prompts to help them get there. In addition to the largely non-verbal techniques in the previous section, you can also help students in these ways:

✔ Tell the student which part of speech or tense they need. For example:

- I came in the bus: Preposition.

- I am here since 2008: Change the tense with 'since'.

- I am eating many bread: Uncountable or countable.

✔ Elicit the correct language by asking leading questions.

- Student: I told the host that I didn't like tomatoes because they're disgusting.

- Teacher: People have different likes and dislikes, don't they? Lots of people love tomatoes. Can you tell me an expression that's quite polite but means you don't like something?

- Student: Is it *not nice?*

- Teacher: That's not quite right. I'm thinking of an expression that means it's OK but not good for me.

- Student: Is it *not my cup of tea?*

- Teacher: Well done! Could you repeat your sentence now please?

Examining echoing

A tendency for some teachers is to just say the correct version of what the student wanted to say, but this isn't usually an effective correction technique.

Giulia has pronunciation difficulties:

> Giulia: I leave in Hackney.
>
> Teacher: You **live** in Hackney.
>
> Giulia: Yes, I leave in Hackney.

Clearly Giulia doesn't even realise that a correction has taken place. She can't actually hear the difference between 'live' and 'leave' because the distinction between long and short vowel sounds doesn't exist in her language. Unless the teacher makes her focus on the error, Giulia's oblivious to it. She hears it as an echo with no particular connection to an error and she'll probably repeat the mistake next time. The teacher needs to recognise that Giulia needs more help to sort out the different sounds by using the phonology of the words and writing the two sounds on the board. In this case /ɪ/ and /iː/. Now she can both see and hear the difference. At the very least it's better to say, 'Not leave but live' and ask her to repeat.

Encouraging Peer Correction

Peer correction is asking students in the class to correct each other's errors. This very practical technique has several benefits:

- ✔ It reduces the pressure on the student who made the mistake, especially if the teacher's attempts to prompt self-correction are unsuccessful.

- ✔ The other students are involved in what's happening rather than just observing.

- ✔ The teacher can tell how widespread the problem is.

You can make use of various techniques in employing peer correction:

- ✔ **Put the error on the board.** Monitor silent work, pair or group activities and make a note of the errors. Then, during the feedback session, you can put the error up on the board.

  It's considerate to conceal the identity of the student who got it wrong, so tweak the sentence a bit in order not to give it away. Then consult the class and ask what's wrong with the sentence on the board.

  Some students have visual memories and may recall the error rather than the correct version. It's important to cross the wrong version out and put the correct word on the board.

✔ **Go round the class asking each student to say a word that some students are pronouncing incorrectly.** If one student gets it wrong, ask another student who did well to say it again, and then ask the student who got it wrong to have another go.

Watch the faces of the other students when one student is speaking. If you see a frown or grimace on a classmate's face when a student makes an error, this is the ideal person to choose for peer correction. At a convenient moment you can ask: Hideki, you were listening carefully. Do you agree with Noako's answer?

Make sure that students offer correction in English. Sometimes they think that their friend understands better if they just translate. At least you can train the students to say something like: 'How do you say . . . in our language please?'

Scheduling Class Feedback

The class feedback session is when teachers usually address errors and give praise, so it's really important to schedule time for this in your lesson plan. (I talk about lesson plans in Chapter 4.) During this part of the lesson you can highlight areas where students got things wrong and deal with the problems by briefly re-teaching a pertinent point or by prompting self and peer correction. Feedback involves the whole class offering suggestions or listening.

A lack of feedback leaves students wondering whether or not they were successful or actually overconfident.

You can carry out class feedback at various times:

✔ **At the end of an activity:** Immediately after the students finish an activity, you can round things up with a review, praise and correction session. Use this as an opportunity to weed out any emerging problems in using the target language before you begin the next activity.

✔ **At the end of the lesson:** Students may be making significant errors not related to the topic of the day that still require attention. Handling this at the end of the lesson prevents going off on a tangent to the detriment of your lesson plan.

✔ **After written homework:** When you've completed the delightful task of marking all your students' written work, make a note of recurring errors and have a dedicated feedback session about them. If several students have the same problems, it may indicate that something got left out when you taught that point.

✔ **At the end of the week:** Repetition is a great way to remember things, so make a note of the errors that came up during the week and have a Friday review. This should help you to assess whether the students really got the point.

Wielding Your Red Pen

Before I say anything about correcting written work, let me address the red pen debate. There are those who believe that the colour red is far too aggressive and confrontational to be used for marking. Others say it is the only colour that really stands out and that other 'friendlier' colours such as green and purple should represent opinions not correction. You have to make up your own mind about the colour of ink you choose, keeping in mind what is appropriate in the local culture.

Chinese students take offence if you write their names in red. They consider it rude, unlucky or both.

Marking with correction codes

Most teachers use a correction code when they mark written work so that the student can do some self-correction. You can devise your own symbols but Table 7-1 shows some possibilities.

Table 7-1	Correction Codes
Mark	*Error Indicated*
∧	A word is missing
/	Start a new sentence
//	Start a new paragraph
Gr	Grammar error
Sp	Spelling error
P	Punctuation error
Art	Error with articles (a, an, the)
c/unc	Countable/uncountable error (you can use a/an before countable nouns but never before uncountable noun)
Wo	Wrong word order
Ww	Wrong word
Wt	Wrong tense
Wf	Wrong form
Irreg	Irregular verb
?	Unclear

You may not want to highlight every error, as this may leave a piece of writing that reads well overall covered in disconcerting marks.

Many teachers gradually wean their students off the code in stages:

- ✔ Put a symbol next to the error
- ✔ Put symbols in the margin only for each line
- ✔ Give an overall assessment without symbols

The advantage of doing this is that the students gradually become more independent and aware of the need to edit their own work. During this process the teacher presents several compositions by other students so that the whole class can practise editing together.

If your students are comfortable with it, you can encourage peer correction of written work too.

Choosing written errors to work with

As it isn't usually motivating to correct everything in an extended piece of writing, you need to give some thought to which points are worth dealing with and which aren't.

Written work includes several areas that may need correction. These include:

- ✔ **Style**. This covers the right degree of formality and the presentation of the work.
- ✔ **Grammar**.
- ✔ **Vocabulary**.
- ✔ **Cohesion.** There needs to be a linking of ideas with appropriate words such as *because, therefore* and *after that*.
- ✔ **Task completion**. Consider whether the piece of writing has really fulfilled the task that you set.At the top of the list of mistakes to correct, many teachers put style. Whenever students write they should have a reader in mind and reflect this in the degree of formality and the presentation. Take the two pieces of writing in Figure 7-1 for example.

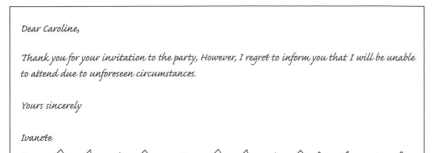

Figure 7-1:
Which
note would
you like to
receive if
you were
Caroline?

The first note doesn't contain any particular errors, but it's inappropriate for the situation. However, the second version has several inaccuracies but it also displays real warmth because of the style. I suspect that Caroline would prefer to receive the second version.

So, when your students write, train them to use appropriate layout, style and register (degree of formality). I talk about appropriate style and register in Chapter 11.

When you correct grammar, try not to get too distracted from the purpose of the text. It's best to focus on expressions that students are likely to use repeatedly.

So, for example, if your class is preparing for higher education, the students probably need to grasp the use of passive sentences in general because these are common to academic writing. If a student wrote: 'First you connect the tube to the cylinder and then you fill it up with liquid.' you may note that he should use passive constructions for describing a process.

After you add your corrections, make it clear whether you expect the student to do the writing over again. Redoing the work helps to fix the corrections in the student's mind, but sometimes he's sick of the sight of it by then and may prefer to transfer the information to a new piece of writing. I encourage students to keep a copy of the original anyway so that they can compare that one, the teacher-edited version and the new improved one.

Marking criteria

A useful tool for students when they attempt longer compositions is marking criteria that inform students what you're looking at and whether they'll receive a grade, percentage or a score. After all students may resent spending all their time checking their spelling if it isn't what you're really looking for.

Areas you may want to focus on include:

- ✔ **Structure:** The composition should include an introduction, body and conclusion.
- ✔ **Content:** Each paragraph should contain a topic sentence and a clearly explained point with examples when necessary.
- ✔ **Verb tenses:** A variety of tenses are used accurately and appropriately.

Marking criteria help students keep their focus.

Praising the good bits

Your red (or other coloured) pen can have a positive function too. If the students' work contains some good aspects, tell them so. It's rewarding for students to see positive remarks and some personal interaction from the teacher. So they'll usually welcome comments such as the following:

- ✔ Good point!
- ✔ Well written!
- ✔ That's better!

And suppose that your students express their thoughts on a matter, you can tell them what you think as well.

> ✔ I agree!
>
> ✔ You surprise me!

When you continue your rapport with a student in writing, the teaching environment becomes friendlier and more encouraging.

Exposing Progress

Quite a number of course books in TEFL have progress tests built in after every three units or so. Such evaluations can be useful for you and the students to see how well you're covering the syllabus. Also the way that you handle the students' errors can lead to more learner independence.

I recommend the kind of procedure listed below for good teamwork and turning the negatives (errors) into positives (reviewing):

1. **Prepare the students to expect the test and encourage them to revise.**

2. **Give them the test.**

3. **Allow the students to compare their answers in small groups and enter into discussion about who's right and why.**

   • Give each group a copy of the answer key so they can mark their answers.

   • Allow the groups a further 5–10 minutes for comparison and discussion.

4. **Encourage the students to consult their course books and clear up any doubts.**

5. **Have a class feedback session where students ask the class for help with any outstanding problems.**

6. **Make sure that everyone in the class understands their errors.**

Apart from tests, another way to measure progress is by continual assessment. This means that you regularly evaluate how each student is performing in class and keeping up with the course. It's very useful to note errors regularly and compare them every few weeks or so to see whether you've remembered to deal with the error and whether the student is improving. In Table 7-2 I show a system you can use for making notes on an individual student's errors. Categorising errors in this way helps you identify particular areas of difficulty for the student, as one column may have more *x*s than others.

Table 7-2 **A form for dealing with common errors**

Description	Error						Action taken	Resolved?
	Grammar	Vocabulary	Pronun-ciation	Lack of cultural insight	Register – too informal	Other		
Can't pronounce words spelt with th, says t or d 02/04/09			X				Unit from Ship or Sheep 05/04/09	Partially, can now hear the difference
Missing articles 05/04/09	X						Grammar exercises from Murphy 07/04/09 as homework	'A/an' okay but needs to work on 'the'
Handwriting – many words illegible 15/04/09						X	Spoke to student. Asked him to be careful 17/04/09	

Chapter 8

Being Materialistic! Using Course Books and Other Materials

....

In This Chapter

▶ Making use of published materials

▶ Identifying popular course books and resources

▶ Adjusting your course book to suit your students

▶ Bringing in real objects

▶ Creating your own materials

▶ Using what's available

....

Depending on the teaching situation you find yourself in, you may have a full library of resources at your disposal or just a piece of chalk and a blackboard. In this chapter, I show you how to make use of whatever tools you have to make a lively lesson.

Wasting No Time Reinventing the Wheel

Some newly initiated teachers resolve to prepare every lesson from scratch, like an organic meal. They believe that their dedication and attention is enough to produce efficient, engaging materials that are going to amaze students in the modern world. Well, even if this is true in rare cases, how long does it take? If you include the time you spend with your scissors and glue when you calculate your hourly rate, you may find that you're working for peanuts by choice.

Face it: The wheel has already been invented, in this case by large publishing houses who've been producing TEFL materials for decades and who have a wide range of research and technology available to them.

Most course books include the four skills – reading, writing, speaking, listening – as well as pronunciation. A good book caters for different learning styles through varied activities, whereas your lesson plans probably tend to play to your own strengths and learning style – it's only natural. So for example, if you like learning visually, you teach most of your lessons that way too. Using a book helps you include activities that suit all types of learners. I mention different learning styles and accommodating them in your presentations in Chapter 5.

Published course books definitely have their place in TEFL and although you may not choose to use one in every lesson, having them around provides some read advantages:

✔ The course syllabus is clearly set out for you and the students.

✔ If each student has a book it reduces your preparation time including photocopying.

✔ It's easy for students to see their progress as they work their way through the book.

✔ Authors and publishers have experience in the field so you feel supported and guided.

✔ Course books often come as part of a set that includes extra resources, so they offer room for expansion and variety.

When you're choosing a book for your students, keep a few points in mind:

✔ Books aren't cheap, so find one that suits your students' pockets.

✔ Consider the cultural suitability of the book. Will the class be able to identify with the images and written content? Is there anything which may seriously offend or upset your students such as constant references to the pub if you're dealing with a teetotal community?

Listing Popular Course Books and Published Resources

When it comes to course books, the majority are written in a series to cover all the levels from elementary to advanced. (I explain the levels of EFL in Chapter 4.) In most cases a school buys five books per level but an individual teacher can make do with less.

Cambridge International Book Centre (www.eflbooks.co.uk) lists more than 12,000 titles in English language teaching.

Common teaching materials can include:

- ✓ **Student's book:** The book the students use in class.
- ✓ **Teacher's book:** This book usually contains the answers to exercises in the student's book and fleshes out the lesson plan for each unit with background information and tips.
- ✓ **CDs**: Sometimes included with the student's book but not always. They can be fairly costly, so check this out before you commit your students to the cost.
- ✓ **Work book:** To save photocopying, you can often get work books that students use as homework.
- ✓ **Resource book:** This book for teachers contains extra, photocopiable activities.

Many books tell you how many hours of study they provide. Compare this with the length of your course before you decide how much material you actually need. Try not to get carried away!

Certain publishers crop up often in the lists of recommended books in the next sections. Representatives from these companies are happy to visit schools to keep you informed of the latest resources. Some even do presentations with students where they explain how best to use their books for effective study. As an individual teacher you can contact these publishers and ask to join their mailing lists. From time to time you can receive sample copies of the latest books and information on any new releases.

Going for general English books

Some of the most well-known and successful general English books for adults from the UK are, in no particular order:

- ✓ *New English File* by Oxenden, Latham Koening and Seligson, published by Oxford University Press
- ✓ *New Headway* by Liz and John Soars, published by Oxford University Press
- ✓ *Landmark* by Simon Haines, published by Oxford University Press
- ✓ *New Inside Out* by Sue Kay and Vaughan Jones, published by MacMillan
- ✓ *Cutting Edge* by Cunningham, Moor and Comyns Carr, published by Longman

- *Innovations* by Dellar and Walkley, published by Thomson/Heinle ELT
- *Language In Use* by Doff and Jones, published by Cambridge University Press
- *face2face* by Redston, Cunningham and Bell, published by Cambridge University Press

Just for back-up in those emergency situations, take a look at *More Grammar Games: Cognitive, Affective and Movement Activities for EFL Students* by Davis and Rinvolucri, published by Cambridge University Press.

Imparting business English

Titles for business English include:

- *English for International Tourism* by Dubicka and O'Keefe, published by Pearson Longman. Includes material for testing students and a video.
- *Business Basics New Edition* by Grant and McLarty, published by Oxford University Press for lower-level students.
- *The Business English Handbook* by Emmerson, published by Macmillan for advanced learners.

Starting off younger learners

Even youngsters learning English can benefit from a book. You can find multi-media resources to work with and all kinds of games and quizzes. Some popular courses for children and teenagers are:

- *Playway to English* by Gerngross and Puchta, a series published by Cambridge University Press for very young children.
- *Join In* by Gerngross and Puchta, a series published by Cambridge University Press for very young children.
- *Backpack* by Herrera and Pinkley, a series published by Longman for primary school children.
- *English World* by Hocking and Bowen, a new series published by Macmillan for primary school children.
- *Top Score* by Falla and Davies, a series published by Oxford University Press for teenagers.

Adapting Your Course Book

Apart from the fact that most teachers like to put their own stamp on a lesson, other reasons may make it necessary for you to tinker with the material the course book presents. One is that course books adhere quite closely to a particular level, so if you have some outstanding students and other extremely weak ones and no hope of moving them up or down, you need to adapt to all your students. Similarly, if all your students are at an intermediate level but a couple are teenagers, a few are housewives, there's a middle-aged businessman and a great-grandfather you need to tailor your lessons to meet everyone's interests – or try to!

Catering to a class of mixed ability

If one student is much better than the rest of the class, she may get bored with lessons using material she already knows. You need to think of ways to extend the exercises in the book to provide a greater challenge.

For the more advanced students, try these options:

- Provide a learners' dictionary so that students can look up words in the course book and prepare to explain them to the rest of the class. This is an alternative to pre-teaching (teaching the meaning of new vocabulary just before students encounter it in the lesson materials) vocabulary yourself.

- While other students are still reading, set an extra activity for the quicker students:

  • Have them transform all the verbs into a different tense.

  • Have them retell the story without using particular 'taboo' words.

  These exercises stretch their grammar and vocabulary respectively.

For weaker students, you can:

- Supplement the book by offering extra information. Plan additional presentations on points that the students find difficult and prepare glossaries of the vocabulary in a particular lesson for easy reference.

- Make the activities easier than the ones in the book. For example, where the book has a fill-in-the-gap exercise, you can give the students a multiple choice option.

- Make greater use of the images as these are less threatening to the student than words. Ask easier questions about what is in a picture and get students to label it.

- Split up a unit to make the content more manageable and less stressful.

For both weak and strong students, include more competitions and games with the same language aims as the syllabus in the book. When the students work together in mixed ability groups they support each other and the group can establish its own pace, whereas exercises in a course book are less fluid.

Dealing with mixed age groups

In a class with different age groups, think about what the task or exercise in the book is aiming to achieve and keep this focus while changing the setting.

In a personal example, in a lesson about expressing figures, the course book presented a graph about profit and loss in a construction company. The teenage students were ready to switch off before they even read the instructions. So, I encouraged them to change the setting to one based on music. Instead of a construction company, their graph was now about a rock star's record sales. The students could come up with reasons for the sales performance, whether based on the serious economic factors or on music trends and concert performances. Once they'd analysed the graph in their own way, I mixed the students up again to summarise their findings because the basic language remained the same – increase, decrease, peak, slump and so on.

There isn't that much difference in the language you teach students of different ages, especially at lower levels. It's the setting in which you put the language that really makes the difference.

Setting tasks

Sometimes students don't engage with the material or feel that it's not relevant to them. In this case, set students tasks based on the book. Get students role-playing characters in the book, and having debates about points made in the text. They can also read a passage aloud in the manner of a particular adverb (quickly, snobbishly and so on) or dictate short sections to each other to practise pronunciation.

When you plan your lesson, include a warm-up activity and maybe a cooldown one too, which have nothing to do with the book. And don't open the book until it's absolutely necessary. Insist that students close the book during the stages of the lesson when it's not needed so that they focus on what you're saying, or so that they try hard to use their own words instead of reading.

Making Use of Authentic Materials

If you're not using a course book for a particular lesson, or at all for that matter, you can make use of *realia,* real objects you take into the classroom to help you teach – anything from a banana to an old shoe. Apart from objects, realia can also be some form of text that wasn't designed for TEFL, such as an article from *The Guardian* or a recording of a sitcom.

When you use realia, often the object sparks the idea for the lesson rather than the other way round. If you have an item that's quintessentially British (or from your culture) that your students may find intriguing, you may wonder how you can use it in the classroom. So, a Dr Martens boot and a Clarks sandal are great props for a lesson on comparisons (*This boot looks much stronger than that shoe,* for example) and since, more than likely, everyone in the classroom has their own shoes you'll find great opportunities to expand the theme.

When it comes to the banana, the obvious lesson to bring it in for is one on fruit and veg, but you can also start a more general discussion on healthy eating, recipes, or idioms ('Don't be such a banana!', a banana republic and so on).

Although the realia won't give you a lesson, it can give you an air of mystery and amusing eccentricity as your students anticipate what you'll turn up with next.

Don't let the desire to show off the realia be the main point of your lesson. If anyone should run into one of your students on the way home and ask what they learnt today, the answer should never be 'I don't know, but she was carrying a boot the whole time!'

With the advent of the Internet, you can harness an endless supply of material in English for your lessons. Hurrah! English speakers also have the advantage of being able to call upon Hollywood movies, decades of famous tunes from the Beatles to the Scissor Sisters and all the science and technology papers conveniently written in English. So it makes sense to use authentic materials like these in the classroom.

Using text other than course books has a few drawbacks though, such as these:

- ✔ It's hard to find materials just the right length for your lesson.
- ✔ Material designed for native speakers is often too difficult for learners in terms of grammar and vocabulary.
- ✔ The text may contain too much slang or irrelevant vocabulary.
- ✔ Students may become overwhelmed by the variety of accents and vocabulary in the English-speaking world.

✔ Authentic materials are so 'of the moment' that you need some knowledge of current affairs and culture to really appreciate them and they soon become out of date.

✔ It takes time to select, adapt and/or prepare them.

However, using authentic materials really motivates students because it gives them a glimpse of what they'll be able to access in English when their language skills improve.

In my case, I learned a foreign language with the help of children's programmes. They were authentic shows at the right level for me and they actually gave me an insight into the culture. I gradually moved on to daytime TV and finally the news. I found that, unlike the lessons in my student's books, the language I learned from TV shows was exactly what 'real people' said. My expressions and pronunciation were not as dry and stilted as friends who'd only studied in the classroom. I'm not suggesting that you take recordings of children's TV shows into your classroom but the principle remains that if your students want to learn to speak like natives, expose them to authentic speech and texts.

Designing Your Own Materials

If you happen to be in a situation where there are few, if any, published materials, or if you're just a creative soul, you can have a stab at designing your own materials to keep and re-use. I say re-use, because it's easy to spend hours preparing the perfect lesson and then forget to file a copy away for another class, effectively loosing the benefit of your work.

To combat this I offer a few tips to help you:

✔ Use cards and laminating so that you won't have to cut things up again next time.

✔ You don't have to make one for each student. Group and pair work encourages speaking so just make enough to share.

✔ To get full use of your materials, build your whole lesson around the theme.

I've seen some beautifully designed materials used for just three minutes in a lesson and then forgotten because the teacher didn't consider how to exploit their design. So, if you've recorded a conversation that you want to use as a listening activity, ask the students to predict what the conversation is going to be about, compare their ideas, analyse the tape-script, imagine the characters who are speaking, describe them, extend the conversation themselves, role play it and so on.

✔ Separate visuals from exercises so that you can use the same visual image in many different ways.

✔ Keep your worksheets and re-use them but make little changes each time so that the examples are more personalised.

✔ Make sure that you present and lay out your material well. Even if your ideas are great, students are put off by anything dull, cluttered or unclear.

✔ Use famous names and brands in your examples as students are likely to use them in real life anyway.

✔ Make sure that your worksheet instructions unfold step by step. So, don't give out all the instructions at once. Give the students what they need to complete one stage at a time.

✔ If you design materials for a school you work in, you should agree beforehand on the future use of this work even after you leave the company.

Using What's at Hand

In training sessions with aspiring teachers, I very often reject published materials in order to demonstrate that you can grab students' attention with just the basic classroom equipment.

Even an atrocious artist can manage the occasional stick figure – witness the one in Figure 8-1. Poor drawings are actually rather good for raising a smile among your students. You may occasionally create confusion when your stick figure horse looks more like a giraffe but your students still have fun guessing what it's supposed to be. It makes a change for them to be laughing at your failings for a change.

Figure 8-1:
A stick figure can be a helpful and amusing visual.

From a simple stick figure you can create an entire back story in collaboration with your students. For example, a class can practice the past simple using a stick man on the board:

> Teacher: What's his name?
>
> Student A: His name is David.
>
> Student B: His name is Abdul.
>
> Student C: No, it's Ramon.
>
> Teacher: Okay, it's Ramon. Where's he from, class?
>
> Students: Colombia!
>
> Teacher: How's he feeling today?
>
> Students: He's happy.
>
> Teacher: I think he's happy because something good happened yesterday. What happened?
>
> Student A: I think he's happy because he met a girl!

The lesson can continue with students drawing their own additions to the story on the board, while their classmates guess what happened. The pictures, along with some key vocabulary that you write up, can serve as the basis for a writing or speaking activity with students telling each other the story.

When you're teaching grammar, a nice clear layout on the board is the best substitute for a worksheet. Use columns and boxes so that everything is clear. Lists and mind maps are also easy to copy down. Mind maps are diagrams which look a bit like spiders because you put the main idea in the centre and then have 'legs' coming out from the middle that point to related ideas and information.

Beyond the use of the board, your most effective tool is your own body. Use your voice well by varying pace and power as much as possible. Use good volume and gestures (Chapter 7 has a section on body language). Acting and mime are great fun and keep the lesson lively.

Chapter 9

Who's The Boss around Here? Managing Your Classroom

In This Chapter

▶ Managing your students

▶ Getting your classroom organised

▶ Setting rules of behaviour

▶ Maintaining control in your class

▶ Taking care of problems

*W*hen you're in the classroom, you do more than just teach. You're the manager and your students look to you for professional handling of their course and the people on it.

In this chapter, I explain how you can deal with problems relating to students and your teaching environment. I also offer suggestions and advice for running your classes and handling difficulties too.

Running Your Classes Effectively

As the teacher, it's your responsibility to maintain order during the course. First, you need to be aware of the time and location of the classes. It may be up to the school to decide this but you should think ahead about your availability to complete the job and be on time. The premises should be suitable for teaching but you may need to make some adjustments. Find out who the students are and how to record their attendance and progress. You need a course syllabus and individual lessons plans but while the lesson is in progress you have to manage your students too. Everyone in the classroom, including you, should behave appropriately, which means being friendly, maintaining a sense of fun but being disciplined at the same time. If students are out of line you need a strategy for dealing with this too.

Some general points of good practice I find very helpful in almost all teaching situations include:

- **Plan ahead.** As far as possible, think about where your course is heading and what possible pitfalls you may encounter along the way. This means knowing where you're teaching, what equipment and resources are available, as much about your students as possible and any personal considerations that may affect your teaching (planned absences, for example). In other words, try to prevent problems before they happen.

- **Ask for and welcome feedback.** The students have their own opinions about how well you teach, but many teachers are too proud or scared to hear them. One of the dangers for teachers is that they can become over-confident because the students appear happy in your class but, to be honest, students don't always have a measure of comparison. You can encourage constructive criticism though by designing feedback forms that ask for specific information. The results of the feedback guide you on changes necessary to make your teaching of the course, the course materials, or any other area under your control more effective. If you invite a colleague to watch you occasionally, his advice can help you to stay on track professionally and avoid getting stuck in a rut.

- **Start off quite strict and ease up later if you can**. Set the right tone from the word 'go'. Students expect you to be in control, so they won't find you unfriendly just because you impose rules. In fact, once they know the rules you won't have to keep reminding them because they remind each other. In this way you're not cast in the role of the bad guy and can get on with making the lessons enjoyable.

- **Start and finish on time.** If you don't respect your students' time, they won't respect yours either. Stick to the scheduled time and apologise if, for some reason, things don't go to plan.

- **Respect your students.** Treat your students as clients and remember that just because they don't know English doesn't mean that they're incompetent or unintelligent.

  Hold your students' cultures in high regard too. There's more than one way to skin a cat and the way you're accustomed to in your own land is not necessarily the best.

- **Maintain a sense of humour**. This is one of the single, most important factors in running a memorable course. Laugh at yourself, laugh with your students when they laugh at themselves, and laugh just to have a good time.

Organising Your Classroom

The layout of your TEFL classroom depends to some extent on the resources available to you. What you do with them is largely up to you. Even if the chairs are fixed to the floor, you can introduce less regimentation with creative wall decorations.

Considering basic equipment

The basic equipment is, of course, a place for your students to sit and a board for you to write on. However, you need to think about a few other considerations such as:

- The size and shape of the room.
- The number of students.
- Equipment such as electrical items that need to be connected to a power socket.
- Special and individual needs your students may have. A partially sighted student needs to be close to the board, and left-handers may need extra elbow room – just two examples.
- The surrounding environment including noise from traffic or other rooms. Check whether you can have the windows or door open.
- Lighting. Make sure that there are no dark corners or a glare on the white board.
- The versatility of the furniture. Some schools nail their furniture to the floor, whereas in others cases you may have a choice of the items to use.
- Where students put their bags and coats. Get a few hooks put up, especially if you want your students to have the freedom to move around.
- Heating and cooling. There should be adequate ventilation and temperature control to enable your students to concentrate.

Most teachers like to personalise their classrooms when it's appropriate by putting up posters, reminders, notices and examples of students' work.

Hopefully your school has a self-access centre for students to do extra work in but if not, make an area of your classroom a mini self-access centre where students can pick up a novel or magazine and use a computer to research their work. If the budget is tight, try using free literature such as holiday brochures for English-speaking countries there, along with some extra grammar and vocabulary exercises.

Arranging the room

When it comes to tables and chairs, each style has its own advantages. I show you the various types of arrangements and talk about their good and bad points in the next sections.

Circling the horseshoe

The most popular layout is a horseshoe formation, shown in Figure 9-1.

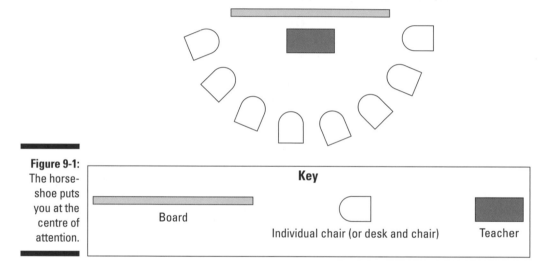

Key

Board

Individual chair (or desk and chair)

Teacher

Figure 9-1:
The horse-shoe puts you at the centre of attention.

The advantage of this layout is that everyone in the room can easily see everyone else and the board. In addition, students usually have room to stand in the middle for more energetic activities.

This layout gives an informal atmosphere to the class but is not for very large groups (much more than 20). It functions well when students work only from their chairs (without a desk) or with tablet chairs (where a mini-desk is attached to the chair).

Grouping students together

Another style, shown in Figure 9-2, is particularly suited to group work. In this case students work at a desk in pairs or fours.

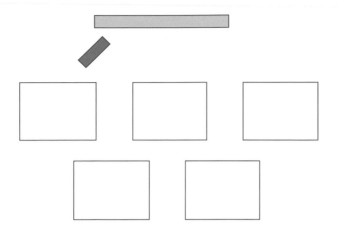

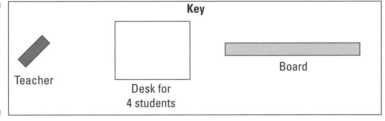

Figure 9-2:
Gathering
students
into groups
aids
interaction.

Make sure that you're able to walk around the desks (large desks or groups of desks) so you can interact freely with students and monitor their work.

In order for students to see the board and you, they can sit sideways on.

Going for traditional rows

The most traditional classroom layout, shown in Figure 9-3, is mainly suitable for exams and tests.

Students in this kind of layout are less likely to feel relaxed and part of a team.

You're likely to find classrooms set up like this unless you ask for something different, but don't accept the room as you find it. Arrive early to set things up in the best way for you and your students.

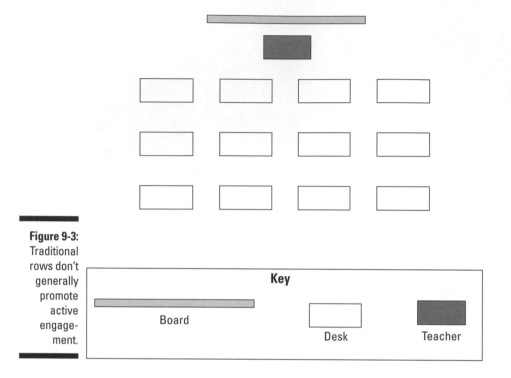

Figure 9-3:
Traditional rows don't generally promote active engagement.

Establishing Classroom Rules

Many language schools have rules for students set out in their terms and conditions, which takes some of the pressure off you because students read and agree to them before entering the classroom. However, as teachers and classmates vary it's a good idea to establish rules at the beginning of the course that reflect the situation of the class. The students can get involved in agreeing some of the rules.

Some common classroom rules are:

✔ Latecomers must not disrupt the class. In some cases you can set a time limit after which the student may not enter the room. In any case, students should display good manners instead of barging in.

✔ Students should bring their own materials (books, pens, paper to write on).

✔ Students should avoid behaviour that's offensive to their classmates and to their teacher. This includes swearing (in English or their mother tongue), styles of dress (highly inappropriate compared with the local culture) and body odour.

✔ No smoking in the classroom.

✔ No eating during the lesson.

✔ Mobile phones must be switched off or on silent. If a student leaves the room to answer a call, he's only allowed to re-enter at the teacher's discretion.

✔ Students shouldn't speak to each other while you're addressing the class and only one student can speak to the class at a time.

Keeping Order

Once you've set up the course and the classroom you need to think about managing the people. Your aim is to build confidence in your students so that they respect your guidance and instructions. At the same time, you should encourage a learning environment that sees all the students treated fairly by you and their classmates. When a student is disruptive you need to deal with the matter efficiently so that there's minimal distraction from the lesson. Learning English is the priority so other matters that students choose to raise shouldn't use up valuable lesson time.

These tips can help you set the right tone and expectations for your students:

✔ **Teach classroom language.** Tell students the words they need to communicate their learning problems to you. It's easy to lose control of a class when they stop speaking English in favour of their mother tongue, but if they know how to say things like, 'I'm sorry, I don't understand. Could you repeat please?' they can let you know when things are going wrong. You can put phrases like this up on the wall or ask students to write them at the back of their course books.

I teach words such as stationery, classroom furniture and several polite requests too. One example is *Would you excuse me for a moment?* because when students lack this kind of vocabulary they fall back on their own language again.

✔ **Don't start until everyone is listening**. There's nothing worse than shouting over boisterous students in an attempt to teach the other quieter ones. It's best to ask for silence and wait for it. Those who want to learn actually help you to maintain order.

Some cultures find speaking over one another acceptable so you may want to point out what you consider to be good classroom etiquette at the start of the course.

✔ **Establish the rules clearly.** If you need to get the rules translated or represented in pictures, go ahead. It's only fair that your students know when and why they're out of line before you pull them up. (The preceding section offers suggestions for rules to set.)

✔ **Don't let problems escalate**. Nip problems in the bud because this helps to maintain a pleasant environment. (I offer troubleshooting advice in the next section.)

✔ **Give ample warning of the consequences of continued rule breaking**. In other words, don't throw a student out for a first misdemeanour. Remind him of what will happen if he does it again. Agree how many warnings you're prepared to give before taking action, a bit like the yellow and red cards in football.

✔ **Be consistent.** There's no point making idle threats. Just do what you say you intend to do. This is one way of gaining respect.

✔ **Be fair and don't hold a grudge**. It isn't right to let one student off and not another. Try to treat your students equally and avoid giving the brightest ones all your attention.

✔ **Don't let other students get involved**. Resolve problems privately in the corridor or after the lesson when others have left. People always react better when they're allowed to save face and when they've no mates around to egg them on.

✔ **Lean on the school for support**. The director of studies should advise you of disciplinary procedures for students and the rules they're expected to abide by. Actually you should only be handling minor misdemeanours yourself. In most cases adult students have a copy of the terms and conditions and as a last resort they can face expulsion.

Troubleshooting

If your course doesn't seem to be flowing, there may be various reasons for this. Teachers find that, typically, a number of difficulties recur.

Some common problems include:

✔ **Students don't bring their books.** Don't keep photocopying everything. If students are slightly inconvenienced by having to share resources they're more likely to bring their own copies.

✔ **A student fancies you or vice versa.** Wait until the course finishes to make your move because things can get very heated if you end up with a spurned lover in your classes. If you don't want to accept the advances of a student at all, allow him to feel that you've rejected him for professional reasons. It's less embarrassing.

✔ **The class is too big.** This comes down to school policy but if you happen to have a class of 30 or 40, identify the more capable students and make them group leaders. Ask them to help you by organising the other students. They may enjoy being used as assistant teachers too.

✔ **Your school says that you have to use a particular course book but it's as dull as ditchwater.** Follow the syllabus but supplement the book with your own ideas whenever you can.

Dealing with disruptive students

Students are disruptive for various reasons. The most common problem is that they're bored because they don't understand or because they don't have enough to do. Students who really are too smart for the level, or not competent enough for it, should move to another class. Ask the school for help arranging this.

Keep a few extra activities on hand to keep the faster workers busy.

Disruptive students come in some familiar forms:

✔ **The 'clever-clogs' who asks questions to show off or just to catch you out.** One solution is to ask them to do their research at home and report their findings to you after the next lesson. They won't be playing to a full house after the lesson so may not bother but if they do and their findings are correct, you can try involving them in presenting the information to the class at an appropriate time.

✔ **The student who wants to have a personal consultation in the middle of the lesson.** These characters ask questions that no one else in the class is interested in or that have no connection to the lesson (or even the course for that matter).

I recommend that when a student says, 'Can I ask a question?' you find out whether it's directly relevant to the situation. You can reply by asking whether the student's question is about the lesson because if not he can ask you later (when he'll probably have forgotten it anyway). If you make it a habit to open up questions to the class, this lessens the focus on you and reinforces the community setting, reminding everyone to do what is best for the group.

If one student is unhappy about the lesson, arrange to talk to him about it afterwards and before he convinces everyone else in the class that he's right and you're wrong. Some students just want to be heard or at least to be satisfied that you're doing your best under the circumstances.

✔ **Students who bully, shun or mock other students in the class.** Employ a zero tolerance attitude in this case. The thing is, these students may not be aware of how strangers see them and are used to getting away with anti-social behaviour. When you show that you just won't accept it, they're forced to analyse what they're doing. Even if they feel that their behaviour is normal in their society, they need to know that in the society they hope to access, the English-speaking countries by and large, it won't wash.

Racial prejudices, sexism and age discrimination may not be law-breaking offences in every land but the way you handle these issues gives students valuable knowledge about how to curb their tongues abroad.

Handling a lack of participation

If your classroom is worryingly quiet, you have a problem on your hands, but fear not, you have ways to increase student participation.

Firstly, it's easier to change yourself than anyone else, so look at your own level of enthusiasm. Keep your energy levels high throughout your lesson (I often have a soft drink on hand, which I can craftily sip to prevent getting dull and dehydrated) and act as though you have full confidence in the success of every activity you present. Cheerfulness is infectious so make sure that you're not a misery guts in class.

Another thing you can do is to ensure that you put your questions simply and create tasks at the appropriate level. Your students are likely to clam up if they don't understand what they have to do.

A nice trick is to drop the level of an activity you present in class so that the students can just concentrate on speaking without grappling with new words and grammar. This may boost their confidence a bit for next time.

Have a look at the pairings and groups you use in class as well. Some combinations amongst the students may not work well. Perhaps two very shy people together don't participate because neither wants to go first. So, rearrange the students frequently by asking them to sit in alphabetical order sometimes, and in order of their birthdays at other times. Just sorting that out requires communication from the students.

You can do speaking activities in concentric circles: in a class of ten students, you have five standing in a circle in the middle, all facing outwards and then five in a circle all around them facing inwards. The inner circle remain still, but the outer circle rotate every few minutes so that they all speak to a different person at regular intervals. It's very helpful for students to do an activity more than once because they improve each time but it doesn't seem boring when they have a different partner for each attempt.

Attending to poor attendance

Poor attendance is a real pain because it affects the progress the class can make. On the other hand, progress also depends on who is turning up to lessons and if you have a hard core of good attenders, You don't need to worry so much about the persistent no show. However, if different people come each time, the only thing you can do is to review previously taught information at the beginning of each lesson.

A course book is a great back-up for students who missed last week or last night as they can at least read through the material by themselves, which allows them to take responsibility for their own learning (if they don't turn up or do their reading, it's their problem not yours).

Of course there may be good reasons why students don't come along, including something you can perhaps change. So try to keep the lines of communication open by asking your students how they're getting on and whether they'd like to suggest any improvements to the course. Of course, you do need to be thick skinned enough to accept constructive criticism.

Part III
Teaching Skills Classes

The 5th Wave   By Rich Tennant

"For the skills part of this lesson I'm handing out the instructions to my smart phone and seeing if they can tell me how to programme it."

In this part . . .

Listening, speaking, reading and writing: the four cornerstone skills of English. Welcome to Part III, which shows you how to master delivering skills skilfully.

I dedicate a chapter to each of these main skills, with a special bonus chapter on pronunciation, since it's such a key component of accurate spoken communication.

Along the way I sprinkle tips on how to keep your lessons lively and how to involve all your students, at whatever level they might be.

Chapter 10

Taken as Read: Teaching Reading Lessons

*R*eading is one of the key skills in language learning. It reinforces the skills students acquire in speaking, listening and writing. On the other hand, it really isn't enough just to put a book or short text in front of students and ask them to read, whether silently or out loud.

You can help students develop a host of sub-skills through activities around reading. And, you can make life easier by selecting reading material that's both at the right level and somewhat interesting.

Many students insist that they prefer to focus on speaking, but before long they want to browse through an English newspaper or read the notices on the Underground. Reading skills help round out your students' English, so in this chapter I focus on this key skill.

Choosing a Text

You can choose from an immense variety of things to read in English – novels, blogs, poems, ads, newspapers, magazines or just flashcards – the list is endless.

Choose a piece of writing that your students are likely to be interested in and is at the right level for them, even if it's just a couple of words long and written on the board. They should be able to understand most of the words on a printed page except for a handful of new words, which you have a strategy for dealing with.

Starting with the ABCs

The alphabet is the most basic reading text you can choose. For EFL (English as a Foreign Language) teachers, using the English alphabet is second nature, but this isn't the case for all EFL students. It may surprise you to know that few students, even those at intermediate level, are comfortable with all 26 letters in their various shapes and sizes – capitals, lower case, handwriting and print.

It never hurts to run through the alphabet at the outset of a course. Make sure that everyone in the class can recognise and say the letters out loud.

Actually you can organise the letters of the alphabet in a memorable way to help students pronounce them accurately. If you're already familiar with *phonemes* (the symbols used to represent all the different sounds in the language), you can use them to group the letters. If not, refer to Chapter 12 for more information.

Even if you don't use the phonemic symbols, rhyming the letters makes things clearer for your students. A good place to start is to analyse the groups and say the letters in Table 10-1 out loud. You can hear that with the exception of the last group the others are similar in the way they're pronounced. This form of analysis based on sound pushes students out of any complacency, as they may believe that they know all the letters based on visual recognition.

Pay particular attention to the vowels. Even higher-level students get them wrong.

Table 10-1	Letters, Sounds and Phonemic Symbols	
Letters	*Sound*	*Phonemic Symbol*
A, J, K, H	**ei** as in day or weigh	/eɪ/
F, L, M, N, S, X, Z	**e** as in egg or let	/e/
B, C, D, E, G, P, T, V	**ee** as in tree or wheat	/iː/
I, Y	**ai** as in my or lie	/aɪ/
Q, U, W	**oo** as in you or blue	/uː/
O, R		

Make sure that your students have a copy of the alphabet in the correct order as well. They need it when using the dictionary.

Practise the alphabet in a fun way by using popular acronyms or abbreviations and see if the students know what they mean. Try these for example:

- ✔ ATM: Automated teller machine
- ✔ BBC: British Broadcasting Corporation
- ✔ BMX: Bicycle motorcross
- ✔ DVD: Digital versatile disc
- ✔ SMS: Short message service
- ✔ UNICEF: United Nations International Children's Emergency Fund

Reading whole words

Remember how you were taught to recognise individual words back in primary school? The teacher would hold up flashcards and the kids shouted the words out. Well in EFL, lower-level students learn word by word too.

Write new words on the board as soon as the class has repeated the pronunciation. At the same time, help your students to read well by pointing out spelling patterns. After all, English is notoriously difficult to spell and pronounce even for native speakers, so reading aloud can be very daunting for EFL students.

These simple examples of English spelling rules make a world of difference to people learning to read in English:

- ✔ The letter *e* after a vowel and consonant together softens/lengthens the vowel sound. Compare rid and ride, mad and made, or cut and cute.
- ✔ When the letter 's' is between two vowels, it's pronounced like a *z* – rise /raɪz/, present /prezənt/ and pose /pəʊz/.
- ✔ At the beginning of a word gn, kn, and pn are pronounced /*n*/.
- ✔ *Wh* is pronounced /*w*/. There's no need to pronounce the 'h'.
- ✔ *Wr* is pronounced /*r*/. The 'w' is always silent.

You probably know all these rules instinctively but your students need you to spell them out. If you think of any other rules, make a note of them as your students will be eternally grateful.

Graduating from words to sentences with the help of punctuation

In order for students to understand complete sentences on paper, they need an idea of sentence structure and punctuation.

From beginner stage, point out what apostrophes, commas and other marks do. Using a slow deliberate change in your intonation as you read often makes this clear.

Make sure that you know the function of all these punctuation marks and how they affect a sentence:

- . Full stop: This mark shows the end of a complete sentence.

- : Colon: You use a colon before you introduce a list, example or the second part of a sentence that gives more detail about the first part.

- ; Semi-colon: When two sentences are very closely related the writer can make them into one sentence separated by this mark.

  I love the Caribbean; I've lived there for years.

- " Quotation/speech marks: You use these to show the beginning and end of what someone actually said, in that person's words.

  He said, 'See you tonight'.

- , Comma: This mark indicates a pause, as if you were saying the words aloud. You sometimes use a comma instead of brackets when giving extra information and also to separate items on list. So a comma can replace the words *and* and *or* to avoid repeating them.

  My favourite dishes, or foreign ones anyway, are curry, lasagne and paella.

- 'Apostrophe: Use an apostrophe to show that some letters are left out or that something belongs to someone.

  She can't (cannot) drive Paul's car.

- () Brackets/parentheses: Brackets show an interruption in the sentence for the writer to add additional information.

  The house (an ugly place) is still for sale.

- - Hyphen: This is used to join two words or parts of words together.

  There was a break-in at the home of his ex-wife.

- ? Question mark: This mark shows the end of a question.

  Is that statement true?

> ✔ **!** Exclamation mark: You use this mark to show that there's stronger emotion than usual, or surprise, in the statement.
>
> *I just don't believe it!*
>
> ✔ **@ :** I know this *at* sign isn't punctuation, but I included it here because it's become so ubiquitous, meaning that it's everywhere!

Don't be lazy about using question marks and capital letters when you write on the board. Many teachers take these things for granted only to wonder why their students read and write so poorly. Students quickly pick up your bad habits.

From the first lessons you're likely to teach whole phrases such as, 'How are you?' and 'I'm from England'. Get your students to repeat whole sentences as they read from the board and you point out the words one by one. That's not to say that students should only read the words one by one. Aim for fluent, connected speech. They then learn to recognise the words and also how to use the appropriate intonation for a statement or question.

You certainly don't want your students to read like robots. So don't slow down too much when you read aloud. You find that you start to sound unnatural if you do and you won't be using the typical rhythm of the language.

Encourage students to chunk words together too. In this way they're less likely to translate word for word, which often leads to them losing the sense of the sentence.

Higher-level students can also work with individual sentences. For example, they can analyse a list of newspaper headlines or short advertisements. The *puns* (jokes based on words that look or sound the same but have different meanings) and other forms of word play in these short texts are a real challenge for learners. On the other hand, when they get the sense of them, students feel a real sense of accomplishment. Collect any good examples you come across for use in your lessons.

Scores of words sound or look the same in English. If students aren't paying attention to the context, they may get completely the wrong end of the stick. Pay attention when teaching:

✔ **Homophones:** Words that sound the same but are spelled differently and have different meanings. For example, both here/ hear are pronounced /hɪə/ and sight/site are both pronounced /saɪt/.

✔ **Homographs:** Words that look the same but sound different and have different meanings. For example, bow /baʊ/ (to bend from the waist as a sign of respect) and bow /bəʊ/ (a decorative way of tying a ribbon).

Looking at length

Once students are comfortable with sentences, give some consideration to the length of the text you want to use in your lessons.

You can use readers, especially designed for language students, containing short stories and novels. These slim, pocket-sized books are written to match the various levels of EFL courses. They're best used at home but can provide short extracts that you can use in the classroom, safe in the knowledge that the level of English is just right.

The majority of texts EFL teachers use in a lesson are between three and six paragraphs long.

The EFL classroom is generally a fun and lively place in which to learn. So think carefully before introducing a long text that requires extended periods of silence while students read. Shorter texts, or texts you can deal with in stages with periods of discussion in between, tend to be more appealing.

Judging interest and relevance

Now we're all proud of Will Shakespeare, but pause for a moment before you reach for a volume of Hamlet. Is the effort of translating 'To thine own self be true' actually worth it for a student who simply wants to serve British holidaymakers in his café?

Ask yourself, 'What's the aim of this lesson?' If the text practises vocabulary or grammar the class has recently covered, and if it seems pretty interesting or relates to something the students need to know in the future, you're on the right lines.

So if you have a nifty recipe for shepherd's pie that you fancy using in class, don't be put off just because your students are unlikely to make the dish. Think about what kind of language your students are practising. Verbs like chop, slice and mix are useful for anyone who cooks. On the other hand, you may be using your recipe to demonstrate how to describe the process of doing something (first . . . , and after that . . . , and finally . . .). Or perhaps you feel your students need a little more cultural awareness. It's perfectly valid to have as an aim something that's not based on grammar and vocabulary, providing that the level of English in the text is appropriate.

Other texts suitable for beginners are timetables – where students need to say what time something happens – shopping lists and menus where the vocabulary is limited but the class can practise saying prices and calling out individual items. You may be surprised how useful authentic English texts can be for practising in class.

Put together a selection of these text types:

- ✔ Diary entries
- ✔ Emails
- ✔ Cartoon strips
- ✔ Food labels and ingredients
- ✔ TV guide listings

Working with the Text

Students should be ready for the text and have a purpose for reading in the form of a task or question. You need to have a strategy for dealing with vocabulary and to design a follow-up activity to expand on the same theme. If you follow these steps, your reading lessons can really open the door to a world of English texts and literature to your students.

Getting ready to read: Pre-reading tasks

Everyone needs a reason for reading, even if it's just to pass the time of day. Don't just hand out a text and expect students to get stuck in. Have them do a bit of preparation first.

A pre-reading task whets the appetite and prepares the mind for the text that follows. As the name suggests, the task doesn't involve reading the text but is connected to the main topic of the lesson.

So what kinds of pre-reading task can you use? You can have a discussion about the author. Find out what the class knows about him or her. On the other hand, if the text represents an aspect of English speaking culture that's unusual for the students, have a pop quiz about it or bring in some pictures.

Before reading an article from *The Sun* newspaper, have a class discussion about what tabloid newspapers are, and how they differ from broadsheets like *The Times*. Identify the new vocabulary in the text and put six or seven of the new words on a worksheet with their definitions. If you mix things up, you can ask students, in pairs or small groups, to match the words to their definitions. You can also ask what the words may have in common too.

List all the numbers or locations in the text. Students can make up their own story with them and then read the text afterwards to see whether their ideas were similar to the text.

Finding your way around

Helping your students to identify the structure of a reading text is a useful way of focusing the mind, so be aware of how the text is put together. This means looking first at the title and pictures that introduce the topic. Next, read any subheadings or just the first line of each paragraph, which should each contain a slightly different idea to the previous one. Is there an introduction and conclusion? Point these out too.

Now that you're aware of how it all fits together, you can make the text less intimidating for your students by showing them these signposts. Reading in another language can seem really daunting but once students know how to find their way around the text they should be more positive about this skill, especially if they're likely to enter higher education in English.

Getting the gist

You get the gist of a text by *skimming* it, or reading through it fairly quickly to form an impression of what it's about. After the pre-reading task, students should glance through the whole text quickly.

An analysis of the structure, which I talk about in the preceding section, involves skimming.

Try giving your students a multiple choice of answers and ask which places, numbers or characters are mentioned in the text. They can find the answer by glancing through without reading each line.

Set a time limit of just a few minutes for all skimming activities.

Getting down to the nitty-gritty

After the students take a good overview of the text it's time for a closer look at the details. This is called *scanning*. Students can't spend as much time as they want analysing every word in the text but they do have more time than the skimming stage. They now read to find specific, not general, information.

A typical comprehension exercise involves scanning, whether it involves true or false questions, multiple choice or filling in missing words.

It's more fun if students read different texts in groups and write their own comprehension questions to test their classmates.

Another more detailed scanning activity is called *multiple matching*. This is where you match a variety of paragraphs and specifications together. Say the class is reading film reviews, the students can then match an appropriate film with the profile of a person you've given them. For example:

> John is a horror fan but he doesn't mind science fiction. His girlfriend Penny likes American films but prefers unknown actors. Read the six film reviews and decide which film they could see together.

With three or four questions like this the students match information together and test their comprehension.

Predicting

Another skill worth making use of in reading lessons is *prediction*. If you can make a fair stab at what's coming next, it shows you've understood what's happened so far and builds up excitement. Any self-respecting novel does this at the end of each chapter. So why not choose a text with a decent storyline? Instead of having long periods of silence in the classroom, the students can read smaller sections and then debate how the plot is going to develop.

For example, here's the introduction to a short story with a prediction question:

> Ravi was awake. He opened his eyes slowly and pushed his arms straight. It was already too hot, at least 30 degrees, and the city streets were full of men and children rushing along to catch the crowded buses. Ravi's stomach was rather noisy this morning, so he decided to . . .

Prediction questions:

What did Ravi decide to do? Compare your ideas.

What did your classmates predict?

Now read the next paragraph to find out what Ravi decided.

Use an overhead projector so that you can uncover one paragraph at a time, or alternatively, fold the text handout so that each fold contains one key section for consideration.

Summarising

Summarising is a valuable skill for students. A summary explains or shows what the whole text is about but in a brief way. You can have them do it verbally, in the form of a diagram or in writing. Even children can summarise by drawing a picture based on what they've read.

Some ideas for summarising are to have students read separate related texts, which they then explain to each other. Give your students a table to fill in with key points or ask them to give a one-minute presentation in front of the class.

Bring in a handful of film reviews. Divide students into groups, with a member for each review and have each student read a different review. Hand out a table such as the one in Table 10-2. As each student tells the group about her review, the others can listen and complete the table with all the films.

Table 10-2		Reviewing Films		
Name of film	*Genre*	*Plot*	*Star*	*Rating*
Vampire Attack	Horror	Vampires invade London looking for more victims.	Brad Cruise	*****
Love In London	Romance	Two tourists from different worlds meet and fall in love in Trafalgar Square.	Denzel Snipes and Jennifer Streep	***

Handling Vocabulary

You can handle new words in a reading exercise in a few ways:

- ✔ Get the vocabulary out of the way from the outset by teaching it in the pre-reading stage.
- ✔ Let the students read first and work on the meaning of individual words afterwards.
- ✔ Don't deal with vocabulary at all so that students learn to find their own coping strategies.

In the first two cases beware of wasting time on words that can just as well be ignored. Even native speakers encounter words they're unfamiliar with and may not look up them up if they're still able to understand what they're reading.

The next sections explore each option in turn.

Before you set off

You can make new words a pre-reading task (see 'Getting ready to read: Pre-reading' earlier in the chapter). This works well if students aren't used to reading in English and need a little reassurance that they can do it. This technique makes sense especially when a new word occurs so frequently in the reading that the meaning is necessary to make any sense of the thing.

Along the way

Get your students to underline new words as they read but without necessarily stopping to check the meaning. They need to read with relative fluency and get an overview of the text. Apart from providing definitions yourself, see if students can help each other. Pooling knowledge is great for keeping everyone involved and interested.

Don't encourage explanations in the students' mother tongue (unless you're totally fluent). They may be barking up the wrong tree.

If possible, make dictionaries available after the initial reading so that students can manage their own learning. Most schools have class sets of learners' dictionaries (English to English ones, which have the key word and definition in English so that students don't use their mother tongue during the lesson) but you can get the students to bring their own.

If students use a dictionary to translate, it's still important that you check their understanding. Ask open questions using *what, why, how, when* so that they can express their opinions and prove that they understand.

Try another route

Context is the biggest indicator of meaning. You can start the investigation by asking students which part of speech the unknown word is – for example, is it a noun, a verb or an adjective?

Then again, perhaps the new word looks familiar somehow. Maybe it's part of a family of words (love, lovable, unloving, lover, for example). Or is it similar to a word in the students' own language?

English words are mainly derived from Latin and German so a large number of students whose native tongues derive from those languages are prepared to take a stab at the meaning.

And of course, loads of foreign words have been pasted into English and vice versa, so it never hurts for the students to have a go.

Working on Skills Associated with Reading

Reading is rather a broad area. Does the fact that students are reading automatically mean that they're improving? Not always. You can adopt various sub-skills as aims of reading lessons to focus the minds of your students and yourself more keenly and mark the difference between efficient and inefficient readers.

Including reading-related skills

Those students who haven't mastered the following sub-skills from reading in their mother tongue benefit a great deal by developing in these areas:

- ✔ Working out the meaning of new words from the context.
- ✔ Recognising high frequency words.
- ✔ Working out what the purpose of the text is (to entertain, inform and so on).
- ✔ Skimming (see 'Getting the gist' earlier in the chapter).
- ✔ Scanning (see 'Getting down to the nitty-gritty' earlier in the chapter).
- ✔ Summarising and taking notes.
- ✔ Learning how texts are organised.
- ✔ Identifying grammar in context.
- ✔ Reading between the lines.
- ✔ Identifying key and minor points.

Doing more than reading

Reading aloud is just one way to use a text. Other ways are for students to answer comprehension questions, extend the dialogue themselves or fill in deliberately placed gaps, even at beginner level.

Ideas for reading lessons

Some authentic pieces of writing you can use in the classroom include:

- ✔ **Classified ads:** Students can discuss things they'd like to sell or buy – a bike or a piece of furniture, for example. First, talk about ways of buying and selling unwanted items. Then, use a page full of classified ads to practise scanning for particular purchases. Give the students a budget and certain specifications to match the ads with. Finally, as a follow on, students can write their ads and make a notice board in class. Lonely hearts columns are great fun.

- ✔ **Problem pages:** Tell students about a problem you have and ask for some advice. Find out if they know what an agony aunt is and if they're common in their own country. Following that, read letters from a problem page and predict what the advice will be. Read the professional advice on the page and get students' opinions on it. Role-play talking about various problems and giving advice.

- ✔ **Tourist information:** Collect or download leaflets on various tourist attractions in an English-speaking country. Find out what students already know about these places or whether they've visited them. Ask students to write questions they'd like to ask a tour guide and then have them read the leaflets to see whether their questions have been answered. They can read different leaflets and pool their answers. They can write their own tourist information to follow up.

- ✔ **Film blurbs:** Examine the *blurb* (the information on the back cover) of a DVD. Skim by looking at the length of the film, the actors and director but scan by reading about the plot. Find out whether students would be likely to watch the film and ask why. A follow-up listening lesson can involve watching a clip or two.

Notice that in each reading source, you can do a follow-up activity that involves a different skill (not reading).

Before long, students can start performing short dialogues from a script using the phrases from a recent lesson. The following is an extract from a beginners' text. Ask the class to tell you what people say when they meet and put their ideas on the board. Students can then compare their suggestions with the text.

En: Hello! I'm a new student and my name's En. What's your name?

Alejandro: I'm Alejandro and I'm from Venezuela. Pleased to meet you En! Are you from Malaysia?

En: No, I'm not from Malaysia. I'm Chinese.

Alejandro: Oh, you're Chinese! Sorry!

Fabio:

En:

Alejandro:

The text is incomplete so that the students can extend the dialogue themselves.

Comprehension questions for this text may include:

- Where does Alejandro think En is from? Is he right?
- Do En and Alejandro speak the same language?
- Is En a teacher?

Notice that good comprehension questions prove that students have got the sense of the text.

Students can now work in pairs to extend the dialogue by completing Fabio's words and the response given by the En and Alejandro. The class then compares its results.

If you intend the students to read aloud and role-play, it's best if you and a strong student perform the dialogue in front of the class first so that everyone can hear it. Lower-level students will enjoy practising short dialogues in pairs or small groups, swapping roles each time.

Reading Case Study

I prepared this lesson to help a class with their reading skills. It's very easy to update and personalise, so do try it.

- **Class Profile:** 10 adult Italian students in Italy. 90-minute evening class.
- **Level:** Intermediate.
- **Materials:** TV schedule for one evening in English. Extra board pens.
- **Problems:** Pronunciation errors (pronouncing each letter). Drilling needed as students are daunted by the idea of reading long texts in English; focus on scanning.
- **Lesson aims:** To practise scanning in a reading text; to revise and increase vocabulary connected with TV programmes.

The sections of the lesson proceed as follows:

1. **Warm-up (6 minutes)**: Show pictures of characters from famous TV shows, made in English-speaking countries, shown around the world (The Simpsons, Friends, and so on). When students recognise one or two, divide the class into teams and hold a quiz to find out how many characters they can identify.

2. **Pre-reading task (15 minutes)**: Ask each student to find ten words associated with TV shows from their notes or general knowledge and then ask them to write the vocabulary on the board, trying not to duplicate any of the words.

Have extra board markers ready for this.

Have the whole class examine the board and identify any words they're unfamiliar with. As the words came from the students themselves, if any problems arise they can ask each other for explanations.

Get suggestions from the class on how to organise the words into categories. Make sure that the students are able to pronounce the words by drilling them thoroughly. You can also indicate which part of speech (noun, verb, preposition and so on) each word is.

Add any necessary words that haven't come up but that you want to pre-teach.

Figure 10-1 shows one category on the board.

TV Vocabulary

<u>TV People</u>

actor/æktə/, (n)

cast/ka:st/, (collective noun for actors) 'a star-studded cast of actors'

presenter/prə'zentə/(n), 'John smith is the presenter of that political programme and he is good at explaining the election'

Figure 10-1:
Sample
vocabulary
words.

contestant/kən'testənt/(n), a person who takes part in a quiz/game show and tries to win

host/hovot/(male) (n v), hostess/həv stes/(female) (n) a person who presents a show where other people are guests. Jonathan Ross is the host of the chat show and his guest is Clint Eastwood'.

When the students have built up the vocabulary and copied it into their notebooks, give each one a copy of the TV schedule.

3. **Skim (8 minutes)**: Ask the students to look at the text quickly on their own and answer three questions. Make sure that the students are aware of the time limit though (2 minutes perhaps), so they don't get sidetracked.

   - How many TV channels are there?
   - Does each channel broadcast 24 hours a day? If not, when are they off air?
   - Does each channel broadcast the news? How often?

Put the students in pairs to compare their answers and then have a short feedback session with the class.

4. **Scan (30 minutes)**: Now have the class to look at the text in more detail.

Have them find programmes that match the interests and routines of particular classmates: 'Is there any football on TV after 9 p.m. for Giovanna?' This is a nice way to personalise the activity and it also encourages the class to make up their own questions.

If the students attach no comment to a particular programme, small groups can discuss what kind of show it may be, based on the title and time of broadcast: 'Property ladder is on once a week at 7 p.m. and lasts for 50 minutes. The name of the presenter is Sarah Beeny. What kind of programme do you think it is? Why?'

Other scan questions you can use may be:

- When can I watch a modern film that's suitable for children?

- Which channel is best for music lovers?

- Are the soap operas shown at the same? Which ones do you think are the most popular? Explain.

- Name someone who is:

 A chat show host

 A newsreader

 A cartoon character

 A TV chef

Comparing answers in pairs or small groups is useful for students.

Have a class feedback session afterwards to check the answers and correct any vocabulary and grammar errors you've noted.

5. **Follow-up (15 minutes)**: Some of the programmes on the TV schedule are also shown in Italy. Have a class discussion on how culture affects the way programmes are made and presented in Italy.

Ask whether there should be more or fewer foreign programmes on local television. Have students form two lines, each person facing a partner. The purpose is to role-play one side of an argument. So, in this case the students in line A argue the case for more foreign TV shows, and the students in line B argue for fewer.

After two or three minutes the students in line B can all move along to form new partnerships in the line. Then they can argue again with new points to consider.

6. **Homework (5 minutes)**: Students can write an essay in four paragraphs on the same argument. Show students how to organise the text – introduction, the argument for more foreign shows, the argument for fewer and a conclusion.

7. **Cooler (6 minutes more or less):** Have the students play hangman using the names of international celebrities. Make sure that they pronounce all the letters correctly or they lose points.

Chapter 11

Write or Wrong? Teaching Writing Lessons

*I*t is rather daunting to produce written work in a foreign language, but with some guidance your students can go from good sentences, to paragraphs, to texts with due attention to style and formality.

You never know just when your students may have to fall back on written communication so try to incorporate writing into your course, even if it's just a little.In this chapter, I show you how to focus a lesson on writing skills.

Putting Pen to Paper

By the time you start getting into writing, your students should have had a chance to listen, speak and read the language to some degree. They have also copied information down, but actually writing in their own words is more of a challenge. After all, proof of progress (or not) remains there in black and white for the world to see. So, teach your students what it takes to make a decent sentence. This will be the foundation for future written texts.

Paying attention to basic writing skills

Most EFL teachers are fortunate enough to have students who can already wield a pen and form all the letters of the alphabet in English. You may take this ability for granted. However, if you encounter students who either have a different writing system in their home country and have had no opportunity to learn the English one, or are illiterate in their first language, you need to start teaching writing skills with the alphabet itself.

It could be embarrassing for students to admit that they are having difficulties starting out, so be vigilant. Students who make no effort to write anything down at beginner level may need special attention.

Right from the first lesson, give your students opportunities to copy from the board. This allows you to start snooping from the outset. Whether you talk to the students directly about their notes or discreetly lean over their shoulders as they write, make sure that they are all able to copy what you have written legibly and accurately.

Point out the errors or else they may become engrained (especially poor spelling) and if a student's handwriting may cause a problem for native English speakers, let the student know. I mention this because national styles vary and the formation of particular letters could be interpreted differently with a foreigner's eye.

Completing sentences

The problem for many students is that they don't understand what a sentence actually is. Without a basic grammar rule they tend to come up with 'sentences' like these:

- The blue bag there.
- Chicken, fish and pork, for example.
- Is very nice here.

With the exception of short *imperatives,* the little action based phrases you tend to yell at people – 'Shut up!' 'Look!' or 'Sit!' – a good sentence needs a noun and a verb at least. You may have learned this rule as 'subject + predicate' at school, but basically the idea is that there is a person/thing doing something or being something. Applying this principle, I made complete sentences from the phrases in the first list:

> ✔ The blue bag is there.
>
> ✔ I like chicken, fish and pork, for example.
>
> ✔ It is very nice here.

After they know to join a noun and a verb, you need to check that students understand the rules of punctuation. For example, have a lesson or two on using capital letters, not just at the beginning of a sentence but for days of the week, months, place names, people's names and all other proper nouns. (I talk about punctuation marks in Chapter 10.)

When students have the hang of basic sentence construction, they can start working on the content by using a wider range of grammar and vocabulary. They can incorporate more adjectives and adverbs to create interest. In addition, you can practise various expressions of opinion such as 'I think' and 'in my opinion' to make their expressions sound more natural.

Higher level students have a problem identifying what a sentence is as well as lower level ones and many make the mistake of having one ginormous sentence where two or three shorter ones would be far better.

Moving on to paragraphs

Your next task after your students can write a good sentence is to show the class how to build sentences into a paragraph and convey the basic rules and tips for doing so.

Each paragraph should contain a separate idea. One sentence sums up what the whole paragraph is about and is generally called the *topic sentence*. It's easiest to teach students to put the topic sentence at the beginning of the paragraph although in other texts they read they might find it in the middle or at the end. The following sentences should support the idea in the topic sentence and/or give examples.

Once you have several sentences for the paragraph, they need to fit together well. For this students need to know *linking words* like the ones listed in Table 11-1 and what kind of punctuation goes with them (some follow a comma, some a full stop and others need nothing at all):

Table 11-1	How to use linking words
Some lower-level linking words	
so and but	You generally use a comma before these words when they join two sentences together. Some people leave out the comma when the two sentences are very short. *Patrick had two bags but he gave one to Nasreen.*
because when before	When these words are first in the sentence use a comma before the second clause (part of sentence which is itself like a sentence with a subject and verb). *Because I like him, I bought him a gift.* You don't need a comma when these words are between the clauses. *I greeted him when I saw him at the party.*
Examples of linking words for intermediate level and above	
however	Use a comma after this word when it links sentences and clauses. *I had a nice day. However, the weather was poor.*
in addition	You use *in addition* or *in addition to this* with a comma then a clause. *There are several styles of dress on display. In addition to this, there are many nationalities costumes.*
consequently	You begin a new sentence with these words and a comma to link the sentence with an idea you have already mentioned. *I liked the cuisine. Furthermore, the museums were very good*

When your students know how to master a sentence and build sentences into a paragraph, they are ready to tackle a more substantial task where they write a complete text.

Structuring a Writing Lesson

For a writing lesson to be successful, you need to set the writing task up so that students are clear about what they have to do and how best to tackle it.

A wide variety of tasks cover various sub-skills too, for example using register, which means the right formal or informal style, and adapting to different kinds of texts.

When deciding on a writing task to set, ask yourself some questions as an initial checklist.

✔ Is it appropriate for the class in terms of level, relevance and interest?

✔ Is it clear what the purpose of the task is?

✔ Is it clear who the imagined reader is?

✔ Do the students have sufficient information to complete the task (vocabulary, layout, background, examples)?

If you have a task which seems to fit the bill, you now need to build a lesson around it.

Energising the class with pre-writing tasks

As writing is often a quiet, solitary activity, a *pre-writing task* is usually necessary because such tasks energise and prepare the students. They allow for collaboration and help students put together ideas which will make the actual writing task more successful.

Fostering discussion

A class discussion is a good way to generate ideas on the writing topic.

To begin the discussion provide an example of the topic. Tell a story, use a visual image or provide a text which gets students thinking along the right lines. You could also put some keys words on the board and ask students what they have in common. Then, ask students to add some more relevant words to the ones you have presented.

If the task you intend to set is a composition about an interesting experience while on holiday, for example, you can begin the lesson with a personal anecdote about one of your holidays and then open the topic up to the students to tell each other similar stories, which should get the creative juices flowing. Alternatively, a short reading about a trip, an exotic piece of music or stimulating photograph from a far away land can stimulate conversation which leads in the direction of the writing topic.

Save vocabulary or key points which come from the discussion and are relevant to the task by writing the words on the board. This gives you something to do and prevents you from hogging the discussion.

Brainstorming tends to raise energy levels as well. Once students are used to the idea of calling out all their ideas on a topic and benefiting from other people's contributions, they can easily do it in small groups with no help from you at all. The class may offer vocabulary or perhaps questions that they think a reader would like the final written piece to answer. Once the groups have something down on paper they can compare with each other for more input.

Some possible topics to brainstorm are:

- ✔ How many words can you think of which are connected with the topic?

- ✔ If you read an article on this topic, what information would you expect it to include?

- ✔ Are there different characters or locations in this piece of writing? What vocabulary do I need to describe them?

- ✔ Does this topic include pros and cons? What are they?

Building structure

Another approach is to focus on the structure of the written work, helping the students conform to the layout needed and remember the expressions that link ideas together. In each case students ought to think through the text beforehand by writing a plan. There should be an outline of each paragraph and the ideas associated with each one. In Appendix A I show examples of formal and informal letters, a review, a report and an essay. I show a template and an example.

Letter writing

All letters need an address, date, opening greeting, paragraphs which each have a main point, a closing greeting and signature. Letters divide into formal and informal, as follows:

- ✔ **Formal letters:** At the top of a formal letter you usually write two addresses. The first is your own address and the second is the address of the person you intend to read the letter. You can't use contractions (shortened forms of words) in formal letters. That means you need to write *do not* instead of *don't*, for example. The purpose of writing the letter must be clear from the first paragraph and you have to stick to formal language with no slang. At the end, you write *Yours sincerely* (if you mentioned the reader by name) or *Yours faithfully* (if you started with *Dear Sir/Madam*) and under your signature you print your name and job title (if relevant).

> ✔ **Informal letters:** The difference between formal and informal letters is that you only need your address at the top. You can use contractions and informal language. You still need to write in paragraphs, but at the end of the letter you use friendlier closing expressions like *See you* and *Take care*. Finally you sign your name, perhaps just your first name, and you don't need to print it clearly below.

Essays

When students give their opinions in writing there are different ways to set out the essay. You can state your opinion in the introduction and proceed to explain your view. You could also have a general introduction, explain both sides of the argument and give your opinion in the conclusion. However, there should always be an and introduction, paragraphs highlighting main points in each, along with examples and ideas which support the point and finally a concluding paragraph which sums up the essay. The language should be formal.

Stories

A story requires creative language in the form of descriptive adjectives and adverbs, and direct speech quoting what the characters say. It is not so important for the students to have great plots in their stories, as time is limited in EFL lessons. Rather, they should be able to describe events, people and places well. Usually, students need to be accurate in using the past simple, continuous and perfect tenses (according to their level) and they also need linking words which show the sequence of events such as *and then, after that* and *finally*.

Reports

A report is a formal presentation of information so it requires formal language. There should be clear headings and subheadings including the division of *Introduction* (followed by the purpose of the report), *Findings* and *Conclusion/Recommendation*. Students should avoid writing their opinions throughout report and restrict their own ideas to the *Recommendations* section.

Reviews

Depending on how many words the review includes, the text might include several paragraphs or just one. However the text should say what the is being reviewed, the good and bad points and a recommendation for readers. The degree of formality that the students use depends on the kind of publication or the reader the student is writing for.

You can provide the students with a kind of template of how the work should look. Ask the students questions about how the piece of writing should look and set out the format on the board. Figure 11-1 shows the template for an essay on having a holiday in your own country. Figure 11-2, meanwhile, is an example of how a student might structure an informal email.

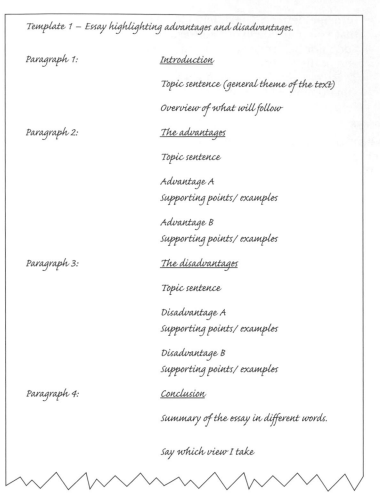

Template 1 – Essay highlighting advantages and disadvantages.

Paragraph 1:   <u>*Introduction*</u>

                                 Topic sentence (general theme of the text)

                                 Overview of what will follow

Paragraph 2:   <u>*The advantages*</u>

                                 Topic sentence

                                 Advantage A
                                 Supporting points/ examples

                                 Advantage B
                                 Supporting points/ examples

Paragraph 3:   <u>*The disadvantages*</u>

                                 Topic sentence

                                 Disadvantage A
                                 Supporting points/ examples

                                 Disadvantage B
                                 Supporting points/ examples

Paragraph 4:   <u>*Conclusion*</u>

                                 Summary of the essay in different words.

                                 Say which view I take

Figure 11-1:
A template
for a stan-
dard essay

You can make a practice activity worksheet out of the template by asking the class to put each heading in the right order until they achieve the appropriate layout.

If you combine this kind of template with some key vocabulary, the students will be in a great position to complete the task effectively.

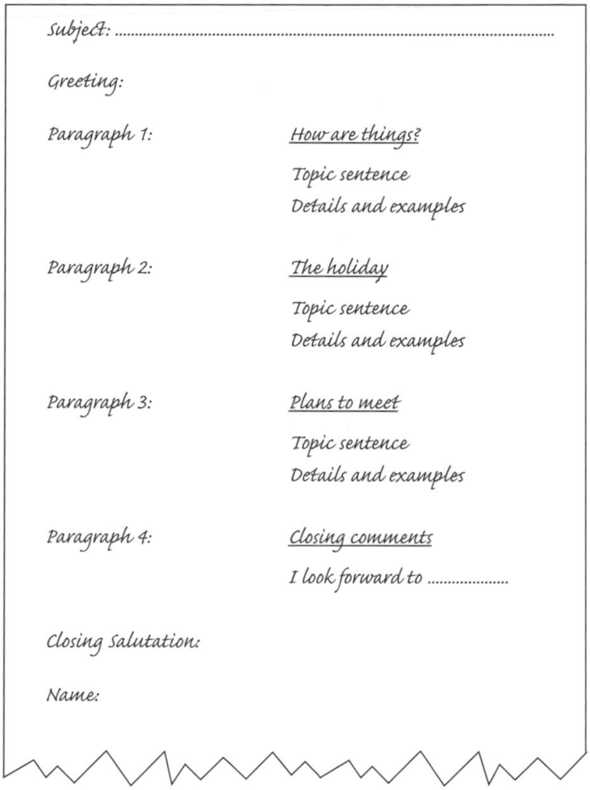

Subject: ....

Greeting:

Paragraph 1:   *How are things?*

                      Topic sentence
                      Details and examples

Paragraph 2:   *The holiday*

                      Topic sentence
                      Details and examples

Paragraph 3:   *Plans to meet*

                      Topic sentence
                      Details and examples

Paragraph 4:   *Closing comments*

                      I look forward to ....

Closing Salutation:

Name:

Figure 11-2:
Structuring
an informal
email.

Setting the writing task and explaining the stages

After preparing the students' minds for the task, you need to tell them what it is, whether they will be working alone or collaborating with someone else, and how long they have to complete it.

Student follow three stages when writing: The first is drafting or planning, the second is actually writing and the third is reviewing. I cover each in the following sections.

Thinking through the drafting stage

For the first stage, drafting, students have already considered how to use a template to good effect (see 'Building structure' a bit earlier in the chapter), but still need time to gather their ideas. At this stage the student should also make sure that each aspect of the task will be covered in the text.

Far too many students pick up a pen, start writing the main text cold and either run out of time or end up with an unsatisfactory piece of work. So although you may meet some resistance when you try to make students take this preparatory stage, it is better than the loss of morale that comes along with continually poor writing.

Set a specific time period for planning so that the students can then pause and compare their ideas. They are likely to notice points their peers have included which they have forgotten about. It also gives you the chance to step in and avert disaster.

Getting stuck in

If you set the task up well, there should be little for you to do at this stage except monitoring – without interrupting too much. Have an occasional look over your students' shoulders but don't say a word unless the student is hopelessly lost or asks for advice.

Have dictionaries available to increase the students' independence. They should not have to depend on you for everything!

Keep the students abreast of the time so that they keep pushing ahead to the end. Students do get stuck on one point or another and end up wasting time, so remind them of where they should be in the task – '10 minutes to go! You should be on your conclusion now, ready to review your work.'

Doing final checks

Before handing in their work, students should be reminded to check it through thoroughly. Provide a checklist with points like these if it helps:

- ✔ Have I answered the question fully?
- ✔ Have I used the right layout?
- ✔ Is my spelling correct?
- ✔ Have I divided my work into appropriate paragraphs?
- ✔ Have I included an introduction and conclusion?
- ✔ Is my work clear (that includes good handwriting) and interesting?

Registering the Right Degree of Formality

The formal word for showing the write degree of formality in English is *register*. It is an aspect of language teaching that you should not overlook. Any errors in this area are particularly noticeable when it comes to writing.

As a general habit, indicate the register of an expression by writing (f) or (inf), that is formal and informal, after it on the board so that students are aware of how to use it.

Additionally, it is best to highlight expressions which are restricted to writing. For example, a very old lady who is not used to many of the advances in technology left me a telephone message ending with 'Yours sincerely, Winnie'. Although a native speaker, she had not worked out the appropriate use of register nor whether the language of messages is transferable from letter to telephone. Do not let your students make this mistake.

Table 11-2 shows some basic differences between formal and informal writing to help you get started. In their notebooks, you could get students to set up a table of equivalent formal and informal expressions which they could fill in as they learn them throughout your course.

Table 11-2   Standards for Formal and Informal Writing

Formal Writing	Informal Writing
Never use contractions. Write the whole word.	Use contractions.
Use verbs derived from Latin.	Use phrasal verbs.
Use passive constructions (eg it is done)	Use active constructions (eg he does it)
Never use slang	Use appropriate slang and common words.

Table 11-3 shows some formal and informal language to share with your students.

Table 11-3   Formal and Informal Phrases

Formal	Informal
Dear Sir/Madam	Hi!
I appreciate…	Thanks
I would be grateful if you could…	Please could you…
Approximately	About
Due to	Because of
A great deal of	A lot of
Sufficient	Enough
Yours sincerely/faithfully	Best wishes

Sample writing activities

Writing activities can begin with a single letter of the alphabet and later develop into formal, lengthy texts. Try this list of activity types with your classes. They can all be done individually but those marked with an asterisk are also well suited to pair and group work.

- Advertisements*
- Application forms
- Articles
- Biographies
- Book/film reviews
- Composition (setting out an opinion or argument)
- CV
- Descriptions of a process or diagram
- Dictation. The students write down what the teacher reads aloud to practise their spelling and punctuation.

- Emails
- Formal and informal letters
- Instruction sheets*
- Memos
- Notices*. Students can prepare notices giving information for use in the classroom, for example about upcoming events.
- Poetry: Get students to write a short poem or limerick. You can provide a list of rhyming words to help them.
- Projects*: Students can do more extensive work over a period of weeks on one topic. They can use English to explore and explain something which interests them.
- Reports: After finding out information on a particular topic students can present this in a concise and formal way as though they were giving feedback to an employer.
- Stories

Choose the activities which your students are most likely to need in the future.

Students who speak Latin-based languages like French and Portuguese tend to favour words of Latin origin instead of more common words and phrases – 'establish' rather than' set up', for example. This makes them sound too formal at times, so you can work on that with them to sound more casual.

Writing Case Study

Many teachers work in UK during the summer months when youngsters from all over the world descend on language schools expecting to learn English in six weeks and be thoroughly entertained in the process. Here is a lesson I used successfully in one such class.

> ✔ **Class Profile:** 12 teenage students from Taiwan, Spain, Brazil and Turkey. 60 minute lesson
>
> ✔ **Level:** Upper-Intermediate
>
> ✔ **Materials:** Two copies of the school rules, tape, a prize, poster-size paper, dictionaries and extra marker pens.
>
> ✔ **Problems:** Several pupils have illegible handwriting, mostly due to laziness. Most feel that writing is too passive and prefer to do lively activities.
>
> ✔ **Lesson aims:** To undertake a collaborative writing activity which requires attention to handwriting and general accuracy. To have fun writing.

Get a copy of the school rules. Make sure they are written in words the students can understand or rewrite them to match your pupils' level. Take the opportunity to embed some key vocabulary or grammar that you want students to notice.

Use normal A4 sized paper so that they cannot read what the document contains unless they are very close up. Prepare two identical copies and stick them to the wall in the classroom.

Then, follow these steps for a successful lesson:

1. **Pre-reading task (5 minutes):** Ask the students to brainstorm ideas about what they love/hate about their school back home individually in their notebooks.

   Put the pupils in pairs of mixed nationalities to compare ideas.

   Use their answers for a quick a short class discussion. Find out how many mention rules as something they hate.

2. **Writing activity 1-Dictation (30 minutes):** Divide the class into two teams of equal size. Arrange the room so that there is a clear space for them to dash to the wall and then back to prepared desks.

   Have the two teams come up with team names and appoint a captain for each to keep order. Give each team a blank sheet of paper.

   Explain that, one at a time, a member of each team will run to their copy of the rules, memorise a section without making any notes. They must then dash back to their team's blank sheet and write down the section they memorised.

   Do the title or the first line yourself as an example. Check that everyone understands the process and set a time limit for completing the dictation.

The exercise continues until the entire document is reproduced accurately.

Whilst the activity is taking place, give encouragement and make sure that the work is legible.

When the teams have finished, award points for speed and accuracy. Decide on a winner and award a prize.

As a class, discuss what they agree/disagree with from the rules and review the language of rules (do/don't, must/mustn't, should/shouldn't and so on).

3. **Writing activity 2 (25 minutes):** Divide the class into four smaller groups. Within these groups students must agree on five things pupils should do and five they should not do when learning English (allow for creative license). Make dictionaries available.

Give each group a large sheet of paper and a couple of markers. Ask them to write up a poster explaining their rules.

When the posters are complete, one representative from each group should give a short presentation explaining it.

Display the posters in class.

Chapter 12

What Accent? Teaching Pronunciation

There's nothing worse than studying a language for years only to find that nobody can understand a word you say. You write with ease but when you open your mouth, you're met with blank stares. This is the experience of many a student whose teachers underestimated pronunciation skills. So in this chapter, I tell you how to teach good pronunciation.

Repeat after Me

Probably the simplest way of making students pronunciation conscious is by getting them to repeat all the new words they learn as well as the words they find tricky. Before you cringe, erase that picture of students sitting in rows reciting dull and meaningless sentences. Repetition can be incorporated into the normal flow of the lesson and can be used to raise energy levels at any level.

Repeating first

The natural order for learning language skills is listening first, then speaking, followed by reading and finally writing. With this in mind, when you introduce a new word students should repeat it after you several times before focusing on the spelling.

Spelling in English is so irregular that if students don't sort out the right pronunciation first they're likely to come up with a letter-by-letter version of how the word sounds. So get them speaking before they read and write.

Whenever students are speaking, pay attention to their pronunciation. You don't have to stop them every time they say something incorrectly, but you can make notes and include repetition of problem words in your feedback sessions. You can also collect data for a whole lesson on pronunciation in which you can address recurring errors.

For example, you may notice that words with 'th' are routinely pronounced with 'd' instead and this may lead to a lesson on analysing the sound, how it's made and a collection of tongue twisters to practise it.

Repeating as a class and individually

The easiest way to get repetition is to ask for it. Just say 'Repeat!' and use gestures to add emphasis. Use your arms like a conductor in front of an orchestra or use your hand to cup behind your ear, indicating that you're listening to them. Students soon get the hang of it and come to expect it.

All together now

When the whole class repeats together this is called *choral drilling*. Students feel more at ease when they work as a team because embarrassment is reduced. However, just as in a musical ensemble, you need to listen very carefully for anyone who's 'out of tune'.

If you hear one poor speaker on the left of the room, ask the students on the right to take a break for a few seconds. Those on the left now work a bit harder because they think that you're starting to home in on them.

Going solo

Individual drilling is another option. This means that one student repeats alone. You can run through the students one after the other and diplomatically ask better speakers to correct the errors of weaker ones by modelling the right pronunciation.

> Teacher gestures: Weak! Repeat please, weak!
>
> Whole class: Weak!
>
> Teacher: Rashid, weak!
>
> Rashid: Weak!
>
> Teacher (gestures to the next student): Weak!

Soraya: Wik!

Teacher: Rashid weak!

Rashid: Weak!

Teacher: Soraya?

Soraya: Weak!

Teacher: Good! Sanjay weak . . .

For a sentence, or a word with many syllables, you can use _backchaining_. This means that students repeat the last bit first and then go backwards until they've done the whole thing. Take the question 'What would you like to drink?'

Teacher: Drink!

Class: Drink!

Teacher: Like to drink!

Class: Like to drink!

Teacher: You like to drink!

Class: You like to drink!

Teacher: What would you like to drink?

Using Phonology: Sound and Spelling

The problem with English is that the spelling is rather misleading. Words such as _recipe_ and _receipt, tough_ and _though_ and place names such as Leicester and Southwark are hopelessly illogical for students to pronounce. So, to combat this problem, you use a whole range of symbols, or _phonemes(pronounced 'foe-neemz', which in the symbols I mention is /fəʊniːmz/)_, to represent every individual sound in this language. They provide a great tool in teaching pronunciation and even in reading the dictionary as most include a phonological transcription. As with many tools, you can get the job done without phonemes and you may find them difficult to use at first, but they do help in the long run. After all, you won't be around your students forever to correct their pronunciation and if they devise their own system of writing pronunciation you can't check it for them.

You teach individual phonemes by drawing the symbol on the board, saying the sound many times and asking the students to repeat it. It helps to tell the students which parts of the mouth, neck or other speech organs (perhaps the nasal cavity, which is the space inside and beyond your nostrils) you use to make the sound and what you do with them. For example, you can tell students to put the tip of their tongue just behind the top of the upper teeth to say /l/. Actually, you can point to the both parts of mouth to make the point.

Getting to know the 44 key sounds of English

Forty-four individual, recognised sounds make up the English language. These are broken down into single vowels, double vowels and consonants. The vowels allow the air to come straight out unobstructed by speech organs – lips and teeth.

All the phonemes that include two marks like this : are long sounds. For example, compare 'it' /ɪt/ and 'eat'/iːt/. There's a long sound in the second word.

The next sections cover the complete list of phonemes with examples.

Focusing on single vowel sounds

A vowel is a sound that comes out of the mouth without any of the speech organs blocking the way. In other words you say them with an open mouth.

Single vowel sounds aren't joined to any other vowel. In the next section I focus on double vowel sounds.

Phoneme	*Examples*
/iː/	tree, easy, please
/ɪ/	trip, is, synchronise
/uː/	food, suit, moody
/ʊ/	put, wood, cook, look
/e/	extra, wedding, said
/ɜː/	early, word, furtive
/ə/	after, important, around
/ɔː/	more, war, awful, floor
/ɑː/	mask, car, afterwards
/æ/	mat, plait, animal, wax
/ʌ/	under, cup, son, thud
/ɒ/	what, not, octopus, along

The phoneme /ə/ is called the *schwa*. It represents the sound that causes the most confusion as it can be represented by so many vowels. However, it only occurs in a syllable that carries no *stress*, or strong emphasis. Some words may include the schwa when the word is not stressed but change the pronunciation when it is stressed. Consider 'can' in these two statements, for example:

> Can we talk?
>
> Yes we can.

You probably stressed 'talk' in the first statement, if you said it at normal speed, and said 'can' very quickly using the schwa. In the second statement 'can' is stressed a lot more so the schwa changes to /æ/.

Doing double vowel sounds

Double vowel sounds are literally two vowels combined to make one sound. You have to move your jaw bone to say them and students find them strange so they often exchange a double vowel for a single one. They may pronounce train /tren/ instead of /treɪn/ However, good use of double vowels really helps in creating a more native sounding accent.

Phoneme	Examples
/ɪə/	**ear**, b**eer**, m**ere**ly, car**eer**
/eɪ/	m**a**te, w**eigh**t, d**ay**time, **a**ce
/ʊə/	p**ure**, s**ewer**, cr**ue**l, f**ue**l
/ɔɪ/	destr**oy**, **oi**ntment, b**oi**ling, b**uoy**
/əʊ/	**oh**, ph**o**to, m**o**tor, l**oa**n
/eə/	r**are**, b**ear**, mal**a**ria, h**eir**
/aɪ/	m**y**, w**i**der, st**y**le, p**i**le
/aʊ/	l**ou**d, c**ow**, pl**ough**, **ou**ch

Saying consonants

Many of the consonant phonemes look exactly like the alphabet but you need to check, as a significant number may be new to you or misleading. So look at the example words to make sure that the sound matches your expectations. Take /j/ for example. It's pronounced like *y* in yacht not *j* in jump.

Different versions of the phonemic chart exist. They always show the same phonemes but in different orders. Say the phonemes out loud in the order I show them here and you notice that they're grouped according to the speech organs you use to make them. For example /p/ and /b/ both use the upper and lower lips.

Phoneme	Examples
/p/	**p**olitics, ha**pp**y, u**p**
/b/	**b**u**bb**le, **b**urn, ca**b**
/t/	dou**bt**, **t**heatre, **t**igh**t**
/d/	**d**i**d**, woo**d**en, mu**d**
/tʃ/	**ch**eese, ri**ch**, **ch**eap
/dʒ/	ju**dg**e, pa**g**e, **g**eneral
/k/	**c**oo**k**, **ch**emistry, bi**k**e
/g/	**g**ood, wi**gg**le, bi**g**
/v/	**v**isit, sto**v**e, **v**oice
/f/	**ph**oto, o**ff**, wi**f**e
/θ/	**th**umb, **th**irst, ba**th**
/ð/	**th**is, ei**th**er, fa**th**er
/s/	**ps**ychology, ni**c**e, **sc**ent
/z/	wi**s**e, ja**zz**, pha**s**e
/ʃ/	**s**ugar, **sh**oot, ma**ch**ine
/ʒ/	mea**s**ure, vi**s**ual, deci**s**ion

Many of the consonant phonemes are paired – voiced and unvoiced. If you were lip reading you'd probably have trouble distinguishing /p/ and /b/, for example, because they both involve the same speech organs (upper and lower lips). However when you put your hand on your larynx (where the adam's apple is on a man's neck) and say them aloud, you can feel that voiced /b/ makes it vibrate a lot, whereas unvoiced /p/ does not. So a voiced consonant is a sound that makes the vocal chords vibrate when you say it, whereas there's no vibration of the vocal chords when you say an unvoiced consonant.

Phoneme	Examples
/m/	nu**mb**, **m**ystery, mi**m**e, autu**mn**
/n/	**n**ow, vai**n**, **gn**ome, **kn**ees
/ŋ/	thi**n**k, la**n**guage, si**ng**er, wri**n**kle
/h/	**h**ospital, **h**airstyle, **h**ello, **h**amster
/l/	**l**essons, whee**l**, **l**eaf, subt**l**e
/r/	**r**omance, bea**r**er, **r**obin, **wr**ong
/w/	**w**atch, fe**w**er, **w**eed, **w**asp
/j/	**y**ellow, la**y**er, **y**esterday, **y**am

Using phonemes in class

If you have a nice, big phonemic chart up in your classroom and you write the phonemic transcription on the board whenever you write a word with potentially problematic pronunciation, your students can pick up sounds as they go along. So you write the word, the part of speech (noun, adjective and so on) and the phonemic transcription:

> bomb (n) /bɒm/
>
> to search (v) /sɜːtʃ/

You can simply point to phonemes and get the class to repeat the sound after you. This is particularly useful when you use *minimal pairs*. This term refers to the comparison of two words with almost the same pronunciation, except for one sound. Students may not hear the difference unless you demonstrate that there is one, perhaps because that sound isn't used in their own language.

> sank /sæŋk/ and thank /θæŋk/
>
> hat /hæt/ and hut /hʌt/

When you compare words, isolate the phonemes and repeat them carefully to raise student awareness so that they make more of an effort to pronounce words as a native speaker would.

If you can include whole sessions on pronunciation in your course, it's worth supplying the students with mirrors so that they can study the shapes they make with their lips, tongues and mouths when pronouncing the phonemes – modelling their pronunciation on yours, of course. It's easier for them to copy you this way.

A cross section of the speech organs is also useful so that you can point to areas at the back or the mouth, for example when you teach /k/.

Adding Emphasis to Words and Syllables

In some languages every syllable you say is equal in emphasis (also called stress) and volume so that no one syllable stands out. In other languages the stress always falls in the same place, perhaps on the first or last syllable in a word. This isn't the case in English. In TEFL you teach which words stand out and which syllables stand out too.

Impotent or important? Placing emphasis on syllables

In addition to the individual sounds or phonemes that make up a word, you also need to know how many syllables there are because if there's more than one syllable, you need to add stress or emphasis. Incorrect placement of the stress can at times change the meaning and definitely hinders communication.

Take the word 'export'. It's a two syllable word (ex + port) and can be used as a verb or a noun. Interestingly when it's a noun, you stress *ex*, but when it is a verb we stress *port*. Figure 12-1 shows the several ways you can show emphasis on the board.

Figure 12-1:
Showing stressed syllables.

'export (n) and ex'port (v)

e**x**port (n) and ex**port** (v)

ēxport (n) and expōrt (v)

- ✔ The accent mark is the style often used in dictionaries.
- ✔ You can write the stressed syllable bigger and bolder than the unstressed one(s).
- ✔ If you draw a line above the stressed syllable, put it above the vowel, not a consonant.

Make it a habit to mark the stress on new words and use one of these visual methods as a means of correction too. It's also fun to illustrate the stressed syllable in an audible way while still allowing the students to work it out. For example, you can show the difference between impotent and important by singing DAdada and daDAda.

Emphasising words

In English, you stress particular words in a sentence more than others, saying them a little louder and with more force. The stressed words are usually those that carry more meaning. Examine the following statements.

Where were **you** at **six o'clock**?

I was at **home**. I **went** to the **club** at **seven** o'clock.

The stress adds meaning but it also makes the speaker sound more interesting than if that person were to use a flat tone throughout.

Stressing words contributes to the distinct rhythm of the English language.

You can teach it by means of poetry recital or rapping.

Take the well-known rhyme 'This is the house that Jack built'. If you say it out loud you find it necessary to stress certain words and cram the others in, in order to keep the beat going. Students find this challenging and enjoyable.

> This is the **house** that **Jack built**!
>
> This is the **malt** that **lay** in the **house** that **Jack built**.
>
> This is the **rat** that **ate** the **malt**
>
> That **lay** in the **house** that **Jack built**.

Notice how quickly you need to say some of the unstressed words. As you stress the words that carry the most meaning and force the other words to fit in, the pronunciation of the unstressed words becomes very contracted.

Students complain that native speakers eat their words but there's actually a reason for this, which they would do well to imitate.

Improving Fluency through Pronunciation

Practice makes perfect and this almost true of pronunciation. I say 'almost' because the aim in teaching this skill should be clear speech instead of a native-like accent. Very few students lose their accents but most can produce the phonemes reasonably well, except for the odd sticky one.

Reading aloud to the whole class isn't something you encourage EFL students to do often. It can be rather dull. However, reading aloud in pairs is less embarrassing and keeps everyone busy reading, correcting or encouraging. Students who've learnt the phonemes can correct themselves using the dictionary and they should always put on an English (or other native speaker) voice. By doing so they can move beyond individual words and emphasis and start analysing how we connect words.

Once students start focusing on pronunciation they may overdo it by being precise about every single word. In fact, native speakers often allow words to elide.

Typically, native speakers pronounce consonants and vowels as though they were joined together. So if a word ends with a consonant and the next begins with a vowel, you pronounce them together. Try this for example:

> teacher and student
>
> vets and animals

Whereas the /r/ at the end of teacher is usually silent, you can pronounce it before 'and' as it begins with a vowel. Similarly, in the second example you allow the 's' of 'vets' to connect with 'and'. Then you connect 'd' of 'and' with 'animals'.

Sometimes sounds disappear or change.

✔ Good game: At the end of 'good' we can't pronounce the 'd' unless we speak extremely slowly and carefully. At the most we say 'goog' because of the influence of the following 'g' in 'game'.

✔ What do you do?: Many native speakers would pronounce /wɒʔdɪə/ instead of 'what do you'. The /ʔ/ represents the glottal stop which is the rather unattractive sound most people make when they stop the air at the back of the throat instead of pronouncing 't' at the end of a word.

These examples highlight the value of sometimes repeating whole sentences at normal speed. Realistic features of the language become evident as long you speak normally and clearly. Use your natural accent to do this and point out alternatives if any obvious ones come up.

Watch Your Tone! – Intonation

Intonation is the method for indicating whether you're uttering a sentence or question, or whether you're in a good mood or bad mood without relying on grammar and vocabulary. When you ask a question your tone tends to rise at the end but when you say a sentence your tone falls at the end to show that you've finished it. In addition, far more rises and falls occur when emotions are running high. Happy intonation sounds a little closer to singing. It's very varied and animated, whereas depressive intonation is very flat. Indeed you can tell a lot about someone's mood and intention from a single word.

Take a fairly versatile word such as 'nice'. Different intonation can change the meaning according to the situation.

Take an innocuous question and response:

> How about cream tea with the neighbours today?
>
> Nice!

Activities to try

Activities to help your students understand pronunciation, stress and intonation may include the following:

- Use a map of local train stations and streets to practise saying place names. You can swap the names for phonemes and see if students recognise them.

- Play a homophones games. *Homophones* are words which sound exactly the same but have different meanings, such as *here* and *hear.* Say the word and see if students can come up with both spellings and meanings. You'll be surprised to find that students often don't know that certain words are supposed to sound the same.

- Have your students put on a mini-play. Drama is fun and encourages students to use good intonation.

- Play 'I spy' using phonemes instead of letters of the alphabet.

Imagine how this dialogue sounds in the following cases, especially the response 'nice':

- A mum is talking to her 14 year-old son who is a computer geek and heavy metal fan.

- An elderly man is talking to his wife who's too ill to travel far.

- A woman is talking to a man who's attracted to her. He had hoped to go for a romantic stroll.

Other words that tend to need intonation to indicate the intention are *okay*, *oh* and *fine*.

When students do listening exercises from a CD or other media they can then use the tape script to role-play the dialogue themselves, copying the intonation. They may need to go through it line by line, repeating after you or the CD, before trying it out. They can also play games where they each have a versatile word and a meaning or mood to convey. They can take it in turns saying their word while the class guesses the meaning or mood from a choice of options.

When you write utterances on the board, you can indicate the intonation pattern by using arrows, such as those in Figure 12-2.

Figure 12-2:
Showing ris-
ing or falling
intonation.

You are waiting for me, aren't you?

You are waiting for me, aren't you?

In this case, the question tag 'aren't you' with falling intonation can indicate that you know what's going on. It may be rhetorical. Then again, with rising intonation, it sounds as though you really aren't sure and need an answer.

Chapter 13

Setting Their Tongues Wagging: Speaking and Discussion

· ·

In This Chapter

▶ Starting the ball rolling

▶ Making the conversation last

▶ Sparking civil discussions

▶ Creating a discussion lesson

· ·

*S*peaking is the most important skill in English language teaching. It's almost impossible to have true mastery of a language without actually speaking it. So in this chapter, I show you how to get your students chatting, arguing and generally wagging those tongues in English.

Getting Students Talking

In general, to encourage speaking in the early stages of a course and with students who are a little timid, give plenty of guidance on what the conversations should be about. You can give students a list of questions to ask each other or specific topics and lots of language input first. So before the activity gets under way make sure that the class knows the necessary grammar and vocabulary with appropriate examples. In this way students don't have to think about what to say, only how to say things. Set speaking tasks for pair group work as often as possible. The tasks should have clear aims and involve taking turns, so say 'Find out what your partner thinks about X and make some notes', rather than just telling them to discuss X. The advantage is that the students are more aware of the need to get the other person's view instead of talking about themselves the whole time.

Warming up

Anyone who speaks a foreign language knows that if you don't use it, you lose it. It's easy to get rusty. And if your mind is full of other matters such as your job, the bills or your love life, it's even harder to get your brain in gear.

This is no less true of your students. In between lessons they may forget what they've learnt or they may just be distracted by life. This is where the warmer comes in. The *warmer* is a very short activity that gets the students acclimatised after the previous lesson. Most warmers are for speaking.

Some of my favourite warm-up activities are:

- ✔ **Last letter, first letter:** This simple game also tests spelling. It works best if the students are in a circle. Basically, one person starts the game by saying a word and the next person has to come up with another word beginning with the last letter of the previous one.

    A chain of words my students recently came up with is: apple, elephant, taxi, interesting, girl, little, eggs, sugar, robot, train.

    As the students get better at the game and improve in their vocabulary, they develop strategies for catching their classmates out by including lots of words that end with the same letter or with a difficult letter like 'x'.

- ✔ **The supermarket game:** This very well-known game involves building up a list of items bought at the supermarket. When it's your turn you have to remember all the items on the list in the right order and then add one more.

    To make it more challenging, you can ask students to attach an adjective to their item, usually starting with the same letter. For example:

    > I went to the supermarket and I bought a crazy camera.

    > I went to the supermarket and I bought a crazy camera and a meaty meal.

    > I went to the supermarket and I bought a crazy camera, a meaty meal and a lovely loaf.

- ✔ **Assemble a sentence:** Sometimes I write a sentence, perhaps with a connection to the lesson for that day, using a different card for each word. I shuffle the cards and give one or two to each student. Then I ask the students to get together and negotiate the correct word order for the sentence.

This warmer is good for getting a team spirit going right from the beginning of the lesson.

✔ **Current affairs:** Noting what's going on in the world often leads to some interesting discussions in the classroom. You can just write a headline on the board, or stick up an image from a newspaper and ask the students what they know about it. Then get their opinions on the story. It works best when you find a humorous story or one with a hint of controversy (but nothing that may offend or hit or a raw nerve).

Talking about communicative activities

This kind of activity has been popular for many years now in TEFL. *Communicative activities* generally involve pairs of students sharing information with each other to complete a task.

Communicative activities come in many different forms but usually involve a Partner A and a Partner B. Each partner needs to ask each other fact or opinion-based questions after receiving initial prompts from you. Sometimes you give them a worksheet which has gaps in it but the gaps are different for each partner. The pair must then hide their own sheet and come up with a question to ask their partner who, as a result, gives them information that they use to fill in a gap. On the other hand the activity may perhaps involve a list of topics or situations to ask a partner about so that the students talk about their own lives.

Communicative activities are practical because they often don't require any imagination or opinions from the participants. They just provide a context for some solid practice of a particular grammatical structure or some new words.

This type of exercise also accustoms students to working with each other and gets them moving about a bit. As in most cases the students aren't allowed to see each others' information, you can get them to sit or stand back to back, for example.

Table 13-1 is an example of a communicative activity designed to practise the phrase 'How much is/how much are the . . . ?'

Table 13-1	Practising 'how much is/how much are'	
Partner A		**Partner B**
Menu		**Menu**
Starter		**Starter**
Spring rolls £2.00		Spring rolls £ . . .
Sesame toast £ . . .		Sesame toast £2.20
Chicken soup £2.50		Chicken soup £ . . .
Main Course		**Main Course**
Prawn curry £ . . .		Prawn curry £4.50
Roast beef £4.70		Roast beef £ . . .
Vegetarian lasagne £ . . .		Vegetarian lasagne £4.00
Dessert		**Dessert**
Chocolate cake £3.00		Chocolate cake £ . . .
Summer fruits £ . . .		Summer fruits £3.15
Apple pie £2.95		Apple pie £ . . .

To make use of this activity in which each partner gets prices for half the items on a menu, use these steps:

1. **Go through the vocabulary to make sure that students understand the food items.**

   If you don't do this first thing, your students are likely to get distracted from the main aim.

2. **Do an example on the board.**

   Get students to suggest what question needs to be asked and make sure that everyone knows how to ask 'How much is?' and 'How much are?'

3. **Divide the class into pairs and give each partner one half of the sheet – Partner A has the left half and Partner B the right.**

   You can tell each partner that his menu is top secret so he can't show his partner.

4. **Ask the students to look at the prices and check which ones are missing, then explain that each partner has to ask the other partner for the prices of these dishes.**

   Check that they all know what to do.

5. **Set a time limit of about three minutes, get them started and monitor quietly.**

   Try not to step in unless a pair is hopelessly lost or silent. Just make a note of any errors to discuss afterwards.

6. **Stop the activity when the time is up and have a feedback session.**

You can use this very simple activity in various ways. For example, if you delete the names of the dishes instead, you can practise 'What costs . . .?'. You can also omit some of the words (such as *apple, curry, chicken*) and practise 'What kind of . . . is it?'.

Lots of opportunities for communicative activities present themselves in the classroom. Even when students are doing a written exercise by themselves, they can compare their answers and opinions in pairs afterwards and explain their reasons for anything that differs from their partner's work. By the time you engage in whole class feedback, the students have had an opportunity to speak and an idea of which answers are likely to present a problem.

How About You? Extending Conversations

Once your students are talking to each other in English, there's no reason to cut them off. In fact, if you can get them to extend their conversations in a more natural way, so much the better.

Communicative activities are rather controlled and often involve repeating the same grammar over and over again, so you need to work your students into more conversational dialogues.

Helping students depart from the script

One of the easiest ways to extend conversations is by teaching students to use phrases that encourage speaking. Try these:

- ✔ How about you?
- ✔ Tell me more.
- ✔ What was it like?
- ✔ Can you describe it?

- Why is that?
- What do you mean?
- What do you think?
- What else?

Once the conversation has opened up it's important to show your interest in what the speaker is saying. You can do this by good body language and expressions that demonstrate interest.

Expressing through body language

Some cultural groups use body language more naturally than others, and individual personalities play a large part too, but students need to be reminded that language is about real communication and that it sometimes goes beyond words. Ask your students to do these things while speaking in pairs or groups:

- Turn towards the speaker.
- Look him in the eye.
- Uncover his face. Don't have hands, hair and hats obscuring the eyes and mouth.
- Smile and nod at intervals.
- Avoid putting physical barriers – your bag on the desk or crossed arms and legs – between you and the speaker.

Showing interest

Another great way to encourage extended conversations in a natural way is to do what native speakers do all the time – you say something to show that you're really listening. It's not always a word, sometimes just 'mmm' with suitable intonation, but you can teach your students to say:

- Really!
- Wow!
- That's interesting!
- Oh no!
- No way!
- Cool!
- What a shame!

Following up

In addition to extending conversations generated from communicative activities, you need to write extended discussions into your lesson plan. Discussions are also communicative, but they don't usually involve filling in worksheets or facts supplied by the teacher. The idea is to get students talking about personal experience and opinions in a natural way. These conversations mimic what someone may tell a friend about in their own language and this is the way most students eventually aim to use English as bilingual speakers. Conversations allow time to explain or ask how?, where?, why? and when?

Usually this kind of activity follows more controlled practice, so by this time the students have had a chance to try out new vocabulary and grammar and they're ready to add this knowledge to all the other English they know in a freer way.

After completing the communicative activity on menu prices (see 'Talking about communicative activities' earlier in the chapter), the follow-up activity may be:

> Discuss in pairs: What is your favourite place to eat for
>
> a) a snack?; b) lunch with friends?; c) a special evening?

Because of the different situations, prices are likely to come into the discussion but they aren't the sole focus of the conversation.

Follow-up activities like these don't only follow speaking practice. You can use them to liven up a reading, writing or listening lesson too. The idea is to take the overall theme of the lesson and develop another area of it in an interesting way, which involves sharing opinions.

Another example is follow-up to a reading lesson in which you read a current news story and analysed it for content and detailed vocabulary. Towards the end of the lesson, you may want to move away from that particular text and widen the topic in the following ways:

> Tell your classmates about a story in the news that you find interesting.
>
> Who or what is the story about? Is it a local, national or international story?
>
> Do people have different opinions about it? Explain.

I find that if you prompt students with some secondary questions, and give them a minute to think about it and make notes, you hear far fewer 'ums' and 'errs'.

Other possibilities for follow-up activities are:

✔ **Role-plays:** Students can create an imaginary dialogue between characters in the previous or related activity and act it out.

✔ **Interview questions:** In pairs or groups students can agree a set of ten questions they'd use to interview a key character.

✔ **Compare and contrast:** Students discuss the similarities and differences between their culture and that of their partner, or that of an English-speaking country in relation to the theme of the lesson.

✔ **Debates:** Assign different groups to represent each side of the argument.

In My Opinion – Agreeing, Disagreeing and Negotiating

The problem with extended speaking activities is that everyone has their own opinion and at times disagreements arise. No problem! Learning to express your opinions in a foreign language is a pretty important skill. In fact if you don't teach the students how to do this, they may just clam up, resort to their mother tongue or, worse still, shout everyone else down using bad grammar.

Expressing an opinion

The way we differentiate between a fact and an opinion is by tacking on little expressions that alert the hearer to what's coming. You say things like:

✔ I (don't) think.

✔ I (don't) believe.

✔ In my opinion.

✔ How about this.

These expressions are quite straightforward to teach because they go neatly on the front of a sentence and don't often change tense.

One of several ways of showing that your expressions are not fact though, is to teach your students some words that show uncertainty such as:

- Maybe
- Perhaps
- Possibly

In the case of *possibly* you need to show the right word order. So you generally say *It may possibly be this* (that's subject + auxiliary verb + possibly + main verb) instead of *Perhaps it's this,* which is easy because you're simply adding a word to the beginning of a normal sentence.

The beauty of these words and phrases is that students immediately sound more fluent without having to do too much work. Sometimes it isn't what you say, but how you say it that counts. That's why, for higher-level students I also teach them how to stall: 'That's an interesting question. I've never thought about that but . . .'.

You'd be surprised how many students have passed their speaking exams by saying very little but saying it elegantly.

Further to this, you can use a number of modal verbs to show that there's a greater or lesser degree of certainty. *Modal verbs* are auxiliary verbs such as: might, may, could, must and can't.

You need to teach these words as a grammar lesson though because the students need to know how the modal verb fits into a sentence:

- Subject + modal verb (+ not) + infinitive verb without *to:*

    It   might   not   be a good idea
- The past form is as follows:

    Subject + modal verb (+ not)+ have + past participle:

    It   might   not   have been a good idea.

Interjecting, rephrasing and summing up

In a conversation you do more than give an opinion then keep quiet. Sometimes you interrupt to add something important, explain in other words to make the point clearer, bring things to a close and so on. These are skills that effective English speakers possess and which you need to teach your students. Let them know how to do these things in accordance with English-speaking culture and in a polite way.

Interjecting

It may seem rude to butt in, but in real life sometimes you need to leave before someone has said their piece or just get them to be quiet! Good classroom management involves giving your students the skills to stop the class show-off hogging the limelight. And if the teacher is rambling on and not making much sense, it's only fair that the students have the language to politely protest, by using phrases such as:

- ✔ Could I stop you there?
- ✔ May I interrupt?
- ✔ Excuse me!
- ✔ Sorry but . . .
- ✔ I understand what you're saying but . . .

Some students of English sound a bit rude because they don't know what to say. When they use these expressions instead of putting their hand in front of your face to stop you, the politeness factor improves immediately. Sadly, a few people just *are* rude in whatever language they use, and giving them expressions like these just brings their personality to the fore.

Rephrasing

Instead of asking for repetition, you can teach your students to check whether they've understood and prove that they're listening by saying something like to following before putting what they heard into their own words:

- ✔ So what you're saying is . . .
- ✔ Do you mean . . .

Summing up

When it's time to signal the end of a conversation or highlight the main points covered in a discussion, some useful little phrases, which students appreciate (especially in business English) come in handy:

- ✔ To sum up then . . ., **or**, in summary . . .
- ✔ In conclusion . . .
- ✔ So the point is . . .

Planning a Discussion Lesson

In Chapter 6 I talk about production activities that encourage students to communicate freely without *you* putting words into their mouths. Discussion can form just one stage of a lesson that focuses on something else (using a grammatical structure or some new vocabulary) or you make discussion the main aim in itself. When you plan a discussion lesson you still need to have presentation and practice stages, which I discuss in Chapters 5 and 6, and then the discussion at the end. Even if the lesson is about discussion skills such as introducing your opinion, there should still be interesting subject matter for the class to talk about.

Choosing the right topic

An error many new teachers make is to expect students to put their heart and soul into discussing something that they'd never even mention in their own language. If you ask your students to have a five-minute discussion on the difference between their own pencil and their partner's, your lesson is unlikely to be a roaring success.

Although it's true that you need to find simple things for your students to talk about, you can't milk a topic beyond its natural length. So my best advice for choosing the topic is to ask yourself a few questions:

- ✔ If you had to discuss this topic yourself, how keen would you be?
- ✔ For how long would you be willing to discuss it?

Personally, I'd be prepared to talk about pencils for two minutes and no longer. So, be realistic. Your students' enthusiasm and goodwill only go so far.

Give some thought to the age and backgrounds of you students too. For example, with children ask them to talk about and role-play things that are relevant to them such as cartoon characters and pop stars.

In general, topics with international appeal are great to get everyone talking. A few famous people are so well known that you can bring them into discussions almost anywhere in the world: Michael Jackson, Jackie Chan, Queen Elizabeth, the Beatles, Mickey Mouse and so on. Issues related to the environment, crime, family life, finding and keeping a job and love transfer very well across ages and nationalities.

If you ask students to discuss their local issues, find out beforehand whether it's possible to translate the words they need into English. If the situation has no real comparison in the English-speaking world, your students feel frustrated trying to express it.

Creating structure in the discussion

A 20-minute discussion doesn't just happen by itself in most cases. Unless you happen to strike on a golden topic, you're likely to find that the conversation dries up within ten minutes.

The best way to avoid this is by using a *slow reveal* method. By this I mean that you can feed in the details one by one, adding another piece of information every so often. It's like putting in another piece of the jigsaw puzzle.

For example, the class begins by discussing how the government should use a piece of land. The options may include a shopping centre, a housing estate, or a nature reserve. After the students give their initial reaction you can give them information about the local population and problems that are prevalent in the area. This may change their minds somewhat. Before they make a final decision you can tell the students about the surrounding towns and other building developments taking place nearby. By adding the information gradually students explore different perspectives and extend the dialogue.

You can also move people around. So, one group can think of all the pros of an argument and another group all the cons. Then you can regroup the class so that each group contains students with both pros and cons. Assign a spokesperson for each group who has the responsibility of reporting to the class the final decision of the group. You'll find this more effective than simply saying, 'Talk about . . . '.

Paying attention without taking over

While the students are having a good old chat, don't just go off to the teachers' room for a cup of tea. You need to monitor the dialogue so that you know when to add a point to fuel the discussion.

Of course, this doesn't give you licence to talk about all your opinions. It's time for the students to speak, remember.

However, as you monitor, you may notice that one student is rather too quiet and needs a prompt from you to get involved. Apart from this, you also need to have your pen and paper ready so that you can note errors and teaching points for your feedback session or for a future lesson.

Chapter 14

In One Ear, Out the Other: Learning To Listen

*W*hen students are able to listen to texts in English and get the sense of them, they feel a real sense of achievement. But how can you train your students to listen without them feeling overwhelmed? In this chapter you find out what to have students listen for and which activities make for an engaging listening lesson.

Structuring Your Lesson

When you teach listening skills, it pays to remember that it takes most people a little time to tune in before they listen well. Students need to pay full attention and have had some practice time before they can cope with detailed information in a foreign language. So, to help your students feel relaxed and prepared you can begin with a warmer activity lasting a few minutes. It doesn't have to be related to the listening activities but is a short game or puzzle that focuses the mind.

Then you need two activities based on the same listening text but the first should be easier than the second. With the first activity you set the task and let students, read, discuss or work on it. Then you play the recording for them to listen to. After that there's a feedback session in which the students compare their answers and discuss them with you. You follow the same order for the second, more difficult activity. In each case the students should be prepared for what they have to do before they listen. It's up to you how long the recording lasts but the second, trickier task should take longer and be more detailed than the first.

Finally, have a follow-up activity that doesn't involve listening to the recording again but is loosely related to it. If the follow-up activity lasts longer than the two listening activities combined, it's too long for a true listening skills lesson.

Choosing a Listening Activity

The first question you may confront is the problem of what your students should be listening to. If you use a course book, quite likely it's accompanied by a cassette or CD with a simple cheesy dialogue. Great! But hold on. Perhaps it's better to give them real recorded conversations to set them up for life outside the classroom. There are pros and cons on both sides, which I lay out in the next sections.

Finding material from the real world

If you happen to be teaching in an English-speaking country or area, you could, in theory, have your students engage in entirely authentic listening by taking them out onto the streets. Realistically though, this isn't your best option, as you've no control over what your students hear in terms of grammar, vocabulary, slang or even good manners.

Having said that, a few real, predictable situations exist, which students can manage with a little preparation. For example, guided tours around cities and museums provide opportunities for quite extended listening. Tours are reliable in that they tend to follow the same pattern each time despite being a little longwinded. Another advantage of a fairly controlled situation like that is that listeners can predict more or less what's coming and this is a key point. In the real world you usually know more or less what kind of information you're about to hear. So it's useful for you to use spontaneous, authentic listening exercises, but they're quite hard to find.

You rarely listen to anything without an expectation of what's coming next. So students also need a bit of preparation before they get stuck into a listening task and they need a reason to listen. (The upcoming 'Motivating students to listen' helps with expectations.)

Short, authentic listening texts work because they provide students with a clear example of real, live English and this is motivating for them because it's what they want to be able to do in the future. However, the activities are hard to prepare and present challenges of unnecessary words and sounds. I give more information on authentic listening texts such as CDs later in this chapter.

Normally your students are confined to the classroom where only your voice provides a realistic listening situation. Being in front of your students is great because apart from the words you say, you give other non-verbal clues.

The environment you're in offers a great deal of context and meaning to the language spoken there. After all, you don't expect to hear an order for fish and chips with a pint of beer in a fast food hamburger place. When you look at the menu in such a place, you realise that there are fairly limited possibilities as to what the speaker can say.

In addition, the speaker's body language varies according to the needs of the situation. Most people use facial expressions such as smiles and frowns to match their words and in addition, it's normal to point at things you're referring to or to use emphatic gestures to stress certain words.

Of course, a film can record the environment and the body language, which is very helpful but the communication is pretty one-sided. Your students can only respond to what's said on screen. So a film is a little more authentic than a tape recording (unless you're practising phone calls or radio broadcasts).

If you're anything like me, the idea of using a video camera, TV and or projector seems quite labour intensive. To do so you probably need a transcript and exercise you've designed yourself. Some schools just don't have the budget for that kind of hardware anyway. Another problem is that when you record people they get nervous and stop behaving naturally, which results in bad acting and stiffness. After all that preparation you lose the authentic air that you'd hoped to capture. But if you just leave the camera running until the subjects forget it's there – a sort of Big Brother approach – you may also get a stream of word whiskers and pausing, which distracts the students.

Word whiskers are the meaningless things you attach to sentences to fill the gaps when you don't know what to say. They include *um* and *err* as well as other annoying, repeated phrases. How much of this kind of dialogue do your students need to understand anyway? Here's an example of how native speakers can really sound: 'So I told her yeah. I went . . . I told her right . . . um "You're out of order!" You know what I mean though. Cause like, she really is'.

Choosing the material from course books

Pre-recorded listening texts that accompany the course book are usually designed to have students practise exactly the language or concept the lesson plan teaches. These texts tend to appear in every one or two units of a course book to balance out the four skills (reading, writing and speaking are the other skills). Listening texts made especially for EFL are:

- ✔ Easily accessible.
- ✔ Appropriate to the level.
- ✔ Focused on the target grammar and structures.
- ✔ Free of slang, distractions and interruptions.
- ✔ Labour saving.
- ✔ The right length for the lesson.
- ✔ Usually accompanied by a tape-script.

Unfortunately they have some drawbacks too. Some of these pre-prepared texts may be unusable because:

- ✔ The initial expense for the CD/DVD/cassette is often quite steep.
- ✔ The dialogues are often so carefully staged that they sound fake or patronising.
- ✔ They give a false impression – in real life people aren't so clear and concise.
- ✔ They may not cover the situations that students actually need.

Ultimately the teacher needs to look at the circumstances of each class and consider the time and resources available before deciding which kind of text to choose.

Using CDs and DVDs for authentic listening

Music, films, podcasts (a video or audio file you can download from the Internet and listen to on your computer, MP3 or other similar device) and broadcasts are very popular with students, except the odd few who prefer grammar tables and 'serious' work. Some broadcasting companies have websites that you can access to look through their archives of programmes and download free of charge.

Try www.bbc.co.uk/iplayer for fairly current BBC shows first broadcast on TV and radio. I also use Channel 4 programme archives, which are free. Access www.channel4.com and register for their 4oD service, which offers a wide variety of shows to download. Another favourite is www.lbc.co.uk offering podcasts from their London radio station. It's a talk station that invites ordinary people to call in and discuss current affairs. You can scarcely find a more cosmopolitan bunch than the residents of London so there's still an international feel to the programmes.

In a lesson you can only usually deal with a few minutes of listening text at a time, so select clips from longer recordings that are appropriate to the level and interesting to analyse. If your students have Internet access you can set longer listening tasks as homework. They can listen to extracts of 20 minutes or so in preparation for a class discussion the following lesson. Although students do sometimes become anxious when they hear the unfamiliar, texts downloaded from the Internet are easy for the students to access by themselves for personal study at another time.

Accommodating accents

Hearing authentic listening material designed for native speakers is very motivating for your students, but you face a serious problem where there are many accents to deal with.

When you teach pronunciation, you generally use whatever is considered to be Standard English in your country and your own accent as models. Suddenly you realise that in the TV clip you want to use there's a heavy Newcastle accent, some Liverpool dialect and a New Zealand speaker too. Well, there's a difference between recognition and imitation.

A good way to deal with unusual accents is by adapting a tape-script for your students. This means turning it into a 'fill in the gaps' type exercise where students can read along and just fill in certain words pronounced in a fairly regular way. Or, they have to put complete lines of the dialogue into the correct order. So even if they don't catch every word just by listening they can still complete the task with the support of their reading skills. The accents then become incidental. In both cases you're connecting listening and reading so that students learn to match the sound and spelling of the language.

When you model pronunciation you actually want them to speak like you or as similarly to you as possible. When you expose your students to other accents, however, you help them to get used to the reality of English as a diverse and global language.

Accents are different from dialects, which feature entirely different vocabulary and grammatical structures.

Correctness in pronunciation is all to do with whether or not people understand you easily. By demonstrating a range of accents students become more accepting of this.

Coping with colloquial language

The extent to which you expose students to informal, colloquial speech may well depend on what they eventually intend to do with their English. For example, if you're teaching business English to students who need to work on an international scale and not necessarily with native speakers of English, they probably won't encounter too many colloquialisms. Compare that situation with Korean students preparing to attend a course at university in Scotland. In the second case, the students are likely to face a constant stream of colloquialisms so it's worth them doing listening activities that get them familiar with everyday speech.

Clichés, expressions that people use far too much so have no originality and little meaning, may be one of the first things to deal with. Footballers are great for this and here are a few classics.

- To be perfectly honest.
- At the end of the day.
- For the record.
- With all due respect.
- Lessons will be learned.

None of these expressions is likely to carry the main message in the sentence or dialogue. Pointing this out, and having students learn to listen out for key words and particular information, makes them feel better about knowing what they can safely ignore.

Slang words are a little different because sometimes they're essential to understanding the message. For example, in the phrase, 'Give 20 quid to the bloke in red', both *bloke* and *quid* are slang words essential to the meaning. So you may want to provide a glossary:

> Quid: British English meaning one pound sterling (£1).

> Bloke: British, Australian and New Zealand English meaning a man.

If students are likely to need the slang words in future, teach them how to use these appropriately. If, on the other hand, the students only need the slang words to understand this text, just provide a glossary for them and leave it at that.

Authentic listening texts give students a chance to hear how normal, natural intonation really sounds. Sometimes students make so much effort that they sound rather over the top. Or alternatively they make no effort and sound dead pan.

Films with robots such as the 'Terminator' series help students to hear the effect of flat intonation.

Whetting Students' Appetites

In the real world listeners usually have a sense of purpose for listening. So before you play your text, you need to prepare your students.

Motivating students to listen

Occasionally teachers bring in a much loved reading or song and proceed with great enthusiasm, only to find that the students have no idea what all the fuss is about. This is why some initial talking up of the activity is ideal – because it raises anticipation. You may have to add some cultural background as well to aid comprehension.

Before you turn on the machine, provide some information on:

- ✓ **Context and background:** Talk to the class about the speakers, the situations referred to, the time period, location and so on. Not only does this generate interest but it reduces the amount of work the students have to do. With some basic questions about the text already answered, they focus more on the specific task you set.

    If, for example, your listening text is a Beatles number, you can begin with pictures of the Fab Four and you can find out what the students know about them. You can ask which Beatle is which? What's so special about them? Are they still alive and if so what are they doing now?

- ✓ **Type of listening text:** As there's a vast array of text type to choose from, try giving the students a multiple choice task by asking them, for example, to identify whether they're listening to a poem, story or play. You can also talk about general features of the genre you're dealing with so that students can pay particular attention to word play such as rhyme and alliteration. They can also listen out for the way the structure identifies the genre. For instance, *Once upon a time* followed by the past simple tense is almost certainly a fairy tale.

> The language in the text:
>
> You may want to remind them of what a particular tense sounds like with its contractions – for example, *I had done it* = *I'd done it* – or what form an irregular verb takes. Then there's vocabulary. If the text contains tricky words, get them out of the way beforehand by giving the students a list of the words and a dictionary.

Another way to keep students' motivation high is to remove the problem of trying to listen while grappling with an unclear task at the same time. So before the listening text is played make sure that students understand exactly what they have to do and that they've read the relevant questions thoroughly. Allow the students to familiarise themselves with the worksheet, if there is one, and ask questions beforehand.

Of course, during the listening stage the students are fairly passive so the pre-listening stage can give them the opportunity to discuss and compare opinions with their classmates. An extended period of listening quietly is just too much for some of the more active students. Fidgety students only disrupt things if you don't allow them to be more active for a time.

After you've done a few of these activities the class should be ready to tune in and listen.

Running through some pre-listening tasks

In this section, I give you some examples of what you can do in the pre-listening stage.

Predicting

When students predict the answers to specific questions or overall content it really raises their curiosity.

If students have an exercise where they need to fill in the gaps, they should first of all try to predict what kind of word is missing. For example, is the word a noun or a verb? Is it a place, a number or a name? This helps them to listen for a few words.

You have an extract from a BBC interview with Madonna. After a short class discussion about favourite pop stars you introduce the activity by saying 'You're going to listen to an interview with the international superstar Madonna. Predict which three of these topics the journalist asks her about:

> Her divorce

> Adoption

> Writing children's books

> ✔ Women in the music industry
> ✔ Living in London

Have them compare choices with a partner and say why they chose these topics.

Making predictions about the text they're going to listen to gives students a reason to listen because they want to know if they were right.

Brainstorming

You can give students a time limit, say two minutes, and then get them to jot down all the words they know on a particular topic. Actually, they can write them straight up on the board for you.

So, for example, before a radio weather report, ask students about weather words: 'How many words can you think of for this kind of weather?'

You can then fill in any gaps in their knowledge by pre-teaching some extra words. You're then at least able to see if they remember the trickier words that are to come in the text.

Discussing

Class, group or pair discussions introduce the topic and feed the imagination. (I talk more about promoting discussion in Chapter 13.)

For instance, before listening to a phone conversation about restaurant bookings students can talk about their own experiences in small groups, responding to questions like:

When was the last time you ate out?

Did you book a reservation?

Did you have a good time? Why/why not?

Questioning

Students can also decide what they hope to gain from the text. I find this useful for students of academic English who may have to listen to longer lectures in the future.

You can ask students to make a personal connection to the topic. For example, if they're going to hear a short lecture on dinosaurs, you can ask, 'What would you personally like to know about these amazing creatures?'

If the lecture doesn't answer what students want to know, they have a ready-made homework project to write about or give a presentation about.

Come Again? Repeating the Text

In most cases you play listening texts twice within the lesson. The first time students get the idea of what the text is about and on the second occasion they listen for more detail.

Listening for the basic idea

A task or activity aimed at getting the gist should be relatively easy but not obvious. So if you're presenting a Madonna interview, there's no point asking *'Who is Madonna?'* It's not even necessary to listen to the text to get the answer. However, if the students had previously predicted which questions the interview would cover, the task may be to listen to the interview and check whether they were right.

Listening and responding to a visual image is a useful way of exercising listening skills because students don't get tangled up with reading and writing, which may create anxiety or distraction.

Listening activities should practise just that, listening. Avoid trying to test reading or writing skills at the same time by using complicated grammatical structures or unnecessarily difficult vocabulary in the questions.

Figure 14-1 is an example of a business English activity I devised along with part of the tape-script. The organisation charts in the figure accompany a listening text about the structure of a company. Students listen for gist and decide which chart best fits the description they hear.

The tape-script is here:

> Mrs Smith: Have you prepared the letters?
>
> Paul: Yes Mrs Smith, but I gave one to Mike.
>
> Mrs Smith: Well, you're a manager too, Paul. You should be doing your own paperwork.
>
> Paul: I know but the client wanted a 35 per cent discount and I'm only allowed to offer 25 per cent. Only you and Mike can agree to bigger discounts so I passed it on to him.
>
> Mrs Smith: I see. Well I'll speak to Mike later. Don't forget that he and I are coming to see you and John tomorrow to discuss the sales figures.

Allow students to get the point through what the speakers infer rather than what they say explicitly, as long as it's not too subtle.

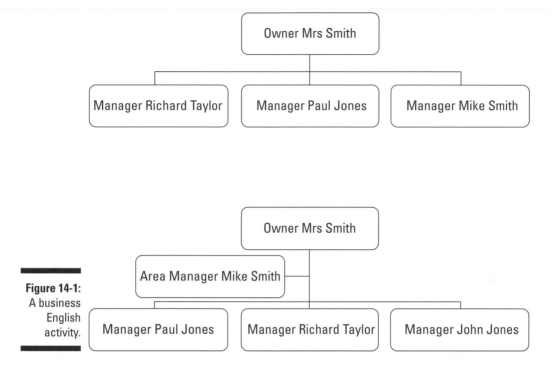

Figure 14-1:
A business
English
activity.

Other simple forms of questions to get at the main idea of a dialogue may be:

✔ Do the speakers in the dialogue agree with each other or not?

✔ How many speakers are there?

✔ Where do you think they are?

Get students to tick off the things they hear, using words or pictures.

I had a class of children listen to the story of Red Riding Hood. They knew the story but didn't realise what it was because they weren't able to translate the title. They were very keen to find out if the English language characters did the same things as the characters in their version. I gave them a worksheet with the words *grandfather, wolf, big ears, big teeth* and *big feet* on it and told them to tick the things they heard in the story.

Listening for detail

After the students have a chance to listen to the text once and get the gist of it, you can prepare to go a bit deeper by setting a more detailed listening task for the students to tackle while listening to the recording a second time. This time the students can listen for more specific information based on particular expressions the speaker uses.

Listening activities to try

Here a few suggestions for you to try in your listening skills lessons:

- Working with a picture. Students can examine a picture to see if it matches up to the listening text. Does the picture show the correct number of people in the right place? Is each person in the picture wearing the clothes the listening text described? In a picture story students can choose the picture that doesn't fit. They may have four pictures that show scenes from a story but one picture shows the same characters doing something that doesn't happen in the story. By listening carefully the students can weed out it out.

- Labelling: Students put labels on various parts of a diagram based on what they hear. Suppose the listening text describes a machine with four of five distinct parts and only one part is labelled on the diagram. As the students listen to the text they hear that Part A is rectangular not round, or that Part D is the only one connected to Part C on the right. By listening to the text the class can identify and eliminate the various parts.

- Following a map: After a description or directions, X can mark the spot.

- Short teacher monologue: Tell a story about an episode in your life while students take notes. They can ask you questions about it afterwards or retell the story to each other.

- Traditional stories: Folk tales and fairy stories are great because there are often similar ones in other cultures so the students may want to tell their own afterwards. If you can't find a professional recording, get a friend to read and record it for you.

- Songs: Music is great for fixing words in your mind. It's a painless way to practice grammar. I recently used Beyonce's 'If I Were a Boy' to practise the second conditional tense.

- Physical response: Get students to follow instructions through movement. They can practice words like prepositions and parts of the body. They can also manipulate objects in accordance with the listening text.

- Dictation: This traditional activity can be livened up by dictating a diagram for students to draw.

- True or false: Have a series of true or false comprehension questions after listening for detail.

- Gap fill: Leave gaps in the tape-script or in the summary you prepare.

- Putting information in order. The listening text may describe a process such as baking a special cake. On the students' worksheet you list all the stages in the wrong order. As they listen, the students can number the stages of the process from first to last.

- Complete information on a timetable or schedule.

Students don't need to understand every word. After all, in real life we often just let phrases go over our heads. You may understand a particular expression only after hearing it many times – this is a natural way to acquire language. So instead of analysing the text to death, just choose specific things you want to highlight.

Keep in mind that you always set the task before playing the text for the second time. Then the students listen, and have a little time to reflect on their answers. After that, have a feedback session. You can carry out reflection and feedback in a variety of ways but it should happen immediately after the listening. It's quite tricky for the students to recall the nuances of what they've heard on the following day, for example.

Your task may be comprehension questions based on the grammar and vocabulary in the text. It doesn't have to be so traditional though. From time to time you can use a text to focus on pronunciation and intonation too. The objective can be for the students to listen carefully and then read a section aloud themselves.

Look for the nearby sidebar, 'Listening activities to try' for examples of activities to use.

Planning Follow-Up Activities

Round off your lesson with a follow-up activity. This helps to conclude the lesson in a balanced way because not everyone is good at learning through listening and some may not appreciate your chosen listening text as much as other classmates. After all, students have different styles of learning.

When you finish with an activity that focuses on a different skill, more students have a chance to shine. You can personalise a theme from the listening text by having students do a quick writing exercise based on the topic the listening text explored.

After having the class listen to an interview with Madonna, you can say something like, 'Now that you've listened to an interview with an American artist, I would like you to think about a very popular musician in your country. Make notes about this musician for two minutes including the reason why she is so popular in your opinion and say whether you have any music by her at home. Then give a 90-second presentation to your group.

This kind of activity is also appropriate for written homework and your follow-up activity may include a plan that leads to composition writing.

Other ideas for follow ups are:

✔ **Making predictions:** Ask students to speculate about what happened after the clip finished. This kind of question lends itself to role-plays, students preparing quiz questions, and story writing.

✓ **Reading a book related to the listening text:** Listening texts that involve a popular personality or event are useful because you can often find other material based on the same topic, such as biographies or conspiracy theories. Books and articles maintain the students' interest after a relatively short listening text. They provide more cultural input and an opportunity to put to good use the vocabulary they encountered during the listening tasks.

Films are often based on books and if you use a movie clip for the listening activity, you can check whether the book exists as a *graded reader* (a short book written especially for EFL students at a particular level) and get students to compare the film and book version of a particular scene. Ask whether the director did a satisfactory job. They can try directing another scene to be acted out by classmates.

Part IV
The Grammar You Need to Know – and How to Teach It

The 5th Wave   By Rich Tennant

ENGLISH AS A
FOREIGN LANGUAGE

GRAMMAR

"Today, we'll break a sentence into its component parts: subject, verb, and rumour..."

In this part . . .

Teaching grammar needn't be a slog, even if you're not much used to it yourself. While this book doesn't claim to be a definitive grammar textbook, Part IV gives you the knowledge you need to be able to teach grammar effectively and suggests ways to make grammar teaching interesting.

Basic sentence structure, the use of adjectives and adverbs, and the many and various verb tenses which help to make learning and teaching English such a joy – they're all here. And of course I show you how to deliver the seemingly driest factual info with a dash of humour and fun.

Chapter 15

Stop Press! Student to Deliver Sentence

In This Chapter

▶ Looking at the building blocks of sentences

▶ Understanding prepositions and articles

▶ Describing adjectives and adverbs

▶ Joining up with conjunctions

A round the world there are thousands of languages, each with its own grammatical system. This means that students can easily get it wrong when they try to put words together to make a sentence in English. So in this chapter you find out about the structure of sentences. Although entire grammar books devote themselves to the subject, this section introduces a few points that students can use to improve spoken and written fluency.

English is basically an *SVO language* – in a simple sentence it's **s**ubject first, then **v**erb, then **o**bject.

Starting with the Basics: Subjects, Verbs and Objects

'Things' and 'doing words' are the explanations for nouns and verbs you may remember from your school days but you have to be a lot more detailed than that to help your students. Actually, nouns are words that tell you the names of people, places and things such as, *office* and *desk*. A verb is word that describes an action such as *to laugh* and *to watch*. Verbs can describe a state of being too, such as *I am happy*. Then there are pronouns, which are words you use to replace nouns in a sentence such as *it* and *they*. I go into these in detail in the following sections.

Thinking about subjects

A *subject* is basically a word telling you what or who is doing something, or what thing, or who, the sentence is about. For example:

> **Peter** loves ice cream.

The word 'Peter' is the subject word because he is the one who 'loves'.

You use the *subject pronoun* when you don't say the name of the person or thing. For example:

> **He** loves ice cream.

Instead of saying 'Peter', the subject word is *he,* which is a subject pronoun.

By the way, subject pronouns are sometimes called personal pronouns and here they all are: I, you, he, she, it, we and they. You should point out that 'I' is always a capital letter.

Students may think that one or two subject pronouns are missing when you first write them out like this. That's because in lots of languages there are different versions of 'you' depending on whether you're talking about one person or more than one, or whether you're speaking to a respected person or a pal. In addition to this, in some dialects and varieties of English, people say 'you all', 'you guys' or 'youse', but you don't teach these as standard English.

Some native speakers use the subject pronoun 'one'. For example they may say, 'One drinks white wine with chicken'. Although the sentence is correct, it doesn't sound very modern and if students say it they can sound rather pretentious. So you're better off not teaching 'one' as a subject pronoun unless your students come across it and ask you for an explanation. Encourage them to use 'people' or 'you' instead.

Students get mixed up for various reasons when they use subject words. For example:

> ✔ In some languages you can make a sentence without using a subject word at all. So, you can effectively say: Peter loves ice cream. Prefers vanilla.
>
> Of course, this second sentence is incorrect in English because in English you must have a subject word, but it may well look fine to a student.
>
> ✔ Sometimes the subject word is not in first place in a sentence. Of course, that's where students expect it to be so they panic when it's not there.

In the sentence, 'Yesterday afternoon Rex went to the supermarket', the subject is *Rex* not *yesterday afternoon*, which appears first in the line up. In this case it's important to show the connection between Rex and the verb – Rex is the person who *went*.

✔ Students repeat the subject word instead of using a subject pronoun. So for a student, Rex's story may continue: 'After Rex finished in the supermarket Rex walked in the park. Rex got a sandwich in the café and Rex ate it on the grass.'

It's therefore important for students to practise replacing the name of the subject word with a pronoun once they're clear about who or what that is. As students progress, you also need to point out that later in the sentence it's possible to leave the subject word or pronoun out, as long as it's there in the first part and the meaning is obvious. So they can say, 'Rex got a sandwich in the café and ate it on the grass' instead of 'Rex got a sandwich in the café, and Rex ate it on the grass'.

Activating verbs

A *verb* is a word that describes an action. It can be manipulated into different tenses to show when something happened. When you talk about a verb in its original, *infinitive* form, you put 'to' in front of it.

Finding verb forms

A main verb can be manipulated into different forms to show which tense it's in or what purpose it serves in a particular sentence. (I talk about auxiliary verbs in the next section.)

Verb forms are:

✔ **Infinitive:** The infinitive form of the verb is the original form before it changes to make a tense. It's the form with 'to' in front of it, for example 'to play'. You usually need to know this form to look up the meaning in the dictionary, although you cut the 'to' off.

✔ **Gerund or present participle:** This is the verb with 'ing' on the end. So the gerund of 'to play' is 'playing'.

✔ **Past simple:** The past simple is a particular tense that describes completed actions in the past. Some verbs have regular endings in the past simple. You add 'ed' to the end (or just 'd' to a verb ending with 'e' already). For example, the past simple of 'play' is 'played'.

Many verbs are irregular though, so they change a lot in this tense. For example: say /said.

- **Past participle:** When you use a passive sentence ('the book was written' instead of 'someone wrote the book') you use another form of the verb called the past participle. You also need this form when you make perfect tenses. For example: I have **seen** it (present perfect), Bob will have **done** it (future perfect), Kenny had **drunk** the beer (past perfect) .

- **Third person singular of the present simple:** When you write a sentence using he, she or it in the present simple tense, you need to put 's' (or 'es') at the end of the main verb – He **plays** guitar.

A verb table is a necessary but hated part of kit for EFL students. It consists of a long list of irregular verbs (verbs that don't conform to usual patterns in English) and you usually find verb tables at the back of course books and in dictionaries for students to memorise or refer to. Verb tables are usually written in three columns:

infinitive	*past simple*	*past participle*
(to) sing	sang	sung

Helping out with auxiliary verbs

Some verbs don't have much meaning all by themselves but when you put them with another verb, a main verb, the sentence has a new shade of meaning. Or even if the verb can be used alone, when you put it in a sentence next to the main verb you can construct a tense.

In the sentence, 'I am drinking coffee', *drinking* is the main verb and *am* has no real meaning; it's just there to make the present continuous tense so you know that the action is happening now.

The auxiliary verbs we use in the English language are:

- to be
- to do
- to have
- may*
- might*
- must*
- ought*
- shall*
- should*
- will*
- would*

The verbs marked with * never change form or tense. By this I mean you can't add anything to the end of them. You don't say, 'He shoulds go', for example.

Others can change because they're sometimes used as main verbs, such as to have (has, had).

In the following sentences I've italicised the auxiliary verbs. They help the main verb in bold.

> ✔ I *have* **finished.**
>
> ✔ They *are* **working.**
>
> ✔ *Can* you **speak** French?

Recognising regular and irregular verbs

Lots of verbs in English are irregular. They don't follow the same patterns as most verbs, especially in the past simple. I discuss the past simple in Chapter 16 – it's the tense we use to say what happened yesterday, for example. Most verbs add 'ed' in the past simple, such as 'looked' and 'washed'. The irregular verbs don't change in this way, for example, 'wore' and 'swam'.

Probably the most important verb and the trickiest one to explain is '*to be*'. Fortunately, most other languages have an equivalent verb so you don't really have to explain its meaning but rather demonstrate how it operates in English. It's the verb with the most changes and exceptions – *am, is, are* for example.

Subject Pronoun	Present Simple	Past Simple
I	am	was
You	are	were
He/she/it	is	was
We	are	were
They	are	were

I talk about the present simple and past simple tenses in Chapter 16.

The gerund or present participle of *to be* is *being*. The past participle of *to be* is *been*. I explain the meaning of these gerund, present and past participles in the following section.

Shortening verbs with contractions

In English, sometimes you can make verbs shorter by omitting letters and using an apostrophe instead. This is very common in conversation and informal writing. You can't use contractions in academic and formal writing though.

am= 'm	I'm tall
is/ has= 's	He's here. He's got a car
will= 'll	We'll help you.
have= 've	You've been there.
had/ would= I'd better go.	I'd like milk please.
are= 're	They're at work.

Not= n't   He didn't come. Notice that when *not* becomes *n't* it's attached to the verb and written as one word. *Cannot* becomes *can't*.

Acting on the object

In the sentence: *Peter loves ice cream,* '*Peter*' is the subject word and '*loves*' is the verb. But what does Peter love? He loves ice cream. So *ice cream* is the object word. It's involved in the action. Peter may love other things too:

> Peter loves *her*.
>
> Peter loves *eating*.
>
> Peter loves *the fact that the town was lively*.

All these endings are the object of the sentence.

In English you don't always need an object word: '*Peter loves*' is actually a complete sentence in itself.

The main reason why students get confused with object words is because they're not sure where to put them in the sentence. In a simple sentence students can just follow the SVO (subject, verb, object) pattern. So even very low-level students can usually manage sentences like

S (subject)	V (verb)	O (object)
The dog	brings	the newspaper.

However, what if the student wants to mention the owner of the dog? There are now two objects.

When you mention the person who receives the action, you're talking about an *indirect object*. An indirect object goes after the verb and before the direct object: The dog brings *its owner* the newspaper.

The indirect object may be a thing not a person but it still receives the action, as in: John made *the book* a new cover.

Placing an object with a transitive verb

However some verbs, called *transitive verbs* need an object. For example the verb 'to drop' is transitive. In the sentence, 'I dropped the cup', 'I' is the subject, 'dropped' is the verb and 'the cup' is the object. If you're not sure whether or not a verb is transitive, use a dictionary to check. Transitive verbs are listed with a *T* or *tr* in brackets next to the verb and the definition often includes *something* or *somebody* to emphasise that you need a direct object.

Standing in with object pronouns

You use 'her' not 'she' as the object. So these are the object pronouns that replace nouns and phrases:

Subject pronoun	Object pronoun
I	me
you	you
he	him
she	her
it	it
we	us
they	them

Proposing Prepositions

Prepositions are words that come before nouns and pronouns and show how words in a sentence relate to each other in terms of amount, direction, time, place, cause, or manner. Here are a few examples:

- ✔ Prepositions of manner: by, via
- ✔ Prepositions of amount: about, over
- ✔ Prepositions of time: before, after
- ✔ Prepositions of direction: into, towards
- ✔ Prepositions of place: next to, in front of
- ✔ Prepositions of cause: because, due to

Unfortunately, prepositions don't translate very well into other languages. Some have fewer; some have 'postpositions' that go after the noun and some just use different expressions entirely. Be prepared for a lot of groans from students whenever they have to get the right preposition because in many cases they simply have to learn the whole phrase by heart .

When an expression needs a particular preposition in a sentence, you should highlight that to students. For example:

> to marry: to be married *to* someone.

> to agree: to agree *with* someone or something.

Introducing Articles

Articles appear before nouns in a sentence. Fortunately for students there are only a three:

- ✔ A: The indefinite article.
- ✔ An: The indefinite article before a vowel sound only.
- ✔ The: The definite article.

You can't teach the students that 'an' comes before a vowel. You need to say a vowel sound or phoneme because they to need to rely on pronunciation, not spelling. For example:

> **a** fire

> **an** aeroplane

> But:

> **a** university /juːnɪvɜːsɪtiː/

> **an** honest man /ɒnist/

Although there are only three articles, quite a number of rules surround them.

Teach the rules for articles whenever you teach the vocabulary associated with them. It's really difficult for students to remember lists of rules but they get a feel for what sounds right if they learn whole phrases. For example, you teach 'to have dinner' instead of just 'dinner', and if the students tend to make errors by inserting an article, you can write it this way on the board: 'to have a dinner' and cross out the 'a'.

Using the indefinite a/an

You use the indefinite articles for non-specific singular nouns, in cases where you're referring to any of the items within a group. For example: *A pet is for life*.

Use 'a' or 'an' for these situations:

✔ Jobs: I'm *a* teacher.

✔ Religions and nationalities in the form of a noun: I'm a Hindu. I'm *a* Briton.

✔ Something you're talking about for the first time: I met *a* doctor at the party.

✔ With *what a/such a* and a singular noun: What *a* shame!

✔ Only one: There's *a* Briton and two Brazilians in the office.

Getting specific with 'the'

By using the definite article, you make clear which particular thing you're referring to. For example: *This food is for the pets*.

Use 'the' for these situations:

✔ Specific things or things mentioned before: In the following example *a* refers to any book but *the* refers to a particular one: I wanted a book so I chose *the* one on the middle shelf.

✔ In geography for the names of rivers, oceans, seas, and also unique places: *The* Thames is beautiful today. That country is near t*he* equator.

✔ Superlatives: This one is the best. This is *the* most expensive.

✔ Ordinal numbers: This is *the* first time.

✔ The activity of playing an instrument: She plays t*he* saxophone.

✔ An entire group of people or animals: *The* Chinese seem industrious.

✔ Decades: I was born in *the* seventies.

✔ When there's only one of something: *The* sun was shining when t*he* Prime Minister met *the* Queen.

✔ Republics and kingdoms: *the* United Kingdom.

✔ Countries made up of separate states, islands and so on: *the* Caribbean, *the* USA.

Foregoing the article altogether

Sometimes you don't need any article at all in English, whereas in other languages you do. Here are some examples of nouns without articles that may surprise your students.

- ✔ Very general ideas: People love humour.
- ✔ Countries: I'm off to France.
- ✔ Languages: I speak Gujarati.
- ✔ Meals in general: I have dinner quite early.
- ✔ People's names: Queen Elizabeth arrived.
- ✔ Single mountains and lakes: Mount Fuji is huge.

Describing Adjectives and Adverbs

Once your students have learnt the basic building blocks of sentences in English they need to work on making them a little more interesting, which is where modifiers come in.

Sprucing up a noun with an adjective

An adjective is a word you use to give more information about a noun or pronoun in a sentence. You can use an adjective to describe, identify or say how much or many in relation to a noun.

When you use a noun in a sentence, it's more interesting to describe that noun and give an idea of what it's like.

The simple sentence, *She sits on the sofa* is grammatically accurate but rather dull. Although the student who wrote it may feel content, you can get him to identify the noun and imagine the details about it, by asking questions about it: What colour is the sofa? What is it made of? How does it feel? and so on.

An improvement would be: She sits on the *cheap, black* sofa. The sentence is already more descriptive because there are two adjectives, *cheap* and *black*.

In English, words made from nouns and verbs but with 'able' at the end are generally adjectives. For example, 'peace' is a noun but 'peaceable' is the adjective and 'adore' is a verb but 'adorable' is the adjective.

Running through the types of adjectives

Adjectives come in three main flavours: describing, identifying and quantifying. The following sections take you through the uses of each variety.

Describing

Many adjectives tell you what the noun is like. For example, instead of just talking about a bag, you can say that it's *a large, leather* bag. The descriptive adjectives tell you that the bag is *large* and *leather*.

Some examples of descriptive adjectives are:

- ✔ **Colours:** Blue, turquoise, pale.
- ✔ **Materials:** Woollen, metallic, granite.
- ✔ **Shapes:** Oval, rectangular, round.
- ✔ **Opinion:** Nasty, tremendous, absurd.
- ✔ **Tastes:** Bitter, tasty, sweet.
- ✔ **Comparatives and superlatives:** Better, best, most exciting.
- ✔ **Nationalities:** British, Jamaican, Irish.

Identifying

At times the adjective tells you who a noun belongs to. These words are called possessive adjectives. So rather than saying the jacket of my brother, you can use 's after the name of the person who owns something (my brother's jacket) or use a possessive adjective, his jacket.

The possessive adjectives are:

- ✔ My
- ✔ Your
- ✔ His/her/its
- ✔ Our
- ✔ Their

Or you can point out which noun you're referring to by using these adjectives, which are a little more specific than using an article:

- ✔ This
- ✔ These
- ✔ That
- ✔ Those

Quantifying

Another use of adjectives is to say how many of an item there are.

Adjectives related to quantity can range from a simple number (one, a thousand, a million) to words like these: each, every, either, neither, both, any, some, none, more, many, all, few and enough.

Using adjectives in order

Once students get the hang of what an adjective is, they put them in all over the place. Unfortunately, that creates another problem because sentences can sound somewhat odd if you don't put the adjectives in the right order.

The sentence 'There's a German, old, ugly car in the street'. is very easy to understand but just doesn't sound right. Surely it should be: 'There's an *ugly, old, German* car in the street'.

You need to teach your students a rule for lining up their adjectives. In reality, you can't cover every line up of adjectives possible, but Table 15-1 offers a guide which works most of the time.

Table 15-1				Example of Adjective Order				
Whose/ Which	How Many	Opinion	Size/ Shape	Age	Colour	Origin	What It's Made Of	What It's For
a	few	great	oval	old	golden	Japanese	acrylic	coffee
his	ninety	awful	narrow	new	white	American	straw	driving
these	two	rude	tall	young	bright	Tribal	ice	bath

For example you can describe items this way: those twenty fantastic, beige, ceramic flower pots and my funny, blue, Aboriginal wall hanging.

Expanding on verbs with adverbs

Adverbs are words that describe verbs. They say how the verb is carried out and, like adjectives, they make sentences more interesting. The same accurate but dull sentence used in the section on adjectives – *She sits on the sofa* – offers no evidence of how she sits. You can ask the student for more information, and may be presented with: She sits *elegantly* on the sofa.

Now you can imagine how she sits because of the word 'elegantly', which is an adverb. She may also sit lazily, well or sleepily as these are all adverbs too.

You can point out to students that most adverbs in English end with 'ly'. But note that many adverbs don't. 'Fast' and 'hard' don't change whether they're adverbs or adjectives and the adverb form of 'good' is 'well'.

Sometimes adverbs describe an adjective or even another adverb. In the next examples the italicised adverb describes the bold adjective and adverb, respectively:

> The statue was *really* **huge**.

> She does that *particularly* **well**.

Looking at types of adverbs

The first adverbs students learn are often *adverbs of frequency* that tell you how often something takes place. They're words such as:

- Always
- Generally
- Often
- Sometimes
- Occasionally
- Hardly ever
- Never

Other kinds of adverbs describe:

- **Time:** nowadays, today.
- **Degree:** quite, rather.
- **Place:** somewhere, here.

Truly, madly, deeply: The rules of using adverbs

What often confuses students is the position of adverbs in a sentence.

Most adverbs go after the verb in a sentence if the adverb is describing the verb. For example:

> They play *professionally*.

On the other hand, adverbs that describe transitive verbs go after the object of the verb. I discuss transitive verbs earlier in this chapter. For example, *to raise* is transitive because you always speak about raising something in particular. In the following sentence the object is *the cup*:

> The winner raised the cup *triumphantly*.

When the adverb shows how strong or weak an idea is (these are called adverbs of degree or intensifiers), you put the adverb before the word it refers to. For example:

How warm is it? It's *fairly* warm.

However, enough goes after the word it refers to:

It's warm *enough*.

Adverbs of time can be used in different positions in a sentence. It's easier for students to go by the rule of thumb that you should put them at the beginning or end of a clause (part of a sentence with its own subject and verb):

This afternoon I'm free/ I'm free *this afternoon*.

Adverbs of frequency go between the subject and the verb as a general rule: I *always* speak to her.

When the main verb is 'to be', in one form or another, the word order is different because the adverb goes after the verb: I am *usually* busy.

In some tenses there's a main verb and auxiliary verb. You fit the adverb between the main verb and auxiliary verb, even if the main verb is a form of 'to be': They were *always* talking. I have *often* been here.

Although you can use adverbs in other positions within a sentence, you should aim to give your students a model that allows them to get it right most of the time. They'll notice other possibilities in time.

Connecting with Conjunctions

You use a *conjunction* to join two sentences or even two words together. Some of the more common conjunctions are: but, and, or/nor, for, yet, so, because, while, since.

Conjunctions can be just one word, but sometimes they're two words. For example: 'so that' – and even three, such as 'in order that'.

Differentiating conjunctions

The family of conjunctions is composed of three members:

✔ **Coordinating conjunctions** join two sentences together when each sentence is as important as the other. So you can teach students to change from writing two short sentences to one longer one:

She sits on the sofa. She reads her book.

She sits on the sofa *and* reads her book.

Michael plays well. He can't jump high.

Michael plays well *but* he can't jump high.

✔ **Subordinating conjunctions** work in sentences with two distinct parts where the understanding of one part depends on understanding the other:

We must go now. We might be late.

We will be late *unless* we go now.

✔ **Correlative conjunctions** work together in pairs, so you can't usually use one without the other:

I don't want milk. I want sugar.

I want *neither* milk *nor* sugar.

Weaving conjunctions into writing and speaking

You teach each individual conjunction one by one. For example, 'and', 'but' and 'because' usually appear in elementary level course books, then when students get used to longer sentences and varied tenses they learn more sophisticated conjunctions such as 'whereas' and 'however'.

Rules surround each conjunction too, which is all the more reason to work through them slowly and progressively, but once you've presented a few, the best way to get students using them frequently is by using practice exercises.

Giver your students sentences with lists and have them write them using 'and' before the last item:

I like tea/coffee/hot/chocolate. Answer: I like tea, coffee and hot chocolate.

He went /bank/ park/ friend's house. Answer: He went to the bank, the park and a friend's house.

She is /big/bold/beautiful. Answer: She is big, bold and beautiful.

You can have students fill in the gaps with an appropriate conjunction:

> I love going to the cinema . . . I don't think I can go tonight . . . I have no money. . . . my dad lends me a few pounds, I will have to stay home. Money is going to be a problem . . . I start my new job.

In addition to written exercises like these you can put individual conjunctions on cards and get students to come up with a sentence about their own lives including the word you give them.

Chapter 16

Feeling Tense? Sorting Out Verb Tenses

In This Chapter

▶ Naming the tenses

▶ Getting comfortable in the past and present

▶ Being perfectly content with continuous and perfect tenses

▶ Focusing on the future

For most new teachers knowing the grammar is one of the most fear inspiring parts of the job. In this chapter you find out how to break down each tense, one by one, and you get ideas for teaching them in context.

With all tenses, you have to know what it looks like. It is never enough to say past tense, present tense or future tense. Actually the tenses are always labelled past/present/future and then simple/continuous/perfect/perfect continuous. In this chapter, we also find out what these terms mean and how we use verbs to put each tense together. Then we discover why and when we use each tense.

I Speak, I Spoke, I've Spoken: Identifying the Tenses

Whereas the terms past, present and future are quite logical in meaning, tenses can be simple, continuous and perfect in the past, present and future as well. So you don't refer to a sentence as just present tense but you say that it's present simple, present continuous, or present perfect.

These tense forms aren't so obvious to decipher, but these pointers can help you:

✔ The **simple tenses** don't use the auxiliary verbs 'to be' or 'to have' with the main verb. The continuous and perfect tenses use these auxiliary (or helping) verbs in their structure. For example, 'I **drink** tea' is in the present simple. 'I drank tea' is in the past simple tense and 'I will drink' is the future simple tense.

✔ The **continuous tenses** always include 'to be' in one form or another (is, are was, were and so on – I go through 'to be' in Chapter 15) and another verb ending with 'ing' (called a *gerund*). So the sentence 'I am eating now' is in the present continuous tense. 'I was eating' is in the past continuous tense and 'I will be eating' is in the future continuous tense. In each case 'to be' and a *gerund* form part of the structure of the tense.

✔ The **perfect tenses** always include 'to have' in some way (has, have, had) and another verb that's a past participle. So the sentence 'I have eaten' is the present perfect tense. 'I had eaten' is in the past perfect tense and 'I will have eaten' is the future perfect tense. In each case the structure of the tense contains 'to have' and a past participle.

There may seem to be an endless number of tenses to remember, but actually there are only twelve and you only need to teach them one at a time.

In Table 16-1 all the tense labels are set out using the first person 'I' and the verb 'to eat', which is an irregular verb, to make model sentences.

Table 16-1		Tense Names	
	Past	*Present*	*Future*
Simple	I ate	I eat	I will eat
Continuous	I was eating	I am eating	I will be eating
Perfect	I had eaten	I have eaten	I will have eaten
Perfect continuous	I had been eating	I have been eating	I will have been eating

Although the table includes all the tenses, I cover other grammatical structures such as 'conditionals' in Chapter 17.

In Table 16-1, I use the subject pronoun *I* in each sentence. Fortunately, in English the grammar changes very little when you use the other subject pronouns. This is much easier than in other languages so don't be surprised if students seem to be overcomplicating the matter. They're usually translating.

1st person singular	*1*
2nd person singular and plural	*you*
3rd person singular	*he/she/it*
1st person plural	*we*
3rd person plural	*they*

The verb 'to be' changes the most according to the subject pronoun used and I list these different forms of the verb in Chapter 15. With other verbs, point out to your students that sentences referring to he/she/it in the present tenses change form. After he/she/it you add an 's' or 'es' .

Present Simple

He/she/it   like**s**/goe**s**/want**s**

Present continuous

I	am	looking/driving
You/we/they	are	looking/driving
He/she/it	is	looking/driving

The verb 'to have' is irregular. The third person singular form *in the present simple tense* is has. You use has for he/she/it *in the present perfect simple* and *continuous* too.

Present Perfect

He /she/it   has gone/has sold

Present Perfect continuous

He/she/it   has been going/has been selling

Beginning with the Present Simple

You use the *present simple tense* to describe an action that happens generally or is generally true.

So it's typical to teach the present simple in the context of hobbies, preferences and routines, along with adverbs of frequency such as: always, usually, often, sometimes, occasionally, rarely and never.

Students can pair up and ask each other questions about their daily lives:

> What do you usually do in the evening?
>
> I often watch TV but I never go to the pub.

The present simple really is as easy as it sounds. Unlike many languages, in English regular verbs don't have to change much for each subject pronoun (I, you, he, she, it, we or they).

- ✔ 1st person singular: I like

- ✔ 2nd person singular/plural: You like

- ✔ 3rd person singular: He/she/it like**s**

- ✔ 1st person plural: We like

- ✔ 3rd person plural: They like

As soon as the students have learnt the verb 'to like' or any other regular verb, they're ready to get started with the present simple, as long as they remember to use 's' or 'es' at the end of the verb in the third person.

I list first, second and third person singular and plural so that you can identify which is which. However, the only one you commonly need to correct in TEFL is third person singular because students often forget to use 's' at the end of a verb in the present simple.

It's unwise to bombard students with grammar jargon. Just use what's necessary to explain the point. So referring to *he/she/it* is clearer than saying third person singular.

The tricky part for students is the negative and question forms where you use 'do', 'does' and 'don't'. In the negative, you put 'do not' and 'does not' before the main verb.

I, you, we, they don't/do not like: What do I/you/we/they like?

He, she, it doesn't/does not like: When does he/she like to drink beer?

We teach the verb 'to be' separately as it behaves in a different way in the positive, negative and question forms:

I am/'m (not) here.

You/we/they are/'re (not) here.

He/she/it is/'s (not) here.

Am I here?

Are you/we/they here?

Is she here?

Staying Continuously in the Present

Whereas the present simple describes a general habit, the *present continuous tense* describes an action that's happening now, at this moment or around this time.

So, you can use the current scene in the classroom to practise. For example, you can have students list everything they're wearing, do 'spot the difference' exercises – because pictures capture a moment in time – or compare first and second languages – 'I speak German but I'm speaking English at the moment'.

In comparison with the present simple, the present continuous is structured with the verb 'to be' and a gerund, a fact that students tend to forget:

> I **am singing**.
>
> He/she/it **is singing.**
>
> You/we/they **are singing.**

I didn't use 'to like' as I did in the examples for the section on the present simple because some verbs don't really describe an action but more of a state, and so can't be expressed in a continuous tense. So we say 'I understand that' instead of 'I'm understanding that'.

As you use 'to be' to make this tense, students should already know how to make questions and negatives based on the way we use this verb in the present simple. For example: Are you staying here? No, I'm not staying.

Even though this isn't technically a future tense, you can use the present continuous for appointments in the future. This use of the present continuous suggests that a particular time has been decided on, rather than a vague intention: *I'm seeing* the dentist at 3 p.m. However, you usually teach this at pre-intermediate level, not to beginners.

We can also express annoying habits in the present continuous: He's always *leaving* his key behind. However, this lesson is generally for upper-intermediate students and above.

Going Back to the Past, Simply

The *past simple tense* is the tense you use with actions that are finished in the past. You often add words like 'ago' or 'last' (night, week, month, year) to show when the action happened.

A typical context for this tense is a story about last weekend or your last holiday: Last summer, I *went* to Florida with my family. It *was* really hot and I *got* a good tan.

The past simple tense is quite easy with regular verbs. Students can easily remember to add 'ed' or 'd' to the end of a verb.

Don't get too comfortable though! The 'ed' ending can be pronounced in different ways. Just compare these three verbs – look*ed*, play*ed* and wait*ed* – and notice that you pronounce the 'ed' as t/, /d/ and /id/respectively, although the spelling is the same.

There's also an array of irregular verbs that students just have to learn by heart. Course books or learners' dictionaries usually include a table of verbs at the back of the book and these tables list the past simple in the second column. Verbs such as 'to drink' and 'to understand' are irregular because they change drastically. Instead of adding '. . . ed', you change them to **drank** and **understood** respectively.

Remembering a Moment in the Past

With the *past continuous tense* you can speak about a particular moment in the past.

All continuous tenses include the verb 'to be' and a gerund (a verb that ends with *ing*). In this case the verb 'to be' is in the past (was or were).

> I/he/she/it **was singing.**
>
> You/we/they **were singing.**

In the negative form you add *not* or *n't* (wasn't and weren't) and for question forms you put *was* and *were* before the subject pronoun (words like I, you, and they). For example: **Were they** singing? No they **weren't** singing.

If a detective wanted to interview someone about a theft that happened the night before, she may ask, 'What **were** you **doing** at 8.30 p.m. last night?'

Whodunnit games are a great way to practise this tense as students can come up with alibis in the past continuous.

Or perhaps two actions happened in the past but one action interrupted the other one. For example: 'At 8.30 p.m. I started making dinner. At 8.35 p.m. my neighbour came round'. The typical way to express that is by combining past continuous, often with 'while' and 'when', and past simple: While I **was making** dinner, my neighbour **came** round.

There may be two actions happening simultaneously too, with each lasting for a reasonable period of time. In this context, use the past continuous twice: While I **was making** dinner, my husband **was watching** TV.

Use pictures with a lot of people and actions to present and practise sentences like these.

Presenting the Present Perfect Simple

The *present perfect tense* is the tense you use to make a connection between the past and present.

Every perfect tense contains part of the verb 'to have' and a past participle (the third column of most verb tables).

So for this tense we use 'have' or 'has' as follows:

> I/you/we/they **have begun** (or **'ve begun**)
>
> He/she/it **has begun** (or **'s begun**)

In the negative form we include *not* (or *n't*) and in the question form we put *have/has* before the subject pronoun (words like I, you and they).

> Why **have you begun** the game? Actually, we **haven't begun** yet.

The present perfect is without doubt the most difficult tense for students to grasp because it doesn't translate well into other languages and is used for many different things

This tense is used in many ways, as I explain in the next sections, but it isn't wise to teach the various uses at once.

Sharing experiences

Use the present perfect simple to talk about experiences and accomplishments in the past without saying when they happened. If you want to speak about times and dates specifically with experiences, switch to the past simple:

> **Have** you **been** to Ireland?
>
> Yes I **have been** to Dublin. Actually I **visited** Margaret there last week.

Quite often we use 'ever' with present perfect questions of this kind and 'never' in an answer.

Have you **ever** studied French? No, I've **never** studied it.

Continuing from the past until the present

Sometimes an action started in the past but is still true now. In these situations we can express the duration of time using the word *for* followed by a period of time or the word *since* plus a date or a point in time:

I **have lived** here for three and a half years now, since July 2005.

This tense can also describe something that is gradual:

Joshua **has grown** as tall as his dad.

Typical words associated with this gradual use of the tense include: today, tonight, this week/month/year, so far, in the last minutes/days/week and so on.

Anticipating expectations

When we ask about things we're expecting, we use the present perfect simple with 'yet'. The answer may include 'already', 'recently' or perhaps 'still', although you use 'yet' in negative sentences(those which include *not*).

Is he here yet?

Yes, he **has** already **arrived,** *or* No, he still **hasn't arrived.**

Noting recent changes

Very often we can see the result of a recent action because of a visible change. We often use 'just' and 'recently' in these sentences but it's important to point out when to put these words in a sentence:

Have you **had** a fall recently? Your arm is all bruised.

I'm blushing again. Jason **has** just **walked** in.

Acting in the Present Perfect Continuous

People use the present perfect simple tense for actions that run from the past to the present and for recent changes. The *present perfect continuous tense* is used for the same two purposes when you want to stress the duration of time a bit more than usual.

Very similar to the present perfect simple, the present perfect continuous includes 'have' or 'has' and a past participle. However, with this tense the past participle is always 'been' and a gerund follows:

He/she/ it **has been singing.**

You/we/they **have been waiting.**

The negative construction adds *not* (or *n't*) after *has* or *have* and in the question form, *has* or *have* comes before the subject pronoun (I, you, we and so on):

Has he **been dancing** again? No he **hasn't been dancing** today.

Moving from the past until the present

Use this tense with the word *for* plus a period of time or the word *since* and a date or a point in time.

I **have been waiting** for the bus for ages!

What **have you been doing** since this morning?

Showing recent changes

When you can see the result of a recent action that was repeated or took a while to complete, use the present perfect continuous:

I think that it **has been raining** in the last half hour. The pavement's wet.

Have you **been dieting** recently? You look great.

Use pictures as contexts for showing the results of recent actions for both the present perfect simple and present perfect continuous and have students guess the cause. For example, a picture of a man who's out of breath can generate sentences such as:

He **has been running**.

He **has** just **missed** the bus.

He **has been playing** with his dog.

Getting to the Past Perfect Simple

You use the *past perfect simple tense* for an action that happened in the past before something else that happened in the past.

Imagine that yesterday I saw you looking rather downhearted. A short conversation follows:

What was up with you yesterday? You looked really miserable.

When you saw me I **had** just **lost** my lucky pen.

Notice the two sets of actions mentioned about yesterday (this works with any time in the past). The first is 'saw' and the second is 'lost'. However, you need to show which action happened first. So, you put the action that happened first in the past perfect (you **had lost** your lucky pen) and the thing that happened later in the past simple (I **saw** you).

Students tend to find the past simple easier and sufficient to convey the idea that an action happened in the past. Sentences using 'had had' may even look strange to native speakers (I had had a bad night, for example) so students avoid using it. However, if you don't push students to use more sophisticated language they remain at a low level, limit themselves and get marked down in exams.

Seeing the structure

All perfect tenses include *have, has,* or *had* and a past participle (the third column of most verb tables).

So, in the present perfect simple you use *have* and *has* to say:

I/you/we/they **have done** something.

He/she/it **has seen** me.

However, in the past perfect you use *had.* So you say:

I/you/we/they **had done** something.

He/she/it **had seen** me.

You can also use the contraction of had, which is *'d*. The negative form uses *not* (or *n't*) and in a question *had* comes before the subject (I, we, they and so on):

> **Had** you **met** him before you went to that party? He reckons he**'d seen** me before but I **hadn't** actually **met** him.

In a sentence you're more likely to stress or emphasise the past participle than 'had'. Help students to practise emphasising the right word by repeating after you. The contracted form is also difficult for students to recognise when they hear it. So, ask them to repeat words like I'd, you'd, he'd and so on.

To teach the past perfect, think of a scenario or story set in the past. Make the sequence of events obvious but don't relate the story in consecutive order. (A story told entirely in consecutive order is best related in the past simple.)

> John was really hungry last night. He had already searched all the cupboards in the kitchen without success and had had no food for hours. Why? Well, the day before he had run out of money and there was not a penny left. Poor John!

Reveal your story bit by bit. Draw John on the board, use a photograph or just tell the story with lots of exaggerated acting.

Your students can use phrases that summarise the story to construct a whole sentence or two:

> Last night /John hungry/no food that day/run out of money.

> Last night John was really hungry because he had run out of money and he had not eaten any food that day.

It's a good idea to work backwards by asking the students questions like

> Why do you think he was so hungry? Because he had . . .

> Why hadn't John bought some food? Because he had . . .

Plotting a timeline

A timeline is a great way to illustrate tenses by showing their relationship to the past, present or future. A *timeline* is a straight line showing time as a continuum. You can plot different actions along the line so that it's clear when the action took place and label it to show the most appropriate tense. It is particularly useful when there's more than one action.

The timeline in Figure 16-1 illustrates the sentence about John:

Figure 16-1:
Timeline showing three actions in the past to demonstrate the past simple and past perfect tenses.

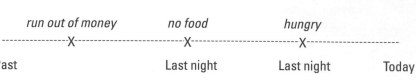

run out of money   no food   hungry
----------------X-------------------------X------------------------X---------------------
Past   Last night   Last night   Today

You can highlight words that are typically used with this tense – *just, already, before, ago, by then* and *never* – but remember to teach students where in the sentence each one goes. For example, you say *I had just/already/never seen that*. So, you use *just, already* and *never* between *had* and the past participle. However, you say *I had seen that before/weeks ago/by then*. So you use *before, ago* and *by then* after the object word(s). I talk about object words in Chapter 15. You can also use *already* after the object.

Focusing on the Past Perfect Continuous

Like the past perfect simple, you use the *past perfect continuous tense* when two actions are in the past and one happened before the other. However, this time you want to emphasise the duration of the action that happened first.

I **had been shopping** for hours when I decided to stop for lunch. In this example, the two actions are 'had been shopping' and 'decided'. The action that happened first and seemed to take a long time is in the past perfect continuous and the action that followed is in the past simple.

The past perfect continuous is similar to the past perfect simple but slightly easier to construct because it always uses *had* plus *been* and a gerund:

> I **had been listening**.

In the negative you add *not* (or *n't*) after *had*. However, in a question you put the subject word (I, you, we and so on) after *had*.

> Where **had** you **been living** before that?

> I **had not been living** in that area.

Here's a context you can use to teach this tense. Show or draw a picture of a boy returning home in wet football gear. Tell your students it happened yester-day. Ask them to suggest why he was wet. Encourage the answer 'He came home wet because he had been playing football in the rain'. Then establish how long it takes to play a match to highlight the duration of time needed.

Draw a timeline to illustrate, such as the one in Figure 16-2.

Figure 16-2:
Timeline
showing
actions in
the past
simple and
past perfect
continuous
tenses.

playing football in the rain   *came home wet*
----XXXXXXXXXXXXXXXXXX---------------------X-------------------------
Past   Present

Students need plenty of practice to get this tense right. The past perfect con-tinuous tense contains three verbs in a row, which is tricky for them, and com-munication doesn't tend to be hindered unduly if you get it wrong. However, at upper-intermediate level students should be aiming to go beyond basic com-munication so don't let them settle for past continuous.

Expressing the Future

Learners find expressing ideas about the future in English very odd and this isn't wholly unreasonable. When people express other tenses they generally add something to the end of a verb. Take 'to wait' as an example:

Present simple	He wait**s.**
Present continuous	He is wait**ing.**
Past simple	He wait**ed.**

In many languages tenses work in this way and also have a special ending that indicates the future, so students may be expecting a new ending. However, in English the structure is rather different. We use another word or words *before* the main verb. For example:

I **will** wait.

I **am going** to wait.

Doing the future simple

Although there's more to the story, when students are at a low level it's enough to start by teaching them to use the future simple to describe an action in the future. Teach separately the other ways of expressing the future, such as in the present continuous, or using 'going to'.

The future simple always includes _will_ and then an infinitive without _to_, which is the original form of a verb before any other endings or irregular forms have been added. The infinitive is usually the first column in a verb table.

Use the future simple with words like _tomorrow, next_ (week, month, year) and _later_.

To make the future simple of 'to go' you use _will_ plus _go_ – _will_ takes the place of _to_. Likewise the future simple of 'to buy' is _will buy_ .

Teach students that _will_ doesn't change in the 3rd person singular (that is: 'he', 'she' and 'it'). We never say _wills'_. In addition, you can use the contraction ('ll) in positive sentences.

> I **will**/**I'll** buy that jacket tomorrow.
>
> You **will**/you**'ll** buy that jacket tomorrow.
>
> He/she/it **will** buy that jacket tomorrow.
>
> We **will** buy that jacket tomorrow.
>
> They **will** buy that jacket tomorrow.

To make the negative form of this tense you use _not_ after _will._

Give some attention to the contraction of 'will not' – _won't_. It looks different from how students may expect it and shouldn't be mistaken for 'want' in terms of pronunciation. The phonemes for _want_ and _won't_ are written like this, so you can highlight the different vowel sounds:

> /wɒnt/= want
>
> /wəʊnt/= won't

And the negatives forms look like this: I **will not** do it. I **won't.**

You can make a question by putting _will_ before the subject word.

> **Will you help** me later?
>
> **How will** I know?

For a negative question, it's best to teach the contraction form, which is far more common.

Won't you help me? (Will you not help me?)

A fun way for teaching this tense is to use predictions. Everybody likes guessing what'll happen to their favourite football or celebrity. Give students the event and ask them to predict in which year it will take place.

When students have progressed to intermediate level they're likely to become more interested in the difference between the future simple and other expressions for the future. Interestingly, other uses for the future simple tense are far more subtle than the reference to when an action takes place.

In reality we don't just use the future simple to stress that an action takes place in the future. We can use this tense to show that we have only just decided to do something rather than having carefully considered it beforehand. Suppose that you go to a restaurant and examine the menu. You're quite likely to say something like: 'I'll have the steak, I think.' Or perhaps the phone rings, and you want to do the honours. You may say, 'Don't worry, I'll get it!

On the other hand, we often use the future simple to express a promise and emphasise our determination to carry out an action, as in: I'll get it right somehow.

We can also make a request in the future simple: Will you help me lift this box please?

Going into the future continuous

Use the *future continuous tense* for an action that's in progress at a particular moment in the future. So when you think of a particular time in the future and imagine that scene, whatever actions are taking place can be expressed with this tense.

The future continuous always includes *will*, along with *be* and a gerund. So for example:

I **will be** listen**ing**.

You **will be** listen**ing**.

He/she/it **will be** listen**ing**.

We **will be** listen**ing**.

They **will be** listen**ing**.

'At 7.45 this evening I will be watching my favourite soap opera.' In fact the soap begins at 7.30 p.m. but it'll still be on TV at 7.45 p.m., so the action will be in progress. A timeline, such as the one in Figure 16-3, can illustrate this.

Figure 16-3:
In a question, *will* comes before the subject word.

Watch soap opera

---------------------XXXXXXXXXXXXXXXXX---------------------------------

Past   7.30   8.30   Future

> **Will** you be listening?
>
> What **will** she be listening to?

It is noteworthy that when a negative question is necessary, the contraction is far more common: '**Won't** they be listening?' instead of 'Will they not be listening?'

When you make a negative statement in this tense you add *not* after *will* or you use the contraction *won't*:

> I will **not** be listening.
>
> They **won't** be coming.

A good way to teach and practise this tense is with the use of a page of diary entries set in the future. Students can then role-play turning down invitations by saying what they'll be doing instead.

You may also combine this tense with 'at this time' and a future time reference. So for example: 'At this time tomorrow I will be doing my shopping'.

Getting to the future perfect

You use the *future perfect tense* when you refer to an action that'll be finished by a particular time in the future, or before another action in the future. For example, if you imagine your retirement and the goals you hope to achieve before that time, you can use sentences on the lines of the following to express yourself:

> By the time I retire, I **will have** completely **paid off** my mortgage. I **will have lived** here for 20 years by then.

Most sentences in the future perfect include *by* and a future time reference (next week, December and so on).

The future perfect tense always includes *will have* and a past participle. This is the same for all subject pronouns (I, you, we and so on):

> I **will have begun.**
>
> You **will have begun.**
>
> He/she/it **will have begun.**
>
> We **will have begun.**
>
> They **will have begun.**

In the negative you use *not* after *will* or *won't* instead.

> I **will not** have begun.
>
> I **won't** have begun.

The question is made by putting *will* before the subject pronoun.

> **Will** you **have begun** by tonight?
>
> Why **will** it **have worked**?

The pronunciation of 'will have' at normal speed poses problems for students. The sound we often use for this is represented in phonemes like this /wɪləv/. It's important for students to recognise what these words realistically sound like, otherwise they won't hear this tense in real life situations.

A timeline, like the one in Figure 16-4, can help illustrate the future perfect.

Figure 16-4:
Timeline illustrating the future perfect.

move in	*pay off mortgage*	*retire*
--X---X--------------------X--		
2009		2029

The idea of goals and ambitions is an ideal context for teaching this tense. Students can set up there own time frames to explain when they hope to achieve these ambitions. They can also make predictions about the world in general.

Looking forward to the future perfect continuous

You use the *future perfect continuous tense* for an action that continues up to a particular point in the future. In the section on the future perfect I used the example of retirement. However, this isn't a suitable example for the future perfect continuous as you only use it to express an action that's completed over a period of time – and the act of retirement happens just once. People arrive at retirement age and just stop. In comparison, 'working' is something we do over an extended period of time and is therefore more suited to this tense.

The future perfect continuous tense always includes four important parts: After the subject comes *will* plus *have* plus *been* plus a gerund:

> I **will have been typing.**
>
> You **will have been typing.**
>
> He/she/it **will have been typing.**
>
> We **will have been typing.**
>
> They **will have been typing.**

In a negative sentence you use *not* after *will* or *won't* instead.

> I will **not** have been typing.
>
> I **won't** have been typing.

You change the word order in a question. So, put *will* before the subject pronoun:

> **Will** you **have been typing** for hours by then?

With so many verbs in a row the pronunciation naturally becomes very contracted. 'Will have been' is reduced and connected to sound almost like one word. This is represented in phonemes like this: /wɪləvbiːn/.

The main verb that follows, carries much more stress (emphasis) when you speak.

There's often little difference in meaning between the future perfect and future perfect continuous except for the emphasis on the duration of time in the continuous form. Both of these sentences are grammatically correct but the second is more likely because 20 years is a long time and would naturally be emphasised.

> I will have lived here for 20 years.
>
> I will have been living here for 20 years.

Expressions typically combined with this tense include: f*or ages, for over* (a week, two days and so on) and *when* plus a verb in the present simple tense.

Talking about 'To be going to'

'To be going to' is not a tense as such but is an expression that shows you intend or plan to do something in the future. It sounds far less spontaneous than the future simple. Compare these sentences:

I'll watch TV tonight.

I'm going to watch TV tonight.

The first sentence is used more often when it involves a new choice or decision:

The party has been cancelled. I think I'll watch TV tonight.

The second sentence gives the impression that you'd thought about the matter previously:

I'm going to watch TV tonight. I always watch the soaps on Mondays.

You can also use *was* or *were going to* to show that something was intended or planned in the past.

Getting the form right is easy! It's the verb 'to be' in the present simple, then *going to* and then a verb in its infinitive form without the *to*.

I **am going to do** something.

You **are going to do** something.

He/she/it **is going to do** something.

We **are going to do** something.

They **are going to do** something.

'Gonna' is a common informal way of saying 'going to'. It's good for students to recognise well-known slang words but don't encourage your learners to use them.

In negative sentences you put *not* after 'to be':

They **are not going to help.**

In a question the word order changes so that 'to be' is before the subject pronoun:

Are we **going to like** it?

In normal speech we don't tend to stress, or emphasise 'to be going to' but rather the verb that follows. It's therefore helpful to get students repeating sentences with the appropriate stress – I'm going to **wait here**.

In addition, you use 'to be going to' when you can see that something is likely to happen based on evidence you have now. For example, when you see black clouds you probably say, 'It's going to rain'.

However, it's best to leave this second usage until at least intermediate level.

Go through the structure making sure that your students recognise all the various parts needed.

Students who are a bit lazy latch on to 'will' and use it whenever they're referring to the future. Others attempt to be cool and informal but end up saying, 'I gonna'.

Here's an idea for using this tense in context. Show or list some ingredients for a popular local dish. Ask students to suggest why you have these items. Now refer to a group of friends, who can be guests, and any other dinner party arrangements. This provides the context for sentences such as:

You're going to have a party.

You're going to invite your friends to dinner.

Students can then organise their own imaginary events and compare ideas using 'to be going to'.

Chapter 17

Exploring More Important Verb Structures

. . . .

In This Chapter

▶ Helping out the main verb with a modal

▶ Adding prepositions for phrasal verbs

▶ Using 'if' and 'when' with conditionals

. . . .

*I*n Chapter 16 I talk about the various tenses in English, which is really the bulk of the grammar you teach students. However, a few other grammar areas tend to give learners the shivers but with a little insight you can make them manageable and maybe even fun. So in this chapter I tell you about modal and phrasal verbs as well as the conditionals.

Knowing Your Modals

A *modal verb* is a kind of auxiliary verb because its purpose is to help the main verb. You can't just use a modal verb by itself because it doesn't have a great deal of meaning on its own.

Modal verbs don't change like other verbs do either. So you don't add 's' at the end when you say he/she/it in the present simple tense, you can't add 'ed' in the past simple tense and there's no gerund form of the verb with 'ing' at the end either.

Identifying modal verbs

Perhaps the easiest way I can help you identify the English modal verbs is to write them all down. So here's the complete list:

- ✔ can
- ✔ could
- ✔ may
- ✔ might
- ✔ must
- ✔ shall
- ✔ should
- ✔ ought to
- ✔ will
- ✔ would

Even though you can create a short sentence with just a modal verb and no main verb, the main verb is understood because of the rest of the interchange:

A: Yes, I can.

B: You can what?

A: Go to the office, of course.

When you put all these modal verbs into a sentence you find that they go between the subject, words such as 'you' and 'we', and the main verb, as shown in Table 17-1.

Table 17-1	Sentence Structure with Modal Verbs		
Subject	*Modal Verb*	*Main Verb*	*Object*
The tourists	should	go	home
They	might	follow	us
She	will not	like	that

In questions, the word order is different though, so the subject word goes between the modal verb and the main verb. Table 17-2 offers some examples.

Table 17-2	Sentence Structure with Modal Verbs and Objects			
Question word	*Modal Verb*	*Subject*	*Main Verb*	*Object*
When	should	the tourists	go	home?
How	might	they	follow	us?
Why	won't	she	like	that?

When you add *have* to a modal verb and then use a past participle (the last column in verb tables) it shows that the action refers to the past:

> They must **have** loved it.
>
> She couldn't **have** watched the movie.

So the order is: subject plus modal verb plus *have* plus past participle.

Comparing the modal verbs and what they do

So how do you explain the way to use modal verbs? Well you can divide them up into specific functions.

Showing degrees of probability

At times you aren't certain about something happening, but you want to make a stab at saying what is the probability or likelihood of it coming to pass. Some of the modal verbs come in really handy in this case.

You can represent each of these modals of probability in the form of a percentage:

- **Must:** He must be happy. It's about 95 per cent certain he is.
- **Might:** He might be happy. It's about 60 per cent certain he is.
- **May:** He may be happy. It's about 60 per cent certain he is.
- **Could:** He could be happy. It's about 40 per cent certain he is.
- **Can't.** He can't be happy. It's about 95 per cent certain he isn't.

Notice that *must* and *can't* function as opposites here. You use *can* to show ability or permission but not probability.

Expressing the future with 'will'

When you refer to future time you can use *will*, although *to be going to* and tenses such as the present simple and continuous are also possible. (I cover these tenses in Chapter 16.)

In a language course, you usually start with *will*, often called the future simple, to teach students how to express the future because it's pretty easy to use. You just put *will* before the *infinitive* (original or unchanged form of the verb) and that's it. For example: I **will** start tomorrow.

Although some people still use 'shall' in the future simple, it sounds a little old fashioned so you really don't need to teach it for this purpose.

Of course there are other ways to use *will,* which aren't really focused on the future. You can use *will* for decisions you make at the moment of speaking. Take this sentence for example: You relax and I'll answer the door this time.

The action of answering the door is really present, not future, but it's a spontaneous decision, not something planned in advance. By comparison, saying 'I'm going to' sounds a bit more planned.

On the other hand, the same sentence without the contraction ('I will answer' instead of 'I'll answer') can indicate that the speaker is really determined or is making a promise.

Giving and gaining permission

Sometimes you need to say whether it's okay to do something or not. In this case you quite likely use *can* or *may* and *could* if you're asking a question. '*May*' sounds a little more formal than the other two.

> Could/may I use your bathroom?

> Of course you can.

Offering

In English there are various ways of offering something; using *would* is one of them, as in: **Would** you like a cup of tea?

Or if you're using 'I' or 'we' you can use *shall* instead: **Shall** I/we make you a cup of tea?

Talking about ability

When you want to say whether or not you're able to do something, you use *can* or *could*. The difference between the two is that *could* also refers to things you were able to do in the past. In this sentence for example *could* and *cannot* reflect ability at different stages of life, childhood and the present day respectively: I **could** speak my father's language at the age of four but I **cannot** really remember it now.

Expressing degrees of obligation

Various modal verbs indicate whether you really must do something or whether you have a choice of doing it or not. For a very strong obligation you use *must*: You **mustn't** smoke here. It's forbidden.

Have to is synonymous with *must* in positive sentences except that you tend to use *have to* when someone else's authority is involved: 'The boss says you **have to** stop that now.'

The problem is that in the negative they no longer mean the same things:

The boss says you **mustn't** stop (meaning don't stop).

The boss says you don't **have to** stop (meaning stop if you want to).

From time to time though, there's a choice or a weak obligation. In that case you can use *should* or *ought to*: You **should** go on a diet. In fact you **ought to** cut out sugar completely.

You use the same words for giving advice.

Using 'would'

Would is generally used to show that a situation is imaginary or hypothetical rather than a present fact: 'I **would** sit down but there are no more seats'.

And *would* is used as the past of *will* too. So when you report what someone else said about the future, you can use *would*:

Bob: I'll go to the post office for you.

John: What did Bob say?

Gary: Bob said that he **would** go to the post office for you. He's gone now.

You can even use *would* for reminiscing about past habits: 'As teenagers we **would** regularly skip school'.

Sorting Out Phrasal Verbs

Phrasal verbs are quite informal expressions that include a verb and at least one preposition.

The meaning isn't always obvious, which is one reason students struggle with them. For example 'pick up' is not too obscure if you understand the individual verb 'pick' and the preposition 'up' but 'keep up' is much harder to guess. Here are a few more examples of phrasal verbs:

- ask someone out*
- back someone up*
- call something off*
- drop out
- end up
- fall out

- grow out of *
- hold on
- keep something up*
- pass away
- run out of*
- show off
- turn up
- wear off

The phrasal verbs in the list marked with * are also transitive, which means that they need a direct object. So basically, you can't just say 'I've grown out of'. You have to add *what* you've grown out of. Likewise, you can't say 'I asked out' because you need to say *who* you asked out.

For most phrasal verbs synonyms exist that are little more formal. For example, 'to back someone up' means to support them and 'to keep something up' means to maintain it. Students tend to latch onto the formal words because they translate better into their own languages (especially Latin languages) but then they don't sound conversational enough when they speak. So remember that, given a choice, most native speakers opt for a phrasal verb in everyday life.

Note that some phrasal verbs are separated by 'someone' or 'something'. This conveniently brings us to another difficulty; phrasal verbs can be separable or inseparable. I deal with this in the following section. The other phrasal verbs in the list are all intransitive so you can't put an object in the middle.

Following the rules about separable and inseparable phrasals

Basically, if you can put 'someone' or 'something' between the verb and the preposition in a phrasal verb, it's separable and *transitive,* which means it requires a direct object. (I talk about objects in Chapter 15.) This doesn't necessarily mean you have to separate it, it just means that you can. For example:

> I have to **call** the party **off**.

> I have to **call off** the party.

If you can't put 'something' or 'someone' in the middle of a phrasal verb, it's both intransitive and inseparable, which means that you can't separate the verb and the preposition: intransitive verbs have no direct object. You don't need 'someone' or 'something' for it to make sense. For example:

The van **broke down**.

She **got up**.

So every time you teach a phrasal verb you need to tell the students whether or not it's separable. The most common way to do this is by writing *s/o* (someone) or *s/t* (something) into the phrasal verb on the board:

To call *s/t* off (pv) (I also include *pv* here to show that it is a phrasal verb.)

In the examples of separable phrasal verbs, I put the object in the middle between the verb and preposition. However, at times you can use an object pronoun instead of a noun.

If the sentence contains an object pronoun instead of a noun, put the pronoun between the phrasal verb and preposition, nowhere else:

I have to **call** it **off**, not I have to call off it.

I need to **back** him **up**, not I have to back up him.

In some cases, a separable phrasal verb must have the object in the middle whether it's a pronoun or not. The phrasal verb 'to tell apart' works in this way:

Can you **tell** the twins **apart**? Not, Can you tell apart the twins?

Some transitive phrasal verbs (the ones that need an object) aren't separable. So for example 'to put up with' needs an object but you can put the object only after 'with':

Why do **you put up with** John's behaviour?

Finally, some phrasal verbs need not one object but two. 'To do out of' needs 'someone' and 'something' to make sense. For example:

That crooked boss **did me out of** my wages!

So here, one object goes after the verb and the other after the preposition.

If you have to use a phrasal verb in a passive sentence, just keep the verb and preposition together, regardless:

He complained that he had **been done out of** his wages by the boss.

Teaching phrasal verbs

With all these rules about phrasal verbs, it may sound a bit daunting teaching them. So here are a couple of tips.

Avoid teaching phrasal verbs as a big topic in itself. Lessons about all the phrasal verb rules tend to be boring and confusing anyway because students don't learn in this way.

Print copies of the rules so that students can use it as a reference, perhaps on a sheet they can keep at the back of their books. However, it's best to teach just a few phrasal verbs at a time, in context and with lots of examples.

One way to teach 'to put up with' and 'to fall out' is by following these steps:

1. **Start with spoken content.**

   'Twins Paul and Paula live together. She is very untidy and likes to have her friends round every day. Paul likes his home to be quiet and organised. He loves his sister but maybe it's time to move out. When he complains, they fall out, but after two years he can't put up with the situation anymore'.

2. **Have students discuss the situation.**

   Ask, 'How do they feel about the situation?'

3. **Display board work.**

   For example:

   - To put up with *s/t* (pv, inseparable)= to tolerate something

   - To fall out (with *s/o*) (pv inseparable)= to argue then stop being friendly

   - Paul can't put up with Paula's friends. They annoy him too much.

   - Paula and Paul fall out whenever they talk about the problem because he shouts at her.

4. **Have students do some practice exercises.**

   Write a sentence about each of the following situations using 'to put up with' or 'to fall out with' in the correct tense. For example: The man gets doesn't complain when the neighbours play very loud music. The man **puts up with** his neighbours' loud music.

   > Last week Evelyn and Debbie argued about where to go for the evening. They got angry and have not spoken since then.

   > Mrs Singh will not allow her son to continue smoking in the house.

   > The reason why the sisters were nervous about seeing each other was because they had had a big disagreement.

5. **Have students discuss similar situations in pairs.**

Ask each other about other situations that result in people falling out and refusing to put up with things. When was the last time you fell out with someone and why?

If I Were You . . . Conditional Structures

Sentences beginning with 'if' are conditional. They're always in two clauses, showing that one situation is dependent on another. Even though native speakers mix conditionals up a lot in real life, you need to teach the students gradually the four basic conditional structures I cover in the next sections.

A *clause* always contains a subject word and a verb.

With all these structures, teach the positive, negative and question forms and don't forget the contractions too. For example, this is a positive sentence; *If I'm unhappy, I eat more.* By comparison a negative version of the question contains *not* or its contraction (short form) *n't.* So the negative version is; *If I'm unhappy, I don't eat more.* Notice that *don't* (do not) is the negative part. The question form is, *If you're unhappy, do you eat more?*

Being general: The zero conditional

You use zero conditional sentences to say that something is generally true. The situation is not just about a particular instance but is more a rule of thumb. In fact, you quite often use this structure to state a fact, principle or truth. For example:

If you cool water below 0 degrees, it freezes.

When you visit a place of worship, you dress appropriately.

Pairing 'if' and 'when'

The zero conditional is the easy one to remember. It comprises two distinct clauses, both in the present simple, but one clause starts with 'if' or 'when'. It doesn't matter which clause goes first.

When I feel tired, I take a nap.

If it's sunny, I sit on the balcony.

When you really want something, you have to work hard.

People usually visit the Louvre, **when** they go to France.

So the structure is: *If* plus present simple tense and a present simple verb in the other clause.

Formulating it for students

You teach the zero conditional at about pre-intermediate level. Generally, students have no difficulty understanding this structure but you break it down into a formula to prepare students for the other conditionals to come.

Try teaching conditionals with a chain story or dialogue. By that I mean that you build up the interaction clause by clause. For example:

Teacher: What do you do **when** you feel ill?

Student A: **When** I feel ill, I stay home instead of going to work.

Teacher: **When** you stay home, do you take medicine?

Student B: Yes, **when** I stay home, I take aspirin.

Teacher: Ask Alex about aspirin.

Student B: Do you feel better, **when** you take aspirin?

Student C: Yes, **whenever** I take aspirin, I feel better. En Feng, what do you do **when** you feel a bit better?

Matching exercises are a useful form of practice for conditional sentences. So, you can divide the clauses and mix them up in two columns, like the one in Figure 17-1.

Match one half of the sentence 1) 2) 3) or 4) with the second half in a) b) c) or d). Write the sentences below.

Figure 17-1:
Matching exercise for the zero conditional.

1) If I meet elderly people	a) it wants to go out
2) When Mark sees Elizabeth	b) I show respect
3) If life is boring	c) he smiles
4) If the dog starts looking at the door	d) people take a trip

Depending on the possible: The first conditional

You use the first conditional for a situation that's quite possible and realistic but still dependent on something else.

Whereas the zero conditional uses the same tense in both clauses, the first conditional doesn't. This time the structure is basically: 'If' or 'when' plus a verb in the present simple with a verb in the future simple in the other clause.

The structure still contains two clauses and one includes' if' or 'when', but it looks like this:

> **If** you aren't nice to me, I'll leave.
>
> Will you help me fix my car, **if** I bring it to your house?
>
> **When** we finish this job, we will not stop.

You can swap 'will' for a modal verb or 'to be going to' as well:

> **If** you aren't too busy, can you come to my office?
>
> He might come, **when** it stops raining.
>
> **I'm going to** take away your toys, if you don't stop spitting.

You can swap 'if' or 'when' for a couple of other expressions too, namely 'whether or not' and 'unless'. In this case, you use a verb in the future simple tense first, then 'whether or not' or 'unless' followed by a verb in present simple (positive, meaning without *not* or *n't*).

> You will have to work late, **whether or not** you want to.
>
> I won't talk to you, **unless** you give me back my money.
>
> **Unless** something extraordinary happens, she'll probably come.

But you can't put 'if' or 'when' in the same clause as 'will', so you can't say something like, 'If I will see him, I will tell him'.

Following the chain activity and matching exercises in the section on the zero conditional, take this a step further by designing some 1st conditional dominoes, like those in Figure 17-2.

They're a little time consuming to prepare initially, but if you use some sturdy card or a laminator, you can keep them for ages. The aim is for students to match sentence clauses together so that they make sense, and the first student to use all his cards is the winner. You may have to act as referee though!

Another way to give students practice in a freer way is to talk about threats, which are generally in the first conditional anyway. Tell the class an anecdote about a time when you were threatened and what happened and then say:

> Write about a time when you were threatened or made a threat yourself. Explain why the situation happened and if the threat was carried out.

when I get home	she'll be ready	if I remind her	will Janet help me	if I do what I promised	Bob isn't going to argue

Figure 17-2:
First conditional dominoes.

if I buy him a drink	it will be cheaper	when the new supermarket opens	there will be queues	if you don't work harder

Imagining the second conditional

The second conditional is a structure you use to express something that's hypothetical, imaginary or unlikely. You usually teach this at intermediate level.

The second conditional confuses students at first because it uses the past simple tense but doesn't actually refer to the past at all. The basic structure is: 'If' plus a verb in the past simple then the subject plus 'would' plus the infinitive form of the verb:

> **If** you won the national lottery, what **would** you buy first?

> **If** I were you, **I'd** stay away from him.

> **If** you found £100 in the street, I'm sure that you **would** give it to the police.

You can use 'were' for all the subject pronouns too. It sounds more formal than when you use 'was' in the normal way:

> If I *were* here, it would be better.

> If we *were* here, it would be better.

Remember that 'if/when' must never be in the same clause as 'would', so you can't say, 'If I'd be rich, I'd live in Miami'.

The structure of the second conditional is difficult to remember at first so you need to find interesting ways to fix it in your students' minds. Here are a few suggestions:

✔ **Use a song.** I have come up with several:

- *'If I Ruled the World'* written by Ornadel and Bricusse and recorded by Tony Bennett

- *'If I Were a Boy'* written by Carlson, Gad and Beyonce Knowles, who recorded it.

- *'If I Were a Sailboat'* written and performed by Katie Melua

- *'If I Were a Rich Man'* written by Zero Mostel and sung in the musical 'Fiddler on the Roof'.

Blank out some words and get students to fill them in while listening to the song. However, the most important thing is to have a good old sing along. That's what they'll find most memorable.

✔ **Lead a jazz chant.** You may not have access to music, so how about a *jazz chant,* which is just words or phrases repeated in a rhythm? You've probably seen footage of army drill sergeants getting the chant in time with the soldiers' marching, often through repetition. Jazz chants are similar. You simply get students to repeat sentences after you in whole or in part and to a beat (everyone should clap their hands). In this way they can more easily remember the structure, and pick up the rhythm of the language while they're at it. Here's an example of an easy second conditional chant:

> Teacher: If
>
> Students: If
>
> Teacher: If I
>
> Students: If I
>
> Teacher: If I were you
>
> Students: If I were you
>
> Teacher: And you were me
>
> Students: And you were me
>
> Teacher: If I were you and you were me
>
> Students: If I were you and you were me
>
> Teacher: We'd be different
>
> Students: We'd be different
>
> Teacher: But still happy
>
> Students: But still happy

✔ **Play a game of moral dilemmas.** You can prepare cards with the dilemmas – some are shown in Figure 17-3 – in one pile and cards for the names of each student individually in another pile. For each round of the game you pick up a card from each pile and ask everyone in the class to write a sentence in the second conditional suggesting what the named student would do about the problem. After everyone has a minute to write something down, have a feedback session when you encourage the named student to confirm or deny what was said.

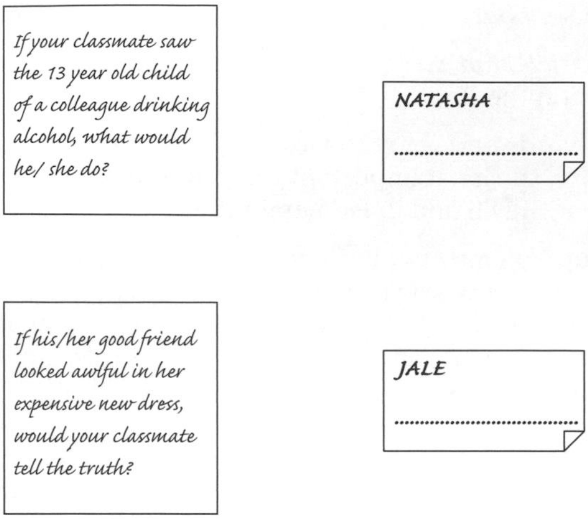

> If your classmate saw the 13 year old child of a colleague drinking alcohol, what would he/she do?

NATASHA
....

Figure 17-3:
Examples of moral dilemma cards using the second conditional.

> If his/her good friend looked awlful in her expensive new dress, would your classmate tell the truth?

JALE
....

Reviewing the past with the third conditional

This tense is used exclusively to talk about the past. You use it to express regrets and imagine how things would be if something different had happened.

The third conditional is probably the most difficult structure your students have to learn. You only teach it to upper-intermediate and advanced learners.

The basic structure is: 'If' plus a verb in past perfect tense, the subject followed by 'would have' plus a past participle verb:

If I had known the shop was closed, **I would not have** come.

If you hadn't studied languages, what **would you have** done instead?

If I had been born poor, I think my life **would still have** been happy.

You can also use past perfect continuous tense in the 'if' clause and the present perfect continuous form after 'would' in the other clause:

If I had been wearing a seatbelt at the time of the accident, I **wouldn't have been** so badly injured.

If you had known I was coming, you **would have been** wearing your suit.

One way to practise this structure is by making excuses.

Put students in pairs and have one student accuse the other of doing something and the other can apologise with an excuse. You just need to provide the students with the situations. For example, students discussing a football match may have a dialogue like this:

Pierre: You arrived late for the game! I'm so annoyed.

Valerie: I'm sorry but if you had given me the right directions, I would have been on time.

Pierre: But you didn't bring my boots.

Valerie: I'm afraid if you had left your boots in the usual place, I would have been able to find them.

Pierre: You don't understand! I couldn't play!

Valerie: Don't worry! Even if you'd played, the team would have lost. The score was 12-0.

Part V
What Kind of Class Will I Have?

The 5th Wave   By Rich Tennant

"Okay, let's go over some of the phrases we've learnt so far. 'Your planet is under attack,' 'Surrender now or face annihilation,' 'All resistance is futile.'"

In this part . . .

Wondering what the experience of dealing with students is like? Wondering how to assess their aptitude and the difference you're making to them along the way? Wonder no more. This part gives you an in-depth guide to assessment, the many types of courses you may become involved with and, most importantly, the sorts of students you'll find yourself face-to-face with. I cover the differences between classes where every student speaks the same language and those where you have as many different mother tongues as speakers.

I also lead you through the intricacies of one-to-one teaching, working with younger students and how to teach specific types of English – English for business, for example – with ease and efficiency.

Chapter 18

Putting Students to the Test

· ·

In This Chapter

▶ Finding out what your students need

▶ Discovering the best course for students

▶ Grading tests

▶ Considering alternatives to testing

· ·

*T*he word 'test' tends to evoke fear in most students, but as a teacher, tests help you gather loads of information that enable you to keep your students happy and progressing.

Testing is useful before students get started so you know what kind of course to enrol them on, but you can also use tests along the way to check progress and find out if the course was successful in meeting objectives.

Testing Early to Discover Your Students' Needs

When a student makes an inquiry about a course, schools and individual teachers see pound signs flash before their eyes. In reality though, the pounds only materialise if you can you deliver the course the student needs. So you start off by checking what she knows and what she needs. I cover the various ways of doing this in the next sections.

Having them test themselves

One kind of test that's really useful for giving you a head start before you even meet the student, is a *self-assessment test* in which you get the student to analyse how good she is at various aspects of the language, usually by rating herself from 1-5 or by completing sentences.

Now, I know what you're thinking, 'If the student can't speak English, how can she complete the test?' Well, if all your students come from the same language base, you can fairly easily organise a test in their mother tongue. You can make the test visual by using pictures of different situations in which they may use English (listening to lectures, using the phone and so on) and ask students how comfortable they are in those situations. Rating systems with smiley faces and frowning faces help to convey the point. Set the test out so that it goes from really easy to gradually more difficult and the students can stop when the questions get too tough.

You can engineer your test to cover areas such as:

✔ **Grammar** by offering a 'complete the sentence' exercise such as: 'If I improved my English, I . . .'.

With this question, you can test whether the student knows how to make a sentence in the second conditional and you can find out a bit about that person's motivation for taking a course at the same time.

If the test contains very direct questions the student is likely to copy from a grammar reference book. It works better when you sneak in the tenses by asking about things you want to know about the student and stating that she should reply with a complete sentence. For example, to test the past simple tense ask:

When was the last time you studied English? Describe your lessons.

✔ **Vocabulary** knowledge centres around the dictionary, so ask something like:

When you talk about the following topics, how often do you use your dictionary?

- Family and friends: a little quite a lot often

- My job: a little quite a lot often

- My hobbies and interests: a little quite a lot often

- Shopping: a little quite a lot often

✔ **Reading** skills depend on comprehension, so ask questions such as:

What do you usually read in English? Say how easy or difficult it is to understand.

✔ **Writing** includes spelling and formats, so present a scale from 1 to 5 where 1 is bad and 5 is excellent, and have students rate their abilities on questions such as:

- How good is your spelling in English? 1 2 3 4 5

- Can you write formal letters? 1 2 3 4 5

- Can you write informal letters? 1 2 3 4 5

> ✔ **Speaking** is a matter of being understood, so ask something along the lines of:
>
> My customers usually understand me. Yes No
>
> ✔ **Listening** is another test of comprehension. Give students the 1 to 5 scale again and ask how well they understand the person speaking in various situations:
>
> - Telephone calls: 1 2 3 4 5
>
> - Presentations: 1 2 3 4 5
>
> - Colleagues chatting in the office: 1 2 3 4 5

You can also find out why students are taking the class by having them fill in a sentence like: I need to study English because . . . Ask them also whether they prefer to study in a class of students or alone and to explain why. The answers that students give help the school or teacher to put students in the right kind of course or to design and sell the courses better.

Assigning levels through placement tests

Rather than designing a course for a student's specific purposes, schools and colleges usually have placements tests so that they can match a student to a course already on offer or planned. In terms of general English, most offer six levels ranging from beginner to advanced and which I talk about in Chapter 4.

Proficiency level is absolutely the highest level, but courses at this level are quite rare. Even beginner and advanced level courses are sometimes tricky to fill. So, before the term begins, or if your school offers continuous enrolment, before you place a student in an existing course, the school has to establish the student's overall level.

Speaking and listening testing

Some establishments offer each student an interview with a teacher, which is basically a test. It's really time consuming to do this but at least you can get a real view of the student's speaking ability, which is the key language skill for most people. Of course, listening is involved too as you interact with the student. You can also take the opportunity to plug the school's facilities and put the student at her ease because the test happens more informally. For example, to try a past simple check question, you casually ask: 'How did you get here today? Did it take long?'

For an interview to be really effective, let everyone in the room introduce themselves. You may have a second teacher who doesn't speak and just assesses, although this makes students more nervous. Explain what's going to happen, personalise the questions if possible and give each student some feedback at the end.

Assessing through the written words

Written placement tests are very common too. They allow a school to test a whole coach load of new students all at the same time, providing there's space. At the end you also have a written record to keep in students' files.

One of the disadvantages of written tests compared with oral ones is that students complain about the results of written tests far more and often ask for another go.

In written tests, students tend to cheat a lot and have warped results because of the pressure of the situation. It's fairly rare that someone in the school can find time to watch a student take the test so the student is likely to sneak a look at the dictionary or ask a friend for help. Sometimes students don't understand the instructions but this only becomes evident later when the marker notices how badly they messed things up.

On the other hand, you can buy published tests or select a section from the course books for each level to form the test. It's possible to include reading passages but it's best not to make the test appear too long and intimidating.

Tests like these should have an easy marking system, usually an answer key, to cut down on administration.

If the school offers exam classes, use questions from past papers to give the students a realistic example of what the exam is like and an idea of how the students measure up to specific exam skills.

Testing for proficiency

Proficiency tests aren't the same as the proficiency level in English, which follows advanced level. A *proficiency test* assesses a student's ability to perform a particular task or tasks that she'll have to accomplish in the future.

So if your student tells you that she's been offered a great job in a restaurant on the condition that her English is up to scratch, you can design a test that covers taking orders and handing complaints. It doesn't really matter whether the student has taken a course before or whether she knows their grammar. You simply need to know how well she may be able to handle that job.

Testing to Establish the Best Course

Once your students are actually enrolled on a course you can continue to use tests to map their progress and measure what you've all achieved.

Testing progress

If a course is of a specific length you can build in one or two progress tests at various stages. Progress tests serve a few purposes:

- ✔ **Providing motivation for the students to study.** Targets and deadlines help some people to get themselves in gear, but for others they can be stressful and de-motivating. You need to decide how to present your test so that you strike the right balance.

- ✔ **Providing a standard level for the class so that students can be changed to a different course that better matches their proficiency level if necessary.** Students sometimes ask to be moved up to a higher level and if you, as the teacher, aren't too keen, the results of the progress test may be the basis on which you decide. Likewise if you have to move a student down, you can use the test as evidence for your decision.

- ✔ **Highlighting gaps in your teaching – or the course materials – that you need to fill**. This can be for your own purposes or for the school to monitor its teachers. The danger of this is that you may end up training your class to pass the test rather than teaching them English.

The way you handle the test depends on the importance you attach to it and your main objective. For example, you may tell the students the topic of the test and ask them to revise particular points that you feel are essential to their progress in the rest of the course. On the other hand, you may decide that the class should have a thorough review, so you don't give the students specific details. This makes them revise everything so far.

A fun and effective way to organise a progress test is to allow the students to design it themselves. Break them into different groups, have each group construct a few questions, or ask each student to submit two or three questions each. As they review the topic and construct the questions, the topic becomes indelibly printed on their minds. There's also an exciting level of competition and anticipation as they wait to see who gets their question right.

Testing achievement

Achievement tests are typically given at the end of the course. You can hold these up against the course syllabus and objectives to see how successful the lessons have been.

The success of a course may not be measured solely in language skills. A student may want to become more outgoing, creative or confident and her success or failure in this is dependent on her own feelings. Formal testing is incidental to her. It's helpful to have class discussions about what each student hopes to achieve and how they expect to do so.

Some of the different ways of testing achievement follow:

- ✔ **True or false questions:** These can be less stressful for students because they test knowledge without necessarily involving writing skills.

- ✔ **Gap-fill exercises:** In this kind of exercise you strategically omit certain words from a text in order to test particular areas of language.

  Suppose you want to test your students' knowledge of English prepositions. You can cut the prepositions out of a text and provide the missing words in the wrong order below the passage, or you can leave out the missing words and make students come up with the prepositions on their own. The words are provided in the following example:

  Goldilocks went . . . the little house and saw a dining table . . . the left. There were three bowls of porridge . . . the table and . . . each bowl there was a chair.

  on   into   in front of   of

  The missing words can be listed in the wrong order below the test as I show here, as a multiple choice or just left out completely.

- ✔ **Cloze:** This is a kind of gap-fill but the omitted words are more random, say every eighth word, so you get more of a feel for the students' overall knowledge of the language. Try this one:

  Teachers select texts from published materials or . . . exercises themselves. The advantage of writing your . . . tests is that you can make them . . . relevant to your students' interests.

  write   own   more

- ✔ **Matching**: At lower levels especially, you can test vocabulary by matching words to pictures or single items to the appropriate categories. You can put a grammar slant on matching exercises by connecting sentences to the right tense label, or perhaps the beginning of a sentence to the appropriate ending. Figure 18-1 shows a matching vocabulary question.

- ✔ **Dictation:** Dictations tend to conjure up bad memories for some but they needn't consist of long dry passages. I find dictations very handy for practising listening, pronunciation and spelling all at once.

  Here is one of my dictation lists: cap, cup, cop, cope, cape, cob.

- ✔ **Transforming and rewriting:** In exams like Cambridge First Certificate in English, students have to show their ability to change a word from a noun into an adjective and rewrite a whole sentence incorporating a particular word. That's why teachers like to get students used to this kind of exercise from early on. Take a look at these examples:

  - Complete the sentence by transforming the word in brackets into the right form:

I am not sure if I should wear my coat because the weather is so . . . (change).

- Rewrite the sentence so that the meaning is the same but include the word in bold.

  Although it was raining, John still went to play tennis. **Despite** . . .

✔ **Translation:** This isn't very common in TEFL but it may be an appropriate test for more advanced students. The text for translation should include idiomatic expressions that reveal a student's ability to understand the more subtle nuances of the language.

✔ **Essays:** Essays test writing skills, as well as spelling, vocabulary and grammar. It's quite important that an essay doesn't become a test of imagination or creativity. During the marking stage, focus on specific language skills rather than level of interest. You can establish the criteria for awarding points beforehand so that you judge fairly.

✔ **Presentation:** Students can prepare a short presentation on a chosen topic. This is an effective way of exercising speaking ability and can balance out the nerves that poor writers have when they take written tests. A combination of tests should give everybody a chance to shine.

✔ **Pair work tests:** When the course is primarily based on speaking, it may be unfair to test achievement through writing, so pairing students to demonstrate communication skills is a good alternative. Students can talk to teach each other to achieve the task while the teacher monitors and supervises. For example:

✔ Discuss which present is best for a new student at university:

money (£50)   two course books   a strong rucksack

Write the number of a shape/shapes next to an adjective it describes

For example: triangular –2

1)   2)   3)   4)

Figure 18-1:
A typical
matching
vocabulary
exercise.

– 3 dimensional

– curved

– symmetrical

Marking Tests

One reason teachers are sometimes reluctant to administer a test to their class is because of their dread of marking and collating results. It can be a tedious and time-consuming task. Now the way you mark has much to do with the kind of test you set but the following are some general points that you can keep in mind.

If your time is severely limited, set a test that has just one or two possible answers for each question and write, or obtain, the answer key. In this way, anyone can help you mark, even a student.

The way you mark a student's sheet itself is something to consider too. These days the red pen is considered a little bit threatening, so teachers often go for friendly green and purple pens instead. In any case, make your marking absolutely clear. Of course, this presupposes that the students are actually going to get their test papers back, or at least see them. Some schools keep test papers so that students can't sell them on and help others to cheat, but they should at least have a chance to see their errors. For the sake of time you can just tick or cross questions.

Ticks and crosses aren't common to every culture so let students know what each symbol means.

Use a marking code for longer answers, if your students are used to one. Highlight a grammar error by writing 'gr' or 'sp' for spelling. This helps them to see what kind of errors they typically make and gives them an opportunity to try correcting the problem themselves. Chapter 7 has more on marking corrections.

For straightforward questions you can allow students to mark each other's work. You need to be careful about cheating though, so you should insist that everyone puts their own pens away and then give everyone a pen in a special colour.

Having their work reviewed by another student can be embarrassing for some students so you need to be quite careful about sharing out this task. Get to know your students' work and their personalities before trying this method.

It's good to have a class feedback session about the test if possible. When you do that, you tackle the tricky questions that everyone got wrong. After all, it may be your fault because you didn't teach that topic thoroughly, or because the test question wasn't clear. You now have the chance to make up for it by re-teaching the point. For students' individual errors you can employ peer correction, which means the students correct each other.

Looking at Alternatives to Testing

Testing carries various disadvantages so you may want to try alternatives such as project work and continuous assessment. These tend to be less pressurised for most students and remove the problem of having a bad day at the time of the test, which results in an uncharacteristically poor performance.

A project in English is a great way for students to express their language skills and creativity at the same time. It is especially appealing to younger learners on short summer courses. By the end of the project they have something to show for their efforts and the opportunity to use the English they've learnt, or picked up, on their own terms.

Instead of filling in the gaps in a test the teacher has written, they choose their own topic and usually they find out what they need to know to achieve the task they set for themselves.

The problem is how to teach project work. Well, you can agree on certain things your students have to include, for example, the history or background, the current situation and future plans of the chosen celebrity, sport or whatever subject they've chosen. This at least pushes the students to use a variety of tenses.

You can also use *continuous assessment* so that every week or so you record the students' progress, performances and achievements. To make the best use of time, the school should organise sheets that you can just tick or grade on each aspect assessed. Writing reports increases the teachers' administration work considerably. However, when you assess students in this way, it's easier to produce a final report at the end of the course rather than just a test score.

Chapter 19

Getting Specific: Teaching Just One Student and Business English

*A*lthough most teachers obtain some training in teaching general English in classes, there's woefully little available in advice and support for teachers making the transition into one-to-ones and business English. So in this chapter I provide advice and tips about these two areas.

Evaluating One-to-Ones

From the outset I can tell you that teaching one-to-ones can be pretty lucrative. As they're often two or three times the cost of class lessons in a school, it naturally follows that people who pay for a private teacher are well off or well motivated.

The typical students fall into several categories:

✔ The student who's reached a reasonably high level of English, at least intermediate level, but who has no desire to commit to another formal course. These students want to maintain their English, probably by studying an hour or so each week, and prefer to have a conversation-based lesson without too much structure.

✔ The student with a specific goal in mind. These individuals have an exam looming or business trip coming up and want to prepare for a specific period of time. They need to develop skills in particular areas and require a needs analysis from you (I give information on needs analysis in 'Working at Teaching Business English' later in this chapter) as well as a syllabus.

✔ The student struggling to keep up with mainstream courses who needs extra support in order to stay level with his classmates. In this case the student often brings you the material that he's struggling with, so part of your lesson is devoted to immediate homework issues and revision of topics covered in class that week.

Some schools set up self-access centres for their students. These take the form of libraries and computers loaded with EFL resources. If you work in a school with this kind of facility, you may find that teachers are asked to man the centre and be on hand to help students with particular problems, effectively giving short one-to-ones and tutorial support.

Listing pros and cons for the student

It's good to think about the various advantages one-to-ones offer a student so that you can promote yourself if you decide to pursue this line of income:

✔ The teacher addresses the individual learning needs of the student.

✔ Shy students feel able to cope with just one other person.

✔ Students can voice their preferences about activities and topics, which they can't do in a class setting.

✔ The lesson is never too fast or too slow. The student can go at his own pace.

✔ The student can have much more input at every stage of the course.

✔ There's usually a great deal more flexibility in terms of time, location, content and so on.

✔ The teacher and student tend to develop a better rapport and understanding of each other.

✔ It's a good way to keep the student's English topped up.

On the other hand, the disadvantages for the student are that:

✔ Students often hope to make friends through the language school. With no classmates they can feel rather isolated.

✔ The student and teacher may not get on too well. Even with the best will in the world, lessons are hard going if you just don't hit it off.

- Many students miss the dynamics of classroom debates, swapping speaking partners frequently and working in a team. Whereas the teacher generally takes the role of the classmate during practice sessions, it isn't possible to engage in the same range of activities as you can in a class.
- Lessons are much more expensive compared to group classes.
- Whereas in a school, the student may have more than one teacher; with one-to-one lessons there's less opportunity for exposure to another accent or style.

Talking pros and cons for the teacher

One-to-ones offer a lot to consider from the student's point of view and this is no less true for the teacher. Your own experience, personality and circumstances affect your decision regarding this kind of work. I look at the advantages and disadvantages in the next sections.

On the whole, one-to-one lessons can be very rewarding as long as you and the student monitor progress regularly, but you need to find out exactly what the course entails for you before agreeing to do it.

Your students are your best advertisements. Give them a few of your business cards to distribute and ask them to mention your services to friends and colleagues. Let local people know what you do too, and try to get some ads up in universities and on other notice boards.

Appreciating the financial rewards

Firstly, the obvious plus is that you can make more money per hour, whether you work for a school or for yourself.

Most students pay at least 30 per cent more due to the increased amount of preparation and the more intense nature of the work, but don't use this rate as the basis for charging your own private students. Remember that the school incurs overheads. So find out what the local schools charge individual students on average and then undercut them (by a considerable amount if you're inexperienced).

Never allow a school to give you one-to-one work without establishing a higher rate of pay than class teaching.

While we're on the subject of money, think about funds you may have to put aside for taxes, factor in the time it takes to prepare your own accounts and don't rely on your one-to-one students always being around. It's hard to predict exactly how much money you'll make from month to month as students tend to stop and start according to their circumstances and finances.

Agree a cancellation policy with your students beforehand so that you don't waste your time. Some teachers ask for payment in advance and others are more relaxed, as long as the students gives them reasonable notice of cancellation, but it's unwise to put up with customers who have no respect for your time.

Finding a place

You need to sort out a place to teach. If you're teaching private lessons in addition to working for a school, and have checked that there's no conflict of interest between you and your employer, ask to use an empty classroom out of hours. If you do this, at least you'll have access to loads of resources nearby. Unless you've built up a good supply of books at home, lack of resources may limit your lesson preparation when you go it alone.

Other locations you may choose to use are your own home or a local library or café. Whilst being very convenient, using your place poses obvious risks, especially if you'll be alone with the student. Because of this, you should think very carefully before taking this option. The same principles apply if you go to the student's home. On the other hand, if you use a public place like a library, you're bound by their opening hours and rules. For example, you may not be able to speak at full volume or play recordings.

One of the nice things about this kind of lesson though, is that you can more easily take the student to different locations. If you're working in an English-speaking country, why not take a few trips to markets, auctions, courthouses or anywhere your student may find stimulating.

Forging a relationship

Your relationship with your student also presents challenges and rewards. Luckily, the majority of students are happy, motivated souls, but if you do get a boring or obnoxious one it can be very hard work.

Private lessons sometimes resemble counselling sessions as students inevitably let off steam and talk about their day-to-day lives.

Now, if you know that you're not the type to put on a smile and feign interest when you're bored witless, be a bit wary of this line of work.

The most successful one-to-one teachers like making other people feel good about themselves. A nice thing about the job is that one-to-one teachers often learn something too. People often pass on information about their specialisms and particular interests, not to mention their culture and traditions.

Enjoying the pace

In the actual lesson, you find that the student who just wants to chat saves you quite a lot of preparatory work. Of course, you should never go to a lesson unarmed but your lesson may be spread over several sessions if the student has other matters to get off his chest. Unlike in classes, students can use their time to talk if they prefer, as long as they don't have deadlines to meet, such as looming exams (in which case try to steer them back to more structured study).

On the point of preparation though, bring along more material than usual for a one-to-one because the student needs a great deal of variety.

Planning and teaching a one-to-one lesson

Planning a one-to-one lesson is largely similar to planning a lesson with a group of students but in order to be effective, you need to keep certain points in mind.

Have clear aims for the short- and long-term. Have a detailed interview with the student before you start the course and review the aims often. This should prevent the lesson turning into a chit-chat every time (unless that's what the client wants of course). A course book that you can dip into may help with this, if you can get your student to buy it, that is. A course book allows you to set homework and have extra material on hand without too much photocopying. Course books also show students how to develop study skills, which may be necessary for those who've been out of education for many years.

Although you need to make your lessons varied and bouncy, remember that your student can only absorb so much in one session. So revise previous topics a lot, after the student has had a day or two to absorb them. Even during the lesson it's not a bad idea to leave the room for a few minutes to give the student a bit of space to think and reflect.

If you do happen to get an intensive course, 15 hours a week for example, you have to pull out all the stops to keep it interesting. I've found that having a running saga is good fun.

What I do is to base a series of lessons (listening, reviewing, narrating and so on) around a film that plays out over the course of the week. The student is keen to know what happens next and is therefore more motivated.

Read a few news headlines each morning and include activities that get your student moving – sorting through cards and objects, doing library research or going on field trips.

By the way, it's easy to stop monitoring the student's errors while you're playing the part of the other speaker in a role play or similar activity. I therefore suggest that you keep your pen and paper to hand all the time, so that you can have some thorough feedback and correction sessions afterwards.

Working at Teaching Business English

The answer to the question about who should teach business English, and how, revolves around *needs analysis,* in other words, finding out in detail what the client needs to do in English and where his wants and lacks are.

The following are some examples of questions for a needs analysis questionnaire, which can help you to assess the needs and lacks of the potential student and determine your own suitability for meeting those needs.

- ✔ What do you need to do in English?
- ✔ Which skills need to be involved (reading, writing, speaking, listening) and through which kind of communication – letters, emails, Skype computer software (which allows you to make free calls using the Internet) or face to face?
- ✔ What do you need to talk about? Tell me about the subject areas.
- ✔ Who are you likely to be speaking to and where are they from?
- ✔ Describe the settings you'll use English in (conferences, lunches and so on)?
- ✔ Do you have any particular time frames? Do you need English now or for a future event?
- ✔ Why did you decide to study English?
- ✔ Is your course being sponsored by your company? What kind of budget is there?
- ✔ What is your educational background?

> ✔ Tell me about your background, culture and interests.
>
> ✔ Do you have a particular location in mind for the lessons?
>
> ✔ How often and how long do you want your lessons be?
>
> ✔ Can you provide a sample of your writing – a recent email for example?

When teaching business English, you do more than check the student's overall grammar and vocabulary, you also get him ready for the particular situations he's to face.

As the spectrum of occupations requiring a certain level of English is so wide, there may be cases where very little specialist knowledge of that industry is required.

If you can get a foothold in teaching people your own specialism in English, so much the better. In addition, for some the most difficult words in the job are similar to English ones anyway. For example, when teaching Italian surgeons I found that their lack was in everyday language for communicating with immigrant patients and for socialising, not the Greek- and Latin- based terminology of medical journals. After all, English is the international language of science and technology now but the words we use often originate elsewhere.

Fortunately, a business English class is sometimes pretty straightforward. If you're teaching a whole class that's enrolled at your school, you'll probably be given a course book or a syllabus to teach from. Some classes are geared towards exams such as Cambridge BEC or LCCI qualifications which a teacher with experience of general English exams can handle with a little extra preparation. (I talk about English proficiency exams in Chapter 21.)

The main difference between general and business English is *register* (formal and informal styles), and the organisation of a *functional-notional syllabus,* which means that instead of learning one piece of grammar or vocabulary after another, getting progressively more difficult, the syllabus focuses on situations and tasks. For example, the first chapter may be about making phone calls and teach whole phrases like, 'Hold the line please. I'll put you through'. The next chapter may cover welcoming visitors to the office and so on. So it's still the English you're used to, but organised in a different way. For this reason, you need to teach chunks of language that students can memorise even if they don't understand the grammar involved.

Use real communications like business letters, faxes and emails you've received and look regularly at the business pages in national newspapers.

Look for business English resources at these websites:

- ✔ E. L. Easton at www.eleaston.com/biz/home.html
- ✔ Macmillan Business English at www.businessenglishonline.net
- ✔ Oxford University Press English Language Teaching at www.oup.com/eltnew/teachersclub/business_english

Chapter 20

Getting Youth on Your Side: Coping with Younger Learners

In This Chapter

▶ Focusing on young learners

▶ Telling stories

▶ Playing games

▶ Singing songs

▶ Connecting with teenagers

---

*T*eaching young learners – from toddlers to adolescents – is a somewhat different experience from the highly motivated and self-disciplined adult students of most lessons. So, in this chapter you get advice on how to make children's lessons fun and stimulating.

Teaching Kids' Classes – Dream or Nightmare?

When you're offered the opportunity to teach children you may delight at the idea of singing songs with cute little pupils or you may envisage screaming, unruly terrors paying you no heed whatsoever. To be honest, you're probably going to encounter both situations and sometimes in the same lesson. It's up to you to decide, but if you take the job it's good to start off by thinking about the way youngsters learn.

Looking at how little ones learn

Most people think that children are superb language learners and that they outstrip adult students. However, more recent research shows that this isn't exactly true. Children have much more time to devote to learning than adults and they can often see a clear need for doing so. So, for example, most bilingual children have a parent or caregiver who speaks to them entirely in another language. Say, a family in the UK are made up of a Twi-speaking mum and a dad who's bilingual, the child eventually speaks Twi to communicate with her mother and English to speak to everyone else. However, when the mother learns English, the child may stop speaking Twi because she doesn't have to. Understanding Twi is sufficient for survival and so English becomes dominant.

Two good points about youngsters learning a language:

✔ Their pronunciation is sometimes better than that of adult students.

✔ They're often less self-conscious about speaking than older learners.

If you work as an au pair to small children, you can just speak your language and the children begin to acquire it because they need to communicate. However, as an EFL teacher you're only likely to have your pupils for an hour or two a week, so acquisition is less likely to happen this way. You need a strategy for helping them learn.

Sorting out what young learners need

Children's and adult's lessons obviously differ in some respects. You really can't just turn up and play a game so here are some things you ought to include in your lesson preparation:

✔ **Shorter activities to match the shorter concentration span:** Even games or role-plays need to be brief and punchy so that the kids don't get bored.

✔ **Extra activities just in case:** Sometimes the children aren't in the mood for a particular activity so instead of forcing them, have an alternative on hand.

✔ **Eccentric behaviour:** Kids love it when you do something out of the ordinary. It gives them a reason to communicate because they want to tell you about it.

✔ **Rewards:** Parents don't always like it if you give their children sweets, except occasionally, but you can have stickers with smiley faces and positive messages. Pre-teens really beam when they get praise and commendation that they can show to Mum and Dad.

✔ **Interest and motivation:** Try to make your activities lively and based on the children's interests so that they really want to get involved.

✔ **Sensory and kinaesthetic activities:** Use all the senses (maybe not so much of taste). If you can't bring in real objects, tap into their imaginations. Ask about how things smell, and what they look or sound like. And get them moving! You can encourage mime and acting out stories. Do activities standing up. Ask them to come up and write or draw something on the board.

✔ **A balance of activities:** Try to alternate between sit-down activities and ones involving movement so that the kids don't end up over excited or bored. It disturbs other classrooms if there's constant noise but short bursts are more acceptable.

✔ **Thorough preparation:** If you're unsure of yourself, youngsters take advantage and start messing about. Know exactly what you want to do.

✔ **Have a starting and finishing routine:** Repeat the same little songs at the beginning and end of the lesson for several weeks. Kids feel secure when they know what's going to happen and when they've picked up the words.

✔ **Revision and repetition:** Repeat information from previous lessons to reinforce the ideas and give the kids a chance to show off what they know.

✔ **Visual stimulation:** Make your classroom and materials bright and colourful with lots of pictures.

✔ **Discipline:** This is an area of concern for a number of teachers. It's best to let children know what will happen if they're naughty. Unfortunately, you may not speak the children's language when you begin but you can always ask for the assistance of the school or a parent to set out the ground rules.

I find it helps when the children know that parents are likely to get involved if problems arise. For minor cases of disruptive behaviour you try getting that pupil more involved by giving them a special responsibility. This can improve confidence and prevent restlessness.

Imagining Once Upon a Time

You should always practise language within a context, and in the case of children, fairy tales and kids' stories in general are ideal. Another benefit of stories is that they encourage the use of the four skills – reading, writing, listening and speaking. Stories improve general linguistic ability because children begin to paraphrase and summarise. In addition, they actually get some cultural awareness through this gentle introduction to world literature.

No doubt you'll read stories aloud in the classroom and this takes a little practice if you aren't used it. Be sure to vary the intonation of your voice as much as possible so that key words stand out and so that the children are gripped by the music of the language. Invent funny voices for different characters and don't insist on silence if the children want to interact with the tale. You can teach booing, hissing and 'He's behind you!' if you like.

Getting the grammar

Grammar is an off-putting word for most students, so when it comes to the little ones, it needs to be sugar coated a little.

Take for example a lesson on adjectives. From beginner level, children learn their colours so they know the basic 'adjective plus noun' structure – a blue ball.

Adjectives of personality are motivating for kids because they enjoy telling you what they think of the various characters in their stories. Fortunately, fairy-tale characters often come with their own adjectives, so you can use them as examples. For instance: **evil** stepmother, **ugly** sisters, **magic** wand, **handsome** prince, **big bad** wolf, **little** pigs.

Students enjoy matching the adjectives to the characters and to their flashcard pictures. And don't forget the dwarfs from Snow White! Six of the seven dwarfs have adjectives for names – Bashful, Dopey, Grumpy, Happy, Sleepy and Sneezy – so you can easily have students practise using a subject, a form of the verb 'to be' and an adjective.

For example they can identify the characters from pictures and show understanding of what the names mean like this:

> I know *he is Sleepy* because he's in bed.
>
> I know he is . . . because he . . .

Most fairy tales are in the past simple tense and can easily become gap-fill exercises where the children choose the missing words from a list under the passage, like this one:

> Once upon a time, there . . . a woman who . . . very sad because she . . . a child but . . . not have one.
>
> wanted was did was

Some famous lines from stories provide a context for introducing other tenses:

- **Future simple:** 'I'll huff and I'll puff and I'll blow your house down', from *The Three Little Pigs*.
- **Present perfect continuous:** 'Someone's been sleeping in my bed', from *Goldilocks*.
- **1st conditional:** 'I'll give you the child if you guess my name', from *Rumpelstiltskin*.

You can use stories to teach modal verbs too. Summarising the moral of the story from fables and fairy tales lends itself to this topic. You may start a discussion like the following:

Teacher: What do you learn from 'The Tortoise and The Hare'?

Student 1: We **shouldn't** rush.

Student 2: We **mustn't** boast.

Student 3: We **can't** judge by looks.

Expanding vocabulary

Many story books for children are designed so that you can just point at the picture and introduce the vocabulary. However, there should be a structure for learning, so it's good to introduce vocabulary within topic areas. Once you decide on the topic you can find a story that lends itself to it.

Some modern TV characters are also shown abroad, not to mention Hollywood movies, which have international appeal. Use any story that's appropriate for the age group. So for example:

- **Food:** Hansel and Gretel
- **Buildings:** The Three Little Pigs
- **Family:** Cinderella
- **Animals:** The Jungle Book
- **Jobs:** Fireman Sam/ Bob the Builder
- **Environment:** The Ice Age

EFL teachers sometimes refer to *inductive* and *deductive* learning. Inductive learning means that students learn through examples and discovering things themselves so that they understand the meaning in context. Deductive learning means that you teach the rules of a subject first so that students refer back to the rules as a point of reference. Using a story to teach vocabulary is a deductive approach when you teach the children the words very directly. But the children also infer the meaning of certain words because of the context, so they learn inductively as well. So in the Hansel and Gretel story the children learn the words for 'woodcutter' and 'witch' inductively; they just pick them up. On the other hand, the food vocabulary is deductive because you tackle it head on. This means that you don't need to worry about students understanding every word before you can use the story. They can work out some of it for themselves.

Of course children have their own imaginations and they enjoy coming up with their own stories too. When they create their own tales and pictures, they're more likely to remember the vocabulary they've used, and they feel a greater sense of achievement if these efforts become posters for the classroom.

Children Only ESL-EFL at `www.childrenonlyesl-efl.com` offers free downloadable flashcards for children's stories.

TEFL Tiddlywinks: Using Games to Teach

Games that have a clear language focus are a real asset to lessons and here I show you list of games you can adapt for TEFL.

Whichever game you play, I find it helpful to teach realistic game-playing vocabulary such as:

It's my turn.

You're cheating.

Pass.

Can I have a clue?

I win.

You lose.

Adapting real games

Very often you can take a game you already know and tweak it for the TEFL market. For example, I use these:

- **Battleships:** In this game, you have a grid onto which you secretly mark off certain squares as the location of your battleships; your partner does the same on another grid. For the purposes of language practice, the grid references can be made up of numbers that sound similar and tricky letters of the alphabet, such as those in Figure 20-1. When the students try to guess the location of each other's battleships they're forced to pronounce their numbers and letters very precisely. For example:

  Student A: Is there a battleship at Q13?

  Student B: Is that Q or K?

	A	E	I	K	Q	G	J	H	W
13									
30						X			
14									
40		X							X
15									
50			X						
16									
60							X		
100									

Figure 20-1: Using 'Battleships' to teach letters and numbers.

- **Bingo:** You can play bingo in lots of different ways. The traditional approach of course, is to have numbers on your card and then to mark them off as soon as they're called out.

  However, you can create your own bingo-style cards with pictures on instead. So if you're teaching children about animals, have pictures of animals on the cards. It works well with food, clothing and furniture too.

  This game gives very good practice in listening skills. Be really crafty and instead of calling out the word, just hold it up in writing. This kind of variation pushes the students to recognise English words in writing.

✔ **Tiddlywinks:** Games like this, which don't actually require speaking, can be used in a slightly different way. If students just enjoy having a go at the skill of the game, tell them that they need to answer a grammar or vocabulary question correctly before they have a turn. You can ask the students to revise a particular topic by going through their notes and making sure that they remember it, and let them play in return for their correct answers.

✔ **Colour by numbers:** This kind of activity really reinforces the names of all the colours (and numbers too), especially if you can get the children to talk about the picture while they work. Ask them whether a particular item is to be blue or green, for example. This works well in very small classes.

✔ **Simon says:** This is a fun game using instructions in command form, for example, 'Simon says, touch your toes'. It practises saying the parts of the body and some useful verbs like 'put' and 'touch'. The advantage of a game like this is that the shy child doesn't have to speak but can still participate.

✔ **Uno:** This is a card game that practises numbers, colours and a series of verbs and phrasal verbs such as 'pick up', 'put down' and 'reverse'. It takes some time to play a whole game, so you may have to reduce the number of cards dealt to each player.

✔ **Snakes and ladders:** Create your own board with various revision questions on it. If the children answer correctly they don't have to go the ladder despite landing on that square.

✔ **Crosswords and word searches:** You can buy some children's puzzle books but it's much more fun if the children create their own to challenge each other, based on different vocabulary areas.

Using games from course books

You can find a number of dedicated course books for young learners. I list some titles in Chapter 8. Most of these include ideas for games and activities within the syllabus but here are two books on the market that are more focused:

✔ *Children's Games Photocopiable Resource Pack'* written by Maria Toth and published by Macmillan is crammed full of activities for young learners at different levels.

✔ *Five-Minute Activities: A Resource Book of Short Activities'* written by Ur and Wright and published by Cambridge Handbooks for Language Teachers is not actually aimed at young learners but many of the games are great for kids because of their short attention span.

Most series of course books are accompanied by teachers' and resource books that contain games and activities. Even those designed for adult learners give you great ideas which you can transfer to children's topics.

When you adapt activities from books, use colourful cards that kids can move around and attach amusing pictures, perhaps something they can colour in afterwards.

Trying other activities

Depending on the resources available to you, you can invent your own activities to practise language.

Here are a couple I use; the first activity is fun if you have English newspapers or magazines around. The second requires no special resources at all. What they have in common is that the children don't need too much involvement from you so they can be more in control of their own learning.

Making a newspaper collage

For this you need a newspaper or two (comics for lower-level students), scissors, card, five or six boxes or envelopes and glue. Make sure that everyone has access to a page or two of the newspaper.

You simply choose a particular part of speech (verbs, nouns, adverbs and so on) and give students a time limit of a couple of minutes to find examples of this kind of word on the page. They can underline the words and you then need to do some feedback to make sure that they've got it right.

Next you get them to cut out all the examples they've found and put them in the designated box or envelope. After a few rounds you end up with collections of nouns and verbs and so on.

Finally, have groups of students pick three words from each collection without looking. They have to think up a short story using all their words, no matter how bizarre, and write it out on a large piece of card. They stick their chosen newspaper words directly onto the card and write the rest in with their own handwriting. Award a prize for the most original.

By the end of the lesson, they'll have learnt several new words and practised sentence structure in English.

That's a good question!

It's always best to let students generate language themselves so here's a game that does just that.

On strips of paper ask students to write down questions they'd like to ask their classmates. They may be about their favourite things or more along the lines of 'What would you do if . . .?'

When they've finished, go through and weed out any that are just too cheeky or inappropriate for other reasons. If you have a good question in poor grammar, put it on the board so that other members of the class can help correct it. Try to include about twice as many questions as there are students so that you retain the element of suspense. And now put the questions in a hat or something similar.

Finally you go from student to student and ask each person to choose a question without looking. On the flip of a coin, decide whether the student has to answer the question or nominate someone else to do so.

By the end of this lesson, the students should have practised asking questions in English and they should also know quite a bit more about each other.

Tuning-In to Songs and Nursery Rhymes

Nursery rhymes are great fun because they contain the kind of vocabulary that's appropriate for children, for example names of animals and parts of the body. They also contain simple actions in nursery rhymes, which kids can do the actions to. However, when children repeat and act out rhymes, they don't see it as learning; it's more of a game.

Choosing the right song

When it comes to choosing a nursery rhyme or song for teaching English, resist the temptation to simply choose your favourites so you can indulge in a bit of nostalgia from your childhood. Think about it! Some rhymes make no real sense at all and certainly won't do well under scrutiny. Take this line for example:

Ring a ring o' roses, a pocket full of posies . . .

Songs that contain words you think are useful are actually a better bet. You may not analyse all the words at this stage but as students progress in English they should be able to recall the rhyme and have some common English words at their disposal. Choose nursery rhymes with an easy, memorable tune and beat so everyone can clap and sing along (or at least hum at first). Rhymes of more than eight lines are hard to memorise unless they're very repetitive. In addition, go for rhymes that are easy enough to pronounce and easy to act out.

Kids also like to perform actions to the rhyme because it helps them remember and adds to the meaning. I'm a big fan of good old Incey Wincey Spider myself, because the hands are moving all the way through.

Teaching your class to sing

So how do you actually teach foreign children an English rhyme? You don't need to break the song down in all its parts. Only certain words deserve a bit of focus. Words that are accompanied by a mime or action are an easy target because the movement helps explain the meaning. You can also highlight words that are part of your course syllabus such as numbers and colours. You should decide what the rhyme is basically about and teach the vocabulary that describes the theme. So for Incey Wincey Spider, focus on 'spider', 'climb' and 'spout'. For Ten Green Bottles teach the number and the colour along with 'bottle' and 'wall'.

The basic steps to teaching your class a song are:

1. **Teach the vocabulary for parts of the body with pictures for the children to label – and lots of repetition.**

2. **Arrange the children in a circle and begin singing the song slowly, doing the actions as well.**

If you sing much more slowly than usual, they can associate the words and actions easily. They can also hear the sounds of the words distinctly so you don't end up with vague, muffled approximations of the words. You may have to repeat a song three or four times when you first introduce it. The kids may not join in with the words but they probably pick up the actions. However, regularity is the key. So if you sing it again the next lesson you should find that they start to sing along with a few of the words they recognise.

'One finger one thumb' is a great nursery rhyme which has actions too. It teaches the parts of the body – finger, thumb, arm, leg, head – and some imperatives (commands): stand up, sit down, turn around.

The idea is to waggle your finger and thumb. Then to push out your arm and leg, nod and follow all the commands in time with the song.

Here's the whole rhyme in case you don't know it. You'll have to ask around for the tune unless you have a recording of it!

One finger, one thumb, keep moving.

One finger, one thumb, keep moving.

One finger, one thumb, keep moving.

We'll all be merry and bright.

One finger, one thumb, one arm, keep moving (repeat twice).

We'll all be merry and bright.

One finger, one thumb, one arm, one leg, keep moving (repeat twice).

We'll all be merry and bright.

One finger, one thumb, one arm, one leg, one nod of the head, keep moving (repeat twice).

We'll all be merry and bright.

One finger, one thumb, one arm, one leg, one nod of the head, stand up, sit down, keep moving (repeat twice).

We'll all be merry and bright.

One finger, one thumb, one arm, one leg, one nod of the head, stand up, sit down and turn around, keep moving (repeat twice).

We'll all be merry and bright

Singing the Happy song

Another great song for young learners is the Happy Song. It goes like this:

> If you're happy and you know it, clap your hands (clap twice and repeat).
>
> If you're happy and you know it, and you really want to show it.
>
> If you're happy and you know it, clap your hands. (clap clap).

The next three verses are the same except that you replace 'clap your hands' with these commands in turn: stamp your feet, shout 'We are!'. Do all three.

This song has simple lyrics and the commands mirror the actions exactly, so you don't need to pre-teach them. The only word you need to teach beforehand is 'happy', which is very easy to do with smiley faces. The procedure is the same, a slow version first then normal speed. Repeat it several times the first day and then regularly after that.

After the song you can then focus on the verbs 'clap', 'stamp' and 'shout'. Whenever someone does well you can ask the class to clap.

I suggest you save shouting exercises for outdoors as you may be unpopular with your colleagues otherwise. You can use 'stamp your feet' when you talk about cold weather too.

If you have a recorded version of the song it's great for you and the children to have some musical accompaniment. If not, go ahead and sing your heart out at normal speed. Be cheery and exaggerate the actions, encouraging the children to join in.

Don't worry about the other phrases in the song unless the children particularly want to know the meaning.

Keeping Teenagers Interested

When you have a class of teenagers, you can have some great discussions providing that you find the topics that really interest them. Whether it's the latest signings by Manchester United, or finding the perfect date, teenagers make the effort to communicate when they feel strongly enough about the subject matter.

Some other points that teenagers look for in a good lesson are:

✔ **Evidence that the teacher is prepared for the lesson and interested in their students' development:** At this age kids are smart enough to know if you habitually throw lessons together at the last minute and they behave accordingly.

✔ **Good classroom management:** There's no point trying to get in with the kids. You aren't one of them! What they like to see is that you're in control of the class and that you're a figure of authority without being too uptight.

✔ **Showing them respect:** Teenagers are moving towards adulthood and they like you to acknowledge this by asking their opinion about various topics and encouraging them to be independent in their learning when this is appropriate.

✔ **Fun activities they can actually learn from:** You can play games at any level and with any age group but with teenagers you need to make your aims and objectives clear so they know why the activities you do are relevant to them.

✔ **Challenging activities:** Take the level up half a notch from time to time so that students feel stretched. Easy activities can lead to boredom.

✔ **An invitation to comment on the course or lesson:** Hand out questionnaires so that students can tell you what they want. You can ask them to suggest topics they'd like to talk or write about.

Have competitive team activities on a regular basis but be sure to mix up the teams regularly.

Intriguing students with international English

If you're teaching in a non-English-speaking country, set your students a challenge. Ask them to find as many examples of English words and slogans as possible over a week. Get them to cut out examples from magazines and newspapers, or take pictures of advertising hoardings (lots of teens have camera phones). This can become a short project resulting in a class poster.

As a result of their findings, students discuss with you with the pros and cons of adopting English words into their language. Discuss questions like:

✔ Are English words used correctly when they're borrowed?

✔ How are they pronounced?

✔ What about the grammar? For example, in many languages words have to be designated masculine or feminine. Who should decide whether a foreign word adopted into your language is masculine or feminine?

✔ Do older people use English words or just the younger people?

✔ What kind of image do companies who use English in their advertising want to have?

Following this, begin another similar task. This time ask students to find out which words from their language have been adopted into English. Make another poster with these international words and discuss:

- ✔ Have the words kept their meaning or have they changed?
- ✔ Does the use of these words abroad create a good image of your country?
- ✔ How do foreigners pronounce them?

Finally have an international word quiz. Get the students to guess the origin of international words used in English. For example:

- ✔ Alcohol (Arabic)
- ✔ Amateur (French)
- ✔ Boomerang (Aboriginal)
- ✔ Bungalow (Bengali)
- ✔ Hamburger (German)
- ✔ Ketchup (Chinese)
- ✔ Taboo (Hawaiian)

Spelling out abbreviations

In this age of text messaging, youngsters are very adept at finding short ways of writing down what they want to say. Why not use some well-known abbreviations to get them thinking? They may already know the gist of some, but not letter for letter and others they may have to investigate.

For instance, these abbreviations from broadcasting, texting and the world at large would make a great quiz activity:

- ✔ AKA: Also known as
- ✔ ASAP: As soon as possible
- ✔ BBC: British Broadcasting Corporation
- ✔ CD: Compact disk

- ✔ Cul8r: See you later
- ✔ GMT: Greenwich Mean Time
- ✔ IOU: I owe you
- ✔ Lol: Laugh out loud and lots of love
- ✔ MC: Master of ceremonies
- ✔ MTV: Music television
- ✔ PTO: Please turn over
- ✔ R&B: Rhythm and blues
- ✔ VIP: Very important person

Even if students recognise the abbreviation, make sure that they can say it correctly. For example, they shouldn't make VIP rhyme with 'skip' but say each letter.

Playing Kim's game

This well-known game tests observation and memory. In the classroom you can use it to teach or reinforce vocabulary.

To play, you gather together 20 objects that teenagers use and lay them out on the desk but cover them with a cloth. Uncover them for two minutes or so to let students look at them, cover them up again, then get the students to write a list of what they were from memory. I like to choose things that students use every day but don't know the name for in English, such as an eraser or ear-phones.

Offering advice with problem pages

Scores of magazines and websites offer advice to troubled teens. I use readers' letters as a basis for reading and writing activities. Students can each become the agony aunt or even submit their own problem for another classmate to answer.

Chapter 21

Making the Grade: Handling Exam Classes

· ·

In This Chapter

▶ Examining the range of exams

▶ Helping students with exam skills

▶ Composing an exam course

· ·

Some students have very fixed goals for their English which often involve passing exams. Exam classes take a bit of getting used to so in this chapter you find out about the most popular exams. I include a section on how to teach the necessary skills; you can consult the chapters in Part III for more tips.

Exploring University Entrance Exams

For a large number of students higher education is the motivation for learning English. They want to take degree courses in an economically strong English-speaking country because this adds prestige to the qualification and opens up more opportunities for their future careers. However, in order to enrol on such courses, students have to prove to universities that they have sufficient language skills and this is why entrance exams in English are necessary.

IELTS (International English Language Testing System)

This exam started in the 1980s and is becoming increasingly well known. As the name suggests, there is a very international feel to this exam. There are a variety of accents and styles of writing in most of the papers.

IELTS is for people who:

- ✔ Want to emigrate to Canada, Australia, the UK or New Zealand.

- ✔ Professional people, especially those in the medical field, who want to practise in the UK, USA or Australia.

- ✔ Want to attend university or higher education courses in New Zealand, USA, Australia, Canada, UK, and South Africa.

- ✔ Want to undertake work experience programmes in an English-speaking country.

Once students have taken the exam, the result is usually valid for two years depending on who needs it. Language skills can fluctuate a great deal over this period of time, so in a situation where competition is intense a university is entitled to set more stringent entrance criteria. However, this is fairly rare.

The exam results are given in bands of 0 through to 9. So, 0 means that the candidate didn't do the test and a 9 means that the candidate is an expert English user.

It isn't usually worth taking the exam unless you can achieve a band 5.5 score at least. However UK universities sometimes ask for a score as high as 7.5, and in the USA some academic institutions ask for 8.5.

Students tend to improve by 0.5 to 1.0 on average in three months of study if they are in an English speaking country and need six months of study otherwise. For example, students who begin an IELTS course with a score of 6.0 (based on pre-course testing) typically achieve 6.5 or 7.0 by the end of the course.

Fortunately you can take IELTS more frequently than most other exams, so students can repeat the exam within weeks if they have a bad day and mess it up. It costs approximately £100 to take the exam each time.

Although IELTS is generally considered to be for higher education, the exam has two versions. One is the Academic exam and the other is the General English version. Most students need the Academic version but emigrants and work experience candidates who are applying for internships take General English.

The listening and speaking elements of the exam are the same in both versions. However, the reading and writing elements are somewhat more difficult in the Academic version which reflects the nature of work and study the exam candidates are in line for. A CB (computer based) Academic version is also offered in some places but this doesn't include the speaking exam.

There is always a recording device in the room but you should advise students not to worry about this because this just supports the examiner's work.

So the four exam papers are:

- ✔ **Listening:** This is a 30 minute test in four sections. There is a conversation between two speakers, followed by a monologue. The third section involves a group conversation and finally there is a lecture or talk. The listening texts are only played once each. The questions take the form of multiple choice, short answers in three words or similar, completing sentences, notes, diagrams and flow charts.

- ✔ **Reading:** This test lasts 1 hour and the question types are similar to those done in the Listening text. However, they also include choosing from a list of headings to identify paragraphs, stating whether a sentence is true, false or has an answer not given in the text, classifying information, and matching lists or phrases.

- ✔ **Writing:** This test lasts 1 hour during which you have to complete two different tasks. You lose marks if you don't finish them.

  - Task 1 consists of a chart, graph or table and the candidate has to write about the information presented. Alternatively you have to describe a process from a diagram, showing how something works. The minimum word limit is 150 words.

  - Task 2 carries more marks and requires you to consider and discuss aspects of a particular topic in a formal way. The minimum word limit is 250 words and the question features international themes.

In IELTS writing, if you restate the question in the same words, those words are deducted from your word count. Hyphenated words and numbers are counted as one word and you shouldn't use contractions.

- ✔ **Speaking:** This test lasts no more than 15 minutes and takes the form of an interview with one examiner. First there is a general discussion about everyday topics. After that the examiner gives the student a topic, a pencil and some paper. The candidate has a minute to make notes about the topic and then gives a two minute presentation.

The Speaking test does not happen on the same day as the other exam papers. It should take place within 7 days of the others though. Candidates have to do Listening, Reading and Writing papers one after the other, on the same day with no break.

Even if a student is proficient in English they might do badly without training because the questions are a little unusual. For example, in the Reading paper candidates have to choose whether information is true, false or not given in the text. Unlike in other exams, you have to read between the lines for the meaning. In the Listening test you have to listen all the way through too because there might be a question which doesn't follow sequentially.

TOEFL (Test of English as a Foreign Language)

TOEFL is designed to show how well a non-native speaker can cope with English in higher education. If the student has already followed a recent course of study in English for two or more years in an English speaking country, they may be exempt from the test. It is not enough to live in an English-speaking country. Many universities in the USA require a TOEFL score to measure proficiency and the exam itself features the American variety of English. Exams fees vary according to which version of the test you take and at which centre but the payment is may be quoted in US currency and is approximately $150.

TOEFL scores are only valid for two years, after that your official report is deleted.

In this exam you need overall skills like:

- ✔ **Note-taking:** Students need to be able to write down key points even if they don't understand the content completely and then rephrase or reconstruct it in writing or speech.

- ✔ **Mind mapping:** This technique of using a diagram to organise ideas around a central point helps students to organise a writing task in just a few minutes.

- ✔ **Synthesising:** This means drawing together information on one topic from different sources to form a new piece of work.

Three versions of the exam exist: the IBT version is internet based, the PBT is paper based and the CBT is the computer-based test, so the version you take depends on where you sit the exam. You only need to take one version.

The IBT lasts 4 hours and has four sections which you do on the same day, as follows:

✔ **Reading:** You have to read three to five passages on academic themes and then answer comprehension questions. It lasts 60 to100 minutes.

✔ **Listening:** You listen to two conversations involving at least two speakers and four classroom based lectures. Then you have to answer multiple choice comprehension questions. It lasts 60-90 minutes.

✔ **Speaking:** Candidates speak about 6 questions based on what they have heard or read for about 20 minutes in total. The information for the six questions is presented during the Speaking test.

✔ **Writing:** There are two writing tasks in this section, one of which involves reading and listening. So after reading or listening to a lecture you write about it. The second is an essay of about 300 words reflecting your opinion on a given topic. The duration of the test is 50 minutes.

Each part attracts a score of 0-30, so the total score is 0-120.

The PBT is a little different from the IBT and involves:

✔ **Reading:** This test lasts 55 minutes and has 50 questions based on general English.

✔ **Listening:** The duration of the test is 30-40 minutes.

✔ **Structure and Written Expression:** This test lasts 25 minutes and is based on using the appropriate language for standard written English.

✔ **Writing:** There is only one topic and candidates have 30 minutes to complete it.

Candidates can take the Test of Spoken English separately.

In TOEFL PBT each paper can attract a score of 31-68 so the total is up to 677.

The CBT papers are:

✔ **Listening:** You get 40 -60 minutes to answer a maximum of 49 questions.

✔ **Structure and Written Expression:** There is an allocation of 20 minutes for this.

✔ **Vocabulary and Reading Comprehension:** This is a 90 minute test.

✔ **Essay Writing:** You get 30 minutes to write one essay.

The score is averaged out so the total is a maximum of 300.

Going for More General English Exams

Some students have goals other than higher education and need a more general qualification which they can show to employers or use as a landmark for their progress in learning English. In this case they are likely to take a general English exam or work through several of these over a period of time. Such exams give students something to focus on and provide motivation. They may also enhance their career prospects.

Cambridge ESOL (English for Speakers of Other Languages) exams

Cambridge ESOL offer a a range of exams in general English which are internationally recognised (see www.cambridgeesol.org). Students in well over a hundred countries take these exams so there is a wide acceptance from employers, educators and other bodies of these qualifications as a measure of students' abilities in English.

The results of Cambridge ESOL exams are valid for life, unlike IELTS and TOEFL results. The exams are:

- ✔ **KET (Key English Test):** This is an elementary level exam which follows the same pattern as PET. The registration fee is about £40.

- ✔ **PET (Preliminary English Test):** This is for pre-intermediate and intermediate level students building up to higher level English exams in the future. The three parts are Reading and Writing (one paper), Listening and Speaking. The registration fee is about £45.

- ✔ **FCE (First Certificate in English):** This one is for intermediate and upper-intermediate level students. It is a very well-known exam and popular with employers and educators. The registration fee is about £80. There are five papers this time:

  - **Reading:** This is a one hour paper based on general fiction and non-fictions texts.

  - **Writing:** This part lasts 80 minutes and comprises two different tasks. You need to train students in letter-writing/emails, stories, essays, articles, reports and reviews. Each style is different and examiners expect candidates' writing to fit the task in style and register.

- **Listening:** This lasts 40 minutes and aims to present realistic contexts such as public announcements and news broadcasts. You listen to the texts twice.

- **Speaking:** Students have to talk about general topics, compare and contrast two pictures by themselves, and discuss a task with another student. This part takes about 14 minutes.

- **Use of English:** This paper is a tricky one which tests overall knowledge of English grammar and vocabulary. It takes 45 minutes.

✔ **CAE (Certificate in Advanced English):** This advanced level exam is almost the same in its format as FCE but of course at a higher level. The registration fee is about £85.

✔ **CPE (Certificate of Proficiency in English):** This level is close to that of a native speaker and the exam consists of the same five papers as FCE. However each one is longer. The registration fee is about £90.

✔ **Certificates in ESOL Skills for Life:** Speakers of English as a second language in England, Wales and Northern Ireland take these state-run exams. Depending on the level the cost of these exams is approximately £10 for the Reading test, £15 to £20 for the Writing test and £20 to £25 for the Speaking and Listening test.

Cambridge offer KET and PET exams 'for Schools', which means they're designed specifically for the interests and experiences of students.

Consult the Cambridge ESOL website at www.cambridgeesol.org for more information about these exams. The British Council website at www.britishcouncil.org gives information about most English exams.

Other exams

Students take other exams, although these are a little less prominent than the ones mentioned in earlier sections. Some of these are specific to the student's (prospective) career or age group. Others are alternatives to the academic and general English exams mentioned above and are also recognised by employers and educators, but are especially favoured by particular EFL colleges.

EDI (Education Development International) offer general English exams and professional English exams through LCCI (www.lcci.org.uk).

✔ English Language Skills Assessment (ELSA): This is a quick, business-oriented English test including Reading, Writing, Speaking and Listening. Students don't need to prepare for the test and they get a score of 1-500 on completion.

✔ Foundation English Language Skills Assessment (FELSA): This is a general English test which is suitable for students at low levels, including elementary, and for different age groups. The format includes a lot of pictures and large text and the student's result is presented as a list of things they can do.

✔ JETSET Certificates in English Language Skills: These are a range of certificates designed specifically for young learners. They cover the four skills of reading, writing, speaking and listening as well as encouraging knowledge of life skills. Because there are several levels, the certificates can provide evidence of continuous progress.

The London Chamber of Commerce and Industry (see www.lccieb.com under LCCI International Qualifications) operate several exams for English in the working environment. They are:

✔ **English for Business (EFB):** All students take reading and writing tests which are related to business English but the speaking and listening components are optional. The exam is offered at different levels.

✔ **English for Commerce (EFC):** This exam is taken by non-native speakers who have a reasonable knowledge of commercial concepts.

✔ **English for Tourism (EFT):** This exam is designed specifically for staff who deal with customers and who manage others in the tourism industry and is offered at two levels.

✔ **Practical Business English (PBE):** This is an elementary level business English certificate.

✔ **Spoken English for Industry and Commerce (SEFIC):** This is an oral exam involving an interview and optional tests in specific areas of work.

City and Guilds run a range of ESOL exams. City and Guilds is an organisation which is largely focused on vocational qualifications helping people to further their careers and their qualifications cater for, among others, migrant workers and non-native speakers settling in the UK (see www.cityandguilds.com).

✔ ESOL for Young Learners: Children from 8-13 can take one paper for Listening, Reading and Writing skills and take another optional test which is an interview to assess speaking skills.

✔ English for Business Communications: These tests at different levels cover areas such as business letters, faxes and emails.

✔ International Spoken ESOL (ISESOL): This is a recorded interview in general English which can be taken at different levels.

✔ International ESOL (IESOL): This is a series of general English qualifications at different levels.

✔ Spoken English Test for Business: The test is a recorded interview at the appropriate level which demonstrates confidence and fluency in business English.

✔ English for Office Skills: This test is especially for office workers who need to show that they can be highly accurate when they write or speak in English.

I mentioned Cambridge ESOL exams earlier in the chapter. Cambridge ESOL is a highly respected examining body who also offer Professional English exams.

✔ BEC (Business English Certificates): These are certificates for people who wish to use English in their careers.

✔ BULATS (Business Language Testing Service): Employers use this service to assess the language skills of (prospective) employees.

✔ Cambridge ILEC (International Legal English Certificate): Workers in the legal profession who need to make contact with English speakers or speakers of other languages through English benefit from this qualification.

✔ ICFE (International Certificate in Financial English): This qualification is for accountants and workers in the financial sector who want to follow international career opportunities.

✔ ESOL for Work):This exam is only for non-native speakers who want to live and work in England, Wales and Northern Ireland.

✔ TOEIC (Test of English for International Communications): This test is similar in format to TOEFL which I mentioned earlier in the chapter. However, it is designed to demonstrate students' readiness for life in the corporate or business world.

Sharpening Study Skills and Exam Techniques

Before anything else, make sure your students are at the right level to attempt the exam within a few months, otherwise they may become demoralised by the amount of work they have to plough through. A general English course is sometimes a better option than an exam class to start off with.

Some general tips to offer students taking exams include:

✔ During the exam, the student has to transfer answers accurately to the official answer sheet. It would be a shame for them to know the correct answer, but lose marks because of failing to do this properly. Towards the end of your course, introduce the answer sheet and get students to practice using it. They should include this in their timing too.

✔ Check whether students need to write in pencil or pen on the mark sheet. It sounds basic but examining boards have different requirements and students need to make sure they have all the right equipment. Correction fluid is usually banned too.

✔ Remind them not to offer alternatives answers in questions where a short answer is required, unless the question invites them to do so. If they're offered two options and choose a third, that answer is automatically wrong, whereas if they guess at the right answer, they have a 50 per cent chance of its being correct. So if a question calls for one word, don't choose two and if it asks for two words, don't choose three.

Tell them to take note of the grammar in the question as it often indicates singular or plural and other clues. Here is an example:

Which person is responsible for the situation?

Answer: Person A or Person B

The question asks about one person but the student has suggested two people. Therefore the answer is automatically marked wrong.

✔ Tell them to pay attention to the word count in short answers too. In some exercises, the student has to write just three or four words per question. If the answer is in good English but contains five words, it's wrong.

✔ Spelling is notoriously difficult in English but there is no excuse for messing up on words which are actually in the exam paper, so advise your students to pay attention to the text. Sloppiness loses marks.

✔ Recommend that they think of their own answer before using multiple choice options. This is an excellent measure of accuracy.

✔ Warn them not to leave blank spaces. Always guess.

Writing especially for exams

The two main things that examiners want to see are good structure and a composition that answers the question in its entirety.

When it comes to structure, the introduction, body and conclusion should stand out at a glance. So, for example, even if the body of the composition is excellent, students are likely to lose marks if they don't have a conclusion. Train your students to include at least one final sentence which sums up or restates the ideas raised in the introduction.

Examiners have very limited time for marking each paper so they won't waste time trying to decipher poor handwriting. When students do homework they should avoid using a computer unless they will be using one in the exam. You need to check that their handwriting is legible and that the punctuation and spelling is accurate.

An additional reason to practise handwriting is to do with word counts. There is no time to count every word in the exam so students need to be able to see what the appropriate number of words looks like for them. Is it half a page or a page and a half, for example? The quickest way to count is to see how many words you write in one line and then count the lines. And never go beyond the word count by much. It's a waste of time which would be better spent checking accuracy. The reality is that the more you write, the more mistakes you make.

English exams don't require complex arguments. Students just need to present a few appropriate points in logical order. The points need to be linked together with expressions such as 'however', 'in addition', 'alternatively' etc.

Many students are repetitious in their writing so flag this when you mark homework. Repetition of ideas reveals poor planning and repetition of words and phrases reveals poor vocabulary.

One overused word is 'say'. Devote a lesson to using alternatives such as state, utter, complain, suggest and so on.

Writing lessons ought to include information on:

- ✔ Opening and closing salutations for letters/emails
- ✔ Saying what the communication is about
- ✔ Apologising
- ✔ Requesting
- ✔ Thanking
- ✔ Giving details
- ✔ Arguing for and against

✔ Contrasting through tenses

✔ Stating opinions

✔ Giving background information

✔ Concluding

Reading for exams

The biggest problem for students when it comes to reading tends to be speed. Very often they run out of time because they attempt to read each text carefully from start to finish. So you need to train your students in speed reading.

After getting an overview from the headings or opening sentences of each paragraph, the students need to know what they are looking for. They can get this information by reading the questions, so tell them to read the questions before reading the text. Teach students to skim through a text until they find an appropriate section and then read that part more carefully. They should practice timed readings in silence (you would be surprised how many people only study to music).

Get students in the habit of reading with a pen or pencil in their hand for two reasons:

✔ Dragging the pen across the page helps to keep up forward momentum and instead of constantly rereading sentences

✔ They can use the pen to underline key words.

Usually answers are in order in the text so it shouldn't be necessary to keep going back to the beginning.

When you tackle reading tasks in class, help students by highlighting new vocabulary but encourage them to guess the meaning instead of always resorting to the dictionary. You should also look at the structure of the text in terms of grammar, layout and expressions which link ideas together.

The questions for Reading exams usually involve:

✔ Choosing headings for paragraphs or parts of a text

✔ Classifying: This involves putting information into appropriate groups or under the right headings.

✔ Completing a table or flow-chart

✔ Completing notes: Students fill in the gaps on an incomplete set of notes based on a reading or listening text.

✔ Completing sentences

✔ Identifying the views or claims of the writer

✔ Locating information

✔ Matching: These questions usually involve matching a heading to a paragraph or a character in a text to activities/attitudes associated with them.

✔ Summarising: Students need to be able to get the gist of and rephrase information in just a few words.

Speaking in exams

In most speaking exams the examiner is looking for intelligible pronunciation, a range of grammar, and vocabulary appropriate for the level and task.

Some students try to memorise a speech or at least set answers. However this doesn't work because they end up sounding robotic and sometimes fail to answer the actual question.

Communication between the candidate(s) and the examiner should be as relaxed and natural as possible. Some tips your students can follow to achieve this are:

✔ **Take your time.** It's no problem to pause for breath before answering. In fact you're more likely to mix up your grammar if you rush.

✔ **Practise speaking on the day of the exam.** If you can have a practise session with your teacher on before the exam, this helps, but you can at least use English before entering the exam room to get 'tuned in'.

✔ **Relax yourself by smiling and using the names of the people with you.** Sometimes two or three candidates take an exam at once. Use their names if they are easy to remember and listen out for the examiner's name too.

✔ **Learn what to say if you don't understand or you need to hear something again.** There are very polite and realistic expressions such as, 'I'm terribly sorry but I didn't catch that' or 'Could you possibly rephrase that for me?'(this isn't always possible but when the request is made in good English you are unlikely to be marked down for asking).

✔ **Realise that the examiner can't give anything away.** The examiner can't let students know how well they have done or put words into their mouths. So, if students know what to expect, they won't be put off by the lack of commendation from the examiner.

✔ **Know how to waffle a bit.** Make sure that you know how to buy thinking time with expressions like, 'That's a good question. Let's see…'

Listening in exams

While listening in exams students have to:

- Circle or tick correct information.
- Complete multiple choice questions.
- Complete multiple matching questions where there are several answers and several categories.
- Complete sentences and other information using no more than three words or numbers.
- Fill in a table.
- Get the gist by stating what the overall purpose of a text is even though it may not be stated explicitly.
- Label a diagram.
- Pinpoint details.
- Write short answers.

Some suggestions for preparing are:

- Tune your ears by practicing English on the same day before the exam.
- Get used to hearing different accents because you never know what kind of voices might be used on the recording. You can do this by practising with authentic materials such as radio broadcasts.
- Read all the questions first so you know what you are listening out for and predict the kind of information required – a name, a place or a number, for example.
- Try to relax but stay focussed. Even if something happens around you, don't lose your concentration.
- Don't get bogged down. If you don't know the answer to one question, just move on. It isn't worth missing the next answer and you can always go back and guess the answer later.
- If you can't hear properly, speak to the examiner immediately. If you have a choice of exam location, choose the one where they use headphones.

Teaching Exam Classes

Most exam classes involve practising actual exam questions from past papers and analysing what went well or badly. There is also a need for general training in grammar, vocabulary, text structure and overall exam techniques.

The first thing to do is get hold of up-to-date information from the examining board on what the exam consists of. Then sit down and take the exam yourself. Don't just answer the questions, make notes on how you found the answer or structured your argument. There is always a reason why one answer is better than another and it's your job to explain it. Did you find synonyms or use a process of elimination, for example?

Find examples of good written texts by students and analyse what makes them successful. Do the same for poor attempts.

Organising your course

After you know what the exam is like, find some course materials. You need a book of past papers or typical exam questions and another book which helps students build up their skills. Ideally students should have their own copies of the book(s) to save you doing photocopies every day and to encourage self-study. Don't worry too much about students looking ahead and cheating, after all they are only cheating themselves. You can also draw on authentic materials from the real world to liven things up and help students to find their own learning resources. So, instead of a text from the course book, use a newspaper article or extract from a popular novel.

Work out how much preparation time is available before the exam and organise the course syllabus accordingly. Students should have a full mock exam during the course, about three quarters of the way through so there is time to put a few things right. Some teachers set a full mock at the beginning of the course so students know what they are aiming for but this can be intimidating. You should definitely go through all parts of the exam though. For the Speaking test, see if you can get a colleague to pose as an examiner as this feels more realistic than when you do it.

Your students must be prepared to do homework. If you plan your lessons carefully you can usually incorporate some of the marking into the lesson time without short changing the class. So for example, if the exam includes a listening or reading component, you can set students a timed exercise and mark work while they do it. Use a marking correction code and get your class to redo their work. (Chapter 7 lists suggested marking codes.)

Remain upbeat and optimistic even if the students are not quite there yet. Let them know if there doesn't seem to be much point enrolling for the exam this time and focus on more appropriate timing. If enrolment isn't optional you can focus on the skills the students will gain by taking it. And beware of the over confident students who rely on being clever rather than practising their techniques. They sometimes fail.

Using English exam papers: Teaching what sounds 'English'

The Use of English paper in Cambridge exams is probably the most difficult to teach. Even if an exam doesn't contain a paper with this name, there is bound to a number of questions based on the same principles. The idea is for students to demonstrate whether they have good overall knowledge of the language and the familiarity to know what sounds correct.

The best way to test this kind of knowledge initially is by using a cloze test. This means that you delete words from an appropriate reading text at regular intervals, perhaps every eighth word, and ask students to complete it. By doing this you take in all parts of speech and get an immediate impression of your students' abilities. From this kind of assessment you may discover that your students have a particular area where they need more study – idioms and prepositions often fall into this category – but on the other hand you could opt for a more comprehensive training regime. This can include:

- ✔ **Synonyms:** Highlight *synonyms* (words that mean the same as other words) all the time. You can do this during reading lessons if you decide to dissect the text, and in addition, do a synonym brainstorming activity before a writing task so that the students are less likely to repeat themselves. As a stand alone activity you can set matching tasks for synonymous pairs or ask the class to find the odd one out which is not a synonym.

- ✔ **Rephrasing:** This is related to the use of synonyms and also *syntax,* or how words in a sentence fit together. As a teacher, your own definitions should include examples of rephrasing so that students become aware of alternative ways of expressing things. A typical rephrasing task is like this one:

Complete the second sentence so that it has the same meaning as the first one. You must use the words in parentheses.

I won't come to the barbecue if it rains. (unless)

I…..….…………………….…..it rains.

Teach grammar rules so that students can more easily work things out for themselves.

✔ **Preposition agreement:** Choosing the right preposition is pretty difficult because there aren't always rules to follow, so highlight which preposition goes with which verb or other part of speech.

✔ **Collocations and chunks of vocabulary:** Sometimes there is no particular rule about which words go together, so you just have to teach a whole phrase at once and highlight to students that those words fit together in a particular way.

✔ **Identify part of speech:** In a *cloze test,* one where you have to fill in the gaps, you can decide whether a preposition or adjective or other part of speech is missing to help guess the answer.

Read the sentence and think of the word which best fits the space.

He would often……**visit**………the forest.

✔ **Prefixes and suffixes:** Once students know which part of speech they need, it's easier to manipulate a base word by adding to it. Here's an example.

Use the word given in capitals to make a new word which fits in the space.At the computer company, all the ……**programmers**……….. take their break at 1pm.

PROGRAMME

✔ **Dictionary usage:** Train students to use dictionaries efficiently. They are a tremendous source of information so if students read more of the entry for a particular word, they will learn about all the associated parts of speech and synonyms too.

✔ **Editing:** Students should be used to editing their own work from your correction code. However, they often have to apply grammar rules to eliminate words from a text in exams. For this reason, always try to explain why a sentence is incorrect.

If a line has a word in it which is incorrect, write that word in the space provided.

1) *Even though my car it was driving smoothly, I took it to the mechanic.*

Chapter 22

Distinguishing Monolingual and Multi-lingual Classes

In This Chapter

▶ Handling classes in which everyone speaks the same language

▶ Teaching multi-lingual classes

▶ Comparing two teaching situations – at home and abroad

---

*E*nglish is English wherever you go but the nature of classes varies tremendously. In this chapter I tell you about learning environments at home and abroad and give you some tips on handling similar and diverse students.

Speaking the Same: Monolingual Classes

In the majority of EFL courses, all the students speak the same native language. These usually run in the students' home land. These classes tend to be larger in size than multi-lingual groups and the students are quite often from the same background and age group as well.

Predicting errors

The advantage of teaching monolingual classes is you can fairly easily predict problem areas, or *L1 interference*. *L1* means first language – mother tongue, in other words. *L2* is a second or foreign language.

Most people who speak another language have an accent which reveals where they're from and usually make mistakes typical of anyone from the same language group. Their mother tongue influences pronunciation, structure and vocabulary. The good news is that because all the students have the same problems it's easier to predict what could go wrong.

Pronunciation errors

If you imagine speaking English with your students' accent you can begin to estimate which *phonemes* (pronunciation segments) they find problematic.

Take a copy of all the phonemes in English and highlight the ones your students struggle with. Then, whenever you introduce words which contain these sounds, make a point of drilling the pronunciation thoroughly.

English has several sounds which don't correspond to Hindi ones. English /t/ seems to fall between a number of similar Hindi sounds but these are said with the tongue between the upper and lower teeth or much further back in the mouth. So students need to see where exactly in the mouth they can make this sound. You could have a diagram up so that you can point out the correct tongue position every time a word with /t/ crops up.

Adopt a similar approach for word stress and intonation patterns. Anything which is markedly different from English should attract special attention from you.

Grammatical errors

You don't have to speak your students' L1 to predict their grammar problems. Just listen to the errors speakers of that language make and then do some research by asking colleagues and checking reference books. In particular, books which teach the students' language to English speakers point out the differences in grammar. It might seem illogical to an English speaker when a student consistently refers to an inanimate object as he or she. For instance, students may say, 'She is a beautiful chair'.

However, knowledge of how gender works for objects in their L1 would cause you to stress that in English objects are neutral. So in Italian a chair is *'sedia'* and feminine because it ends with the vowel 'a'. It probably wouldn't occur to you to point out that a chair is not 'she' without this kind of background information.

Vocabulary errors

False friends are words which look or sound similar in two different languages but have entirely different meanings.

For example, 'byte' in Swedish means prey or victim; in English it's a group of binary digits

Find out as much as you can about false friends and note them down whenever you come across them so you can help your students avoid pitfalls.

Or how about words which function differently when you translate them? For example compare English and French: 'langue' in French means language or tongue, so you can say 'I speak a language' and 'I speak a tongue', but you can't say 'I taste with my language' so you have to pay attention.

Literal translation from L1 to L2 is risky so point out any traps you are aware of.

Apart from the practicality of the thing, when you are living abroad it is to your advantage as a teacher to start learning the local language.

Using the students' language

Although most EFL professionals are against the use of the students' L1 in the classroom, there are those who point out the advantages of its use in small measure.

For one thing, weaker students who have no option but to attend the class at that level (there is no lower level to move to for instance) do not feel as lost as when only English is in use. For true beginners L1 use might build confidence especially if the teaching methods are just as new to them as the language. In both cases there is a reasonable argument in favour of using the L1 just to give instructions.

Suppose you are struggling to convey the ins and outs of an activity in English. Is it a wise use of time to persevere or should you allow another student to whisper the explanation in L1 to someone who doesn't get it so that everyone can proceed?

A more extended use of L1 is for grammar explanations. A bilingual teacher might be able to switch to L1 for detailed comparisons of structure. There is also the option of team teaching with one partner the native English speaker and the other a native L1 speaker. In this way the native English speaker can concentrate more on conversation and cover the grammar only lightly.

Ultimately the aim of TEFL is not to erase the L1 but to help learners become bilingual. In reality bilinguals switch from one language to another all the time so you could reason that it should be allowable in class.

The problem is, of course, that use of L1 reduces the use of English and that as the teacher you may not understand what the students are saying. How do you know if their translations are even correct? And anyway, it isn't possible to accurately translate every English phrase into L1. Sometimes students have to just adopt an English speaking mindset to really get the point when they learn the language.

So it's up to you to decide whether to allow L1 in the classroom. Perhaps you need to take each situation as it comes.

Pointing out the pitfalls of monolingual classes

The trouble with monolingual classes is that when students know that everyone speaks the same language (except perhaps the teacher) there just isn't a great need to communicate in another tongue. There is no urgency to learn English or at least to speak it. Especially for younger learners, there is not as much natural curiosity as when their classmate comes from a far flung, exotic land.

Another problem is that there isn't so much to ask classmates about when they all come from the same area and have similar backgrounds. Even worse, perhaps the students have taken the course just to get out of the house and make some new friends. This is hardly ideal for linguistically focused lessons. Your class might just as well be a coffee morning.

If your students are school age or perhaps taking English as a compulsory course in university, they may be lacking in motivation and at times downright resistant to learning because they have no choice in the matter.

Creating an 'English' environment

You can employ various strategies to get students using English together. The physical environment can encourage use of the language if it promotes the culture typical of English speaking countries. So students should see and hear lots of interesting things in English. You should also use the English language so consistently and efficiently in the classroom that students view it as inappropriate to speak any other language in this environment. The idea is for the classroom to become a place where students can suspend disbelief and forget that there is any other language which offers a viable means of communication. During the lesson they are in an outpost of an English speaking country and must behave accordingly.

Use these tips to create the kind of atmosphere in class that makes students want to speak English.

> ✔ **Make activities interesting, but not too fun.** Believe it not, if an activity is too fun, students may simply forget to speak English in the heat of the moment, and the activity becomes more important than the language point you're practising.

Now, I'm not suggesting the elimination of fun from your lessons but perhaps you could highlight the aim of the activity, teach additional phrases we use when we are having fun such as 'That's great!' and offer subtle reminders to use expressions in English throughout.

✔ **Explain the benefits of pair and group work.** As teaching methodology varies from country to country, it could be that students don't understand that this kind of work has a serious purpose.

✔ **Forestall use of L1.** If you don't want students to resort to L1, teach them everything they need to say in English. This includes classroom language like asking for clarification and even asking for the translation of a word, but in English: 'Does anyone know how to say that in English?'

✔ **Give clear instructions.** Communication in English will definitely break down if students don't know what they are supposed to do. So make sure everyone knows what they're doing before you start and check with the weaker students directly because they are the ones most likely to resort to L1.

✔ **Give your students some quiet time to prepare.** Before actually speaking in English, give the class a chance to switch languages. This should help to focus everyone on the task and it gives them time to ask you a question if they're unsure about the lesson, which builds confidence.

✔ **Encourage teamwork and cross-communication.** Make all the activities you do communication activities. So encourage discussion and set tasks which students cannot complete unless they speak to someone else who has the information they need and vice versa – information gap exercises, which I talk about in Chapter 6 are excellent for this.

✔ **Sit the students back to back for some activities.** You tend to concentrate on verbal communication more when you can't see your partner's face or body language. There is less chance of the students just copying down the information they need from each other and then chatting in L1.

✔ **Collect money for a local charity (or a class visit to the pub) from anyone who speaks in L1.** If money isn't appropriate, collect names and make frequent offenders do a forfeit of some kind.

✔ **Decorate the room with English.** Fill the classroom with posters, magazines and brochures from English speaking countries.

✔ **Play English music.** Have some English language music playing when students enter and exit the room.

✔ **Have students use English names.** If students are in agreement, tell them the English equivalents of their names and use them. Some students like choosing an English name or descriptive title for themselves. 'Hunter' was one of my favourite Chinese students.

Diversifying with Multi-lingual Classes

Classes made up of students with different languages tend to be in English speaking countries. There are several advantages to this situation:

- **Motivation among students is high.** Either they have paid a considerable sum of money to attend a language course abroad or they have moved to that country lock and stock and barrel so they need English to get on with lives.

- **English is the only way to communicate with everyone else**. Even if you speak the language(s) of some of the students, you're unlikely to do so in that setting or else the others will feel alienated.

- **An English speaking country offers lots of opportunities for learning outside the classroom.**

- **Students have a natural curiosity about their classmates' lives and have much to discover about them.**

Unfortunately multi-lingual classes have their downsides too. If you had 12 students who each spoke totally unrelated languages, all things would be equal. However, this is not often the case. Certain schools are popular with particular nationalities because of strong word of mouth and very active agent promotion. As a result, there tends to be large groups of students from just a few nationalities, perhaps 4 or 5 nationalities amongst 12 students. Some of these nationalities might speak the same language, or at least share similar cultures. The upshot of all this is that students may form cliques to the exclusion of others in the class.

For younger learners particularly, cliques can result in negative peer pressure. Say, there are four students who can speak Russian in one class. One diligent student might want to speak English throughout the class whereas the Russian speaking friends insist on using their mother tongue most of the time. They might make fun of the 'goodie two shoes' who insists on doing what the teacher says.

Something similar happens when one friend in the language group is weaker than the others in English. This person often feels too embarrassed to get help from the teacher and instead relies on friends to translate. Consequently they all end up speaking their mother tongue.

Building rapport

Students are usually quite apprehensive when they begin a new course and this is magnified when the only thing they appear to have in common is their poor English.

With a class of students from different language groups and backgrounds, breaking the ice is key to getting the course off to a good start. By using these activities, you can help students make friends, feel comfortable and avoid them gravitating towards speakers of the same language.

Chuck a monkey (or whatever toy you have)

A useful tool in an EFL classroom is a stupid looking cuddly toy (I use a monkey myself), or if you just can't bring yourself to have one of those with you, try a bean bag. I have tried doing the following activity with a pen but found that one student complained on the grounds of health and safety. She said I could have someone's eye out!

The icebreaker goes like this:

1. **Arrange the chairs into a circle if possible.**

   Students can sit or stand for this.

2. **Introduce yourself according to the class level.**

   For example, with absolute beginners you might just say your name and point to yourself or at advanced level you can explain your background in teaching and any interests you have.

3. **Now throw the toy to someone else and ask them to introduce themselves.**

   Sometimes a raised eyebrow and expectant look does the trick.

4. **After the student speaks, indicate that they should throw the toy to someone else.**

5. **Keep going until everyone has introduced themselves, then retrieve the toy.**

6. **This time you throw the toy to someone else and you introduce that person.**

   So, you say their name and whatever you remember about them.

7. **Indicate to the student to throw the toy to someone else whose name they remember and keep going until you've covered everyone.**

   Encourage the rest of the class to help if someone gets stuck.

8. **The activity ends when someone finally introduces you again.**

Make a map

Get students working in pairs or threes for the first time.

Draw or point to a map on the board to illustrate your background – where you're from, places you've lived in and/or countries you've visited. Explain the story with drawings, mimes and dates as necessary. Now get each student to draw a map too.

Pair or group the students up and get them to explain their own stories. Even if they have to mime to each other they will still enjoy breaking the ice.

Ask the students to reorganise themselves in order of their birthdays (not age). Now they get a chance to meet someone else.

Guess the numbers

This one is not suitable for beginners because it involves asking questions.

Write some numbers or facts on the board which relate to your life and get the students to guess what they mean. I sometimes write the number of siblings in my family or the year I began teaching. You can only answer yes or no to the students' questions. Now they can play the same game in pairs/groups.

Names and actions

Try this memory game with a twist with the students in a circle.

Have everyone think of a unique action or gesture – maybe stamping your left foot. So first of all you say your name and perform your action. The next person has to say your name, stamp their foot, say their name and perform their own action. This continues around the circle until the last person has a nightmare of names and funny moves to recall. It really gets people laughing.

Managing learning

After breaking the ice you need to get on with the day to day business of teaching your class English.

Speakers of European languages have a distinct advantage over other students because of the similarities in structure, vocabulary and culture between their tongue and English. Even amongst European languages there is the potential for some students to grasp a concept almost immediately while others take a little longer.

Take the word 'television'. Although the concept is not at all difficult for the German speaker, the other nationalities barely have to translate.

- ✔ Czech: televize
- ✔ Dutch: televisie
- ✔ German: Fernsehen
- ✔ Italian: televisione

✔ Portuguese: televisão

✔ Spanish: televisión

This example highlights three problem areas in multi-lingual situations:

✔ You need to be prepared for the different speeds at which learners are likely to grasp language, given their different backgrounds.

✔ If only one person is lagging behind, this individual may feel too shy to speak up.

✔ You may overlook the one student who doesn't get it because the others so enthusiastically express that they do.

The solution to all three problems is that you never take for granted that the whole class understands. If you draw or show a picture before using the word, everyone gets the idea at once. Additionally, you can ask questions to make sure that students understand (I discuss concept check questions in Chapter 5). Even if the student understands already, they have an opportunity to express themselves and help their fellow students understand.

Concept check questions for 'television' are:

What shape is a television?

Do you have a television in the garden?

Where is the television in your house?

What do you watch on television?

Use students who are faster on the uptake to help model the language. Good speakers can show classmates how to pronounce a word in small groups. They become your assistant teachers which is motivating for them and helpful for the classmates.

If one student has a linguistic problem which is more complex and not relevant to the other students, give them more personal attention. For example, a student from Libya could be slower at doing his work just because it is more difficult for him to use the English alphabet and script. Instead of partnering him with a classmate who reads and writes well, be his partner yourself so that you can assist with some of the more difficult words and give encouragement.

In the long run, you may have to accept that some students will have to change class in order to move ahead more rapidly or to repeat the course again. This isn't desirable but there is no point ignoring the needs of one or two students just so that you can keep the group together. Your class should proceed at a pace which is comfortable for the majority of learners.

Going beyond language: Teaching culture

Some of us are fortunate enough to have been brought up in a multicultural society so that it's nothing new or strange to have a mixture of races, cultures and languages around us.

There is a knack to showing interest without appearing ignorant or acknowledging differences without alienating anyone. In a class with many different nationalities you sometimes find that students from mono-cultural societies lack these skills and are in danger of making gaffes.

Unfortunately, students sometimes bring their prejudices with them to the learning environment. Some problems I have encountered so far are:

- Students from neighbouring countries can display animosity towards each other based on historical or political factors.

- Some males feel that they are superior to female students (and female teachers).

- One student's religious beliefs may be undermined by others, for example the observance or non-observance of particular festivals or the need to pray at particular times.

- Differing opinions on sexuality might be offensive to some.

- Stereotyping might result in a failure to accept as a native speaker, a teacher who doesn't fit the student's perception of Britishness (a black teacher for example) or a student whose physical characteristics are not typical of his nationality.

- Students may use inappropriate gestures or expressions to refer to someone of another race.

- A dodgy sense of humour with inappropriate jokes which the student feels the strange compulsion to translate into English.

By all means, deal with problems as they arise but there are also some preventative measures which might help: Promote an atmosphere of mutual respect by asking students to share information about their backgrounds at a class level and showing real interest in what they say.

Occasionally you encounter students who resent the dominance of the English language and the political histories of English speaking nations. When you enquire about the student's culture and demonstrate that you view it as equal to your own it helps to break down these barriers.

Teach students the right words for describing other people in the community (Oriental, mixed race etc) and let them know what is acceptable behaviour. If necessary you can discuss how the law of the land reflects on these issues so students are clear that this is not just your opinion.

Have clear guidelines for classroom conduct and explain the consequences of breaking these rules if you have offensive individuals in your class. Fortunately, most objectionable attitudes come from a position of ignorance so when you teach students another way, they tend to adapt.

Applying Case Studies

In this section I take one 90-minute lesson for 12 students and comment on how it differs for two different classes. It appears to be short in length but this allows time to incorporate the needs of each class.

- ✔ **Level:** Upper-intermediate

- ✔ **Materials:** IELTS speaking test practice material (IELTS Masterclass, Haines and May, OUP pages 171, 172 which includes a speaking test on theme of reading). A video of students taking the exam.

- ✔ **Lesson aims:** To practise the three stages of the IELTS speaking exam. To teach a strategy and expressions useful for Part 3, which is a discussion between the examiner and exam candidate.

The structure of the lesson for each group is as follows:

1. **Elicit from students the stages of the IELTS speaking test and length of each (5 minutes)**

   Put the following information on the board. These are the parts of the test:

   - Part 1: General chat about home, work, study, and general life (4 minutes)

   - Part 2: Presentation (1 minute for preparation and notes; 1-2 minutes describing given topic)

   - Part 3: Expansion on Part 2 (3 or 4 minutes)

2. **Brainstorm what the examiner is looking for and put ideas on the board. (5 minutes)**

Make sure they cover these necessary points:

- Fluency and coherence

- Range of vocabulary

- Range of grammar

- Accuracy

- Clear pronunciation

3. **Have each student think of four questions suitable for Part 1 of the exam.** Then have a brief class feedback session in which they tell you the questions they have thought of. (5 minutes)

4. **Pairs ask each other their questions and give answers** on these general topics. (5 minutes)

5. **Reorganise the pairs and assign partner A as examiner and partner B as exam candidate.** Ask students to prepare their note books with the marking criteria set out so they can assess each other more formally, as the examiner would. (5 minutes)

6. **Students practise and role play**, alternating the roles of examiner and student. (6 minutes)

7. **Students give each other feedback on Part 1.**(4 minutes**)**

8. **Students each practice Part 2, which is the presentation.** They switch roles after giving feedback to their partner based on the marking criteria. (10 minutes)

9. **Class feedback.** Students say what they find easy or difficult in Parts 1 and 2 (5 minutes)

10. **Focus on Part 3, which is the topic expansion discussion related to Part 2.** Brainstorm ways to comment on a question and think of sample phrases to use during the test. (15 minutes)

Some suggestions may be:

- Say something about the question

- Make a connection to your life

- Answer in two parts

Possible phrases to use in this part may include:

- That's an interesting/a difficult/ an important question.

- I have (never) thought about that.

- That's quite relevant because I . . .

- It's funny you ask because recently . . .

- There are two sides to this.

- I'll mention the pros first and then the cons.

11. **Students watch a video of other students taking the exam, assess these other students and give feedback.** (15 minutes)

12. **Students practise asking and answering a few questions each for Part 3. on the topic of reading.** (5 mins)

13. **Give students an envelope full of questions typical of Part 3 but on various topics, one for each pair.** Together they practice asking and answering the questions using the phrases on the board. (5 minutes)

The English class in Italy

The students in this class are all Italian and vary in age from late teens to mid- twenties. They are generally quite communicative and tend to focus more on getting their message across than accuracy. As I speak their language to upper-intermediate level, I can anticipate some particular difficulties.

General skills

Ask students to pay particular attention to accuracy when they speak and also in the examiner role. Make sure that they don't interrupt when someone else is speaking. It's more acceptable for speakers to do this in Italian culture but it would be a disaster to do so in the exam. Use a 'wait' gesture to remind students about this throughout the lesson.

Vocabulary problems

The course book discusses different kinds of reading material but there are two words which might be false friends:

- The Italian *romanzo* is very similar to 'romance' but means *novel*.

- *Magazzino* means warehouse, not magazine, which is actually *rivista* in Italian.

Pronunciation problems

In Italian, most words carry stress (emphasis) on the penultimate (the second-to-last) syllable. Students tend to use the same stress patterns when speaking English, which makes it more difficult to understand the accent. On the list of reading material, get the students to mark the stress for each word.

There is usually some confusion with the correct stress on compound nouns such as different kinds of books. Drill several examples with students making, sure they stress the first noun **–sports** books.

Science books are on the list of reading material. The letters *sci* are pronounced /ʃɪ/ as in 'ship' in Italian so students are very likely to mispronounce *science*. Be sure to drill it.

Many words in Italian end in a vowel so the students often add an extra vowel sound to the ends of words. They pronounce the words 'read' and 'reader' almost identically, for example. Use the cutting gesture during the lesson to remind them to cut the ending.

Grammar and syntax problems

There is a recurring error caused by students confusing the infinitive form of a verb (such as to go) when it should be the gerund (going). Remind students how to use 'enjoy' as it comes up in the lesson: 'I enjoy reading'; not 'I enjoy to read'.

The English class in London

In this class there are four nationalities among the students in equal numbers. They are Brazilian, Japanese, Colombian and South Korean. I don't speak the languages of any of these students so I can only use my observations of them and fellow countrymen to predict errors. In addition to linguistic problems faced by the students due to L1 interference, there are other cultural characteristics which I need to take into account to get the best out of everyone.

Most of the students need to broaden the range of tenses they use and include more modal verbs, so while monitoring I will make an effort to check their progress in these areas. I can also encourage them to modify the examples they give me to include these points.

As the students all have different problems they should be able to assist each other. It's important to mix them up so that each pair is made up of different nationalities, ideally one South American and one Asian. Before the role play, students can inform their partners of particular problems they have so that the acting examiner can be on the look out for these points. The peers can correct each other during feedback sessions too.

Problems for Korean students

Most of the Korean students make mistakes with /p/ and /f/, getting the two sounds confused. They need to practise drilling these words but I can use the Colombian and Brazilian students to help model words such as *favourite* /pevrɪt/ and *fiction* /pɪkʃən/.

This group of students have a tendency to focus more on grammar than fluency. Remind them to be coherent and use linking words. Ask the examiner in the role play stage to listen out for this.

Problems for Japanese students

The Japanese students pronounce every syllable with equal length and stress, so they can sound a little like robots. Monitor and drill intonation and get students to mark the stress on all the vocabulary listed in the course book. They can also underline key words in their notes so they give them more emphasis when speaking.

Read /liːd/ is a key word in this lesson but these students have difficulty with the letter 'r', so show and exaggerate the mouth position for this word.

Being overly polite is a hindrance for some of the students. Encourage them to be bold and not to apologise too frequently. Explain that formal and traditional gestures like bowing and receiving things with both hands are unnecessary but not objectionable.

When they're unsure, some of the Japanese students say 'Huh!' in what looks like a startled manner from an English speaking perspective. This response needs to be softened. Memorising some of the expressions from this lesson will give the students something to say in response to any question.

Problems for Colombian students

My Colombian students are all university undergraduates from the same college. They stick together a lot and break into Spanish whenever they can get away with it.

Students put an initial /e/ before words which begin with 's', such as *sports* /espɔːrt/ and *science* /esaɪɛns/. Apart from the initial vowel, I predict that students will pronounce *science in* a Spanish way because of the Latin connection /ʃiːens/.

Problems for Brazilian students

Collectively the Brazilians are the most outgoing and vocal. They sometimes intimidate the other groups, especially the Asian students, simply because they speak up more readily. If others wait for a convenient moment to speak they find it difficult to get a word in sometimes. This manner brings a lively atmosphere to the classroom though.

They have some ingrained bad habits that will lose them marks such as:

- Omitting the auxiliary verb: *What you think?* instead of *What do you think?*
- Making adjectives plural to match nouns: *bigs books* instead of *big books*

Part VI
The Part of Tens

The 5th Wave   By Rich Tennant

Cartoon English

☆ Yikes! POW

⑥★#!M

"Remember, it's ⑥ before ★ except after M."

In this part . . .

It's a *For Dummies* book, so it's bound to have a Part of Tens. This part consists of a couple of chapters containing ten bite-sized chunks of valuable info you can dip into as and when you feel the need. Here I touch on how to liven up your lessons with games and activities and how to make the best use of the multitude of TEFL resources out there.

Chapter 23

Ten Ways to Liven Up an English Lesson

In This Chapter

▶ Varying your resources

▶ Giving students a chance to show off

▶ Adapting your teaching style

*T*his chapter contains suggestions for injecting something different into your lessons when you feel things have become a bit a flat. It happens to the best of teachers sometimes, but with a little thought you can get things back on track.

Bring in Real-World Objects

In TEFL, sometimes you want to bring real items – called realia in the biz – into the classroom to help teach a particular point. These items may include clothing, food, household items or even a musical instrument.

Lugging these things into class isn't as easy as showing a picture or offering a definition, but the advantage is that students are more likely to remember the day the teacher came to school with a potato in her handbag than the day she pointed to one in a book. Students will want to pick the item up, play with it and generally make a connection with something three dimensional.

As well as using realia for teaching new vocabulary, you can also use it to practise what the students already know. Take prepositions: A toy car moving through a Lego town is very engaging for young learners, and as one child plays with the car, the others can describe what's happening or give instructions inevitably using prepositions. Even adults prefer using real maps from places they dream of visiting than pretend ones mocked up for the classroom.

If you are working for a language school, find out if there a stock of realia and keep it topped up by bringing in things you don't need anymore.

Step Outside the Classroom

Whether you can leave the classroom behind for a while and get out into the real world depends on the context you find yourself teaching in. However, in most cases you can at least escape to the garden or local town.

The fact is that when the language you are learning is associated with a new situation it can suddenly feel fresh again. So, it may never have occurred to a student to ask the word for sky, traffic light or market stall before because there had never been anyone to speak English to around these things. By getting outside, the students associate English with a wider range of situations, not just a classroom.

If you are teaching in an English speaking country, you do a lesson or two building up to a visit to the local courthouse, a place of historical interest or even a café offering typical dishes. Even something as mundane as an English breakfast is fascinating to someone from overseas. The opportunity to speak English to a 'real' person under the watchful eye of their teacher is enough capture the students' attention. The motivation to learn comes much more easily when the grammar or vocabulary you are teaching concerns a real event.

In a non-English speaking country, you can still find examples of English words on hoardings and notices. Or perhaps the students can take you for a traditional drink or snack. They are likely to be very proud of their culture and make every attempt to explain and translate to initiate you. As long as you create a structure by noting the vocabulary/grammar appropriate to the situation and going over it beforehand or afterwards, the students will see the lesson as purposeful.

Take your students out on the street in their town. Have them find as many English words as they can in ten minutes, then see whether they understand what the words they mean.

Browse the Net

The worldwide web is an absolute gift to teachers and a large proportion of it is in English! As with the two previous points, the internet is a way to bring the real world into your lessons.

Students can do their research online instead of using a dictionary or depending on you. In addition, they can interact with other people in selected chat rooms and discussion forums. It gives students a thrill to know that outsiders understand their English too and that they can post information in their new found second language for all the world to see.

If you have internet access in the classroom, or if you have taken your class to the Information Technology room as part of your lesson, it is your responsibility to make sure that students are not looking at offensive websites.

Start a Project

There comes a time when students want to take more control of their learning. Perhaps your students have their own interests which they would like to explore in English – anything from football, movies, music, fashion and more.

Whatever their interest, it is liberating for students to do a presentation or wall display around it then share their efforts with their classmates.

You can also have student tackle projects in small groups with each student adopting a different role. Teenagers, for example, often enjoy putting together a class magazine with a wide variety of articles, interviews, surveys and artwork.

Establish a regular time for sharing or preparing project work. Make it part of the class routine.

Let the Students Teach

English lessons tend to follow the same pattern: teachers teach and students practise. But for a change, how about giving the students the board pens and seeing how well they rise to the challenge?

There are always restless individuals who struggle to sit still and listen. And what about those know-alls who interrupt you at every turn? Well, these students are ideal candidates for a bit of role reversal. Or, you could give all the students a chance to have a go by giving everyone a 10 minute teaching slot over several lessons.

Students don't need to teach the whole class; more timid students can teach their partner or a small group.

To be fair, you need to back up whatever they teach by thorough checks and feedback sessions.

Starting Out with 'Once Upon a Time'

Story-telling is part of every culture in the world and is something you do frequently in day to day life. It combines human interest and clear settings for language practice. So, help your students develop this skill by giving them lots of opportunities to tell their favourite anecdotes and tales.

To be honest, because most people struggle to make a story interesting in a foreign language, the first attempt at storytelling might be rather subdued. Interestingly though, things start to change if the same story is repeated two or three times. Students increase in confidence and fluency, and in between each telling they tend to check or note points which they have realised they need. Whereas most people don't mind repeating their favourite tales, it is rather boring to hear the same story over and over. So, the best way to get around this is to change the pairings of students each time the story is told. You will find that with each re-telling they get livelier and more accurate to boot.

Use traditional fairy stories, urban legends, jokes or your autobiography as resources.

When you think about it, native speakers learn to appreciate stories right from when they are toddlers and long before they are able to tell stories themselves. What does this imply? Basically that if you tell your students stories, even ones which contain some new words or grammar, they will enjoy it because the overall meaning is clear and interesting.

Open Up Your Life

As you're from a different background (race, nationality, religion, and so on) to your students, they are bound to be more than a little curious about what goes on in your life. Feed them a few simple titbits about your life and you'll find that students can't wait to learn more.

You might wonder what kind of information is safe to reveal. Your hobbies and interests are a good place to start. Bring in some realia or photographs for the class to examine. Even if the class don't share your passion for, say, hiking, they will have something to talk to you about. It is surprising how a lack of cultural knowledge can really stifle conversation. So your students may need to know which topics are safe to discuss with you.

Then again, a bit of junk mail which you would otherwise throw away could fascinate the students. If you are sure there is no classified information in it (the 'Dear Homeowner' kind is useful), you can even let them open it (from a new envelope if you want to conceal your address), have a go at filling in forms or planning a reply.

Move Around

A *kinaesthetic learner* is someone who learns by actions and movement. Although some people just seemed to be wired that way (you know, the fidgeters who are always asking when the next break is), almost everyone benefits by getting out of the chair and shaking off the cobwebs from time to time.

Try to adapt your activities so that they become more physical.

Whenever possible, get students to:

✔ Change seats

✔ Stand up

✔ Do pair work (even back to back)

✔ Act things out

Play a Game

Most students, even serious business types are up for a challenge in the form of a game, puzzle or quiz. It makes sense to have an armoury of these at your disposal to use as warmers at the beginning of a lesson, coolers at the end or just to break things up when the atmosphere has become rather flat. Another approach is to see how you can turn your existing lesson material into something more competitive or entertaining by pitting teams against each other, setting time limits and awarding points.

The games and puzzles we native speakers play are often easy to adapt for classroom use. All the children's games below require speaking in simple statements and no props at all.

✔ **Simon says:** In this game one person gives orders such as 'Simon says touch your toes'. However, you don't follow the order unless the speaker first says 'Simon says'. If you forget and follow the order anyway, you are out of the game.

✔ **I spy:** This popular game in one in which players take it in turns to secretly identify something in the room and the letter that the object begins with, for example 'L' for lamp. You then say, 'I spy with my little eye something beginning with . . . L!' Then all the other players have to guess what the thing beginning with L is.

- **I went to the supermarket:** This is a memory game based on shopping lists. The first person says, 'I went to the supermarket and I bought . . . '. This person chooses an item and says the word. It might be a pen for example. The second person must now say the introduction, the word pen and then add another item of their own. 'I went to the supermarket and I bought a pen and some cheese'. Move from student to student as they repeat the ever increasing list and add an item.

- **Chinese whispers:** Stand all the students in a line or a circle. Whisper a short message in the first student's ear. That student whispers the message, as they have understood it, to the next student and so on. The challenge is to see whether the message remains the same by the time it reaches the last student

Then there are other games which, with a little adjusting can fit snugly into a lesson. Chapter 20 has more on games and don't be put off because the chapter is directed at teaching children – the games can be adapted for any age.

Get Musical

Music generally puts a smile on people's faces and reduces stress too, so if you can find a song to illustrate the piece of language you want to practise you will find your lesson much livelier than when you use a simple worksheet.

Songs are generally seen as a listening activity and older, professional students may not want to sing along too often. There is an alternative though if you want to get musical and this means using jazz chants. A *jazz chant* is a cross between speaking and singing (a little like rapping) which involves repetition and rhythm. While chanting sentences you want to practise, you can snap your figures or clap your hands which really helps learners to hear how English pronunciation and intonation works.

If you are still not sure what chanting sounds like, take a look at `www.onestopenglish.com` under Listening skills: jazz chants. You can download and listen to some jazz chants on MP3.

Chapter 24

Ten Great Resources for TEFL Teachers

▶ Making use of books and other reading materials

▶ Visiting helpful websites

▶ Calling on real people

▶ Getting your hands on real stuff

*J*ust in case you find yourself lacking in time or inspiration, in this chapter I list resources to help your lessons and your career along. With these at hand you should be able to deal with many a tricky situation.

Making the Most of EFL Reference Books

A high proportion of EFL teachers are nomads who try not accumulate too many weighty objects in their backpacks. However, if you decide to invest in any EFL reference books apart from this one, the two here are real classics. They both deal with grammar, as this is the area where you tend to get caught out in either understanding it or teaching it.

A grammar reference to fall back on

Few EFL teachers have not been caught off guard by a grammar question they just could not answer. There you are with your perfect lesson plan, or so you think, when some clever clogs student raises their hand and suddenly reveals your Achilles heel. The best way out of this is, of course, to look confident and promise to go through the answer in the next lesson, giving you a chance to do your research and save face.

One of the most popular grammar reference books for EFL is *Practical English Usage* written by Michael Swan and published by Oxford University Press. All of the trickier grammar areas are there from intermediate to advanced level. The book contains examples of what you can say and of what you cannot say as well. This very well laid out publication is well worth the investment. As a matter of fact, this is a book which you can even recommend to your more advanced students.

A book with grammar lessons to save the day

Ok, so you know what that tense is called, the form and the function, but you are still a little clueless about what to actually do with it in the classroom. *Teaching Tenses: Ideas for Presenting and Practising Tenses in English* written by Rosemary Aitken and published by ELB Publishing/ ABAX Ltd is a great book with ideas, explanations, timelines and photocopiable illustrations which you can use time and again. You basically get entire lessons which present and practise the tenses in a practical, thorough and enjoyable way. In addition to this, you get superb examples of what a good lesson consists of.

If you have more room, try these other books too:

✔ For pronunciation practice drills and comparisons, pick up *Ship or Sheep* written by Ann Baker and published by Cambridge University Press, along with *English Pronunciation Illustrated* written by John Trim and published by Cambridge University Press. This second book also offers thorough practice but has particularly amusing cartoons to make your students smile.

✔ The photocopiable ELT Games and Activities series published by Longman are spiral bound teachers' books for practising language skills in a fun and engaging way. Included in the series are the Communication Games books for different levels. Written by Jill Hadfield, they're a staple for EFL schools around the world.

Looking It Up! Making Use of the Dictionary

Some great learners' dictionaries out there offer more than just definitions.

The *Macmillan English Dictionary for Advanced Learners,* for example, includes colour sections with clear diagrams showing various vocabulary groups. It indicates how frequently used a word is, the pronunciation in the form of phonemic transcription (symbols that show how to pronounce an English word), what kind of word it is (noun, verb and so on), what collocates or typically goes next to that word(for example *pitch* and *black* are collocations because the usually go together as one phrase) and the different meanings. It offers whole sections on different varieties of English, metaphors, phrasal verbs (verbs which include a preposition or two and have a special meaning such as *to set off* and *to get on with)* and other useful areas.

If you either recommend one particular dictionary to all your students, or have a class set of dictionaries, you can plan lessons and whole activities based on dictionary skills. In most cases, accompanying websites offer exercises for the students to do with you or as self-study for homework. You can also write to the publisher and ask for resource packs.

Another two popular dictionaries for EFL students are:

- *Oxford Advanced Learners' Dictionary* comes along with a range of online resources from the Oxford University Press (OUP) website www.oup.co.uk
- Various editions of the *Longman Dictionary of Contemporary English* come in paperback or hardback format and also with CD roms.

Browsing Websites

Just as in many other industries, the internet has revolutionised the world of EFL. From job-hunting to lesson planning, you can find loads of help and encouragement from colleagues on a variety of websites.

Finding work

Before ever you find yourself in the classroom, you need to get a job. So, if you are currently in Warsaw but hoping to find yourself a position in Beijing, for example, you need to get on the internet, CV at the ready.

For many years www.tefl.com has been an essential website for job seekers in EFL. It lists vacancies from all over the world and allows you to save a CV online which can be forwarded to potential employers at the click of a mouse. It also offers advice on training courses, franchise opportunities and living costs in particular cities.

Planning lessons

Take a look at www.onestopenglish.com, an excellent site for teachers maintained by MacMillan, the largest publisher of educational books. Countless pages cover many different kinds of lessons including business English, ESOL (English for Speakers of Other Languages) and exam classes. In addition, the site has articles on methodology and new developments in the industry. Downloading a worksheet or lesson plan is quick and easy too.

The British Council is a well established organisation which, among other things, runs English language training programmes around the world. It also tries to promote understanding among different cultures and promotes the UK to other nations.

As well as job vacancies, the British Council website at www.british council.org has a section on teaching English with ready made lesson plans and links to other useful sites offering resources. This site is also ideal for students interested in travelling to Britain to study or need some extra guidance on funding or exams.

Your first exam class is always a daunting experience. However, if you happen to be teaching one of the Cambridge suite of exams you can get a head-start by looking at the tips and sample exercises on their website www.cambridgeesol.org. Each exam is broken down paper by paper and there are classroom activities to help you teach all the skills and sub-skills your students will need.

Reading the English Language Gazette

The *English Language Gazette* is the most well-known industry journal and has been running for over 20 years. You can subscribe to the newspaper with an online edition at affordable rates and visit the website www.elgazette. com. All of these will tell you about vacancies, upcoming events and the latest EFL books to hit the market. You can make use of lesson plans too and get information about colleges and universities offering further development courses such as masters programmes.

The *EL Gazette* presents articles from all over the world and reports on the global EFL market, which is useful if you are considering teaching abroad but need some up-to-date inside information about your chosen destination.

Attending Professional Seminars

In countries where EFL is popular, publishing houses, larger teaching institutions and examining boards organise yearly lectures and sessions for teachers to update themselves on methodology and resources. They can be very refreshing, not least because you get to discuss your problems with other teachers who may have found solutions. Some offer free sessions as long as you register and for others you need to pay (or ask your employer to – it's worth a try, anyway).

Regular seminars are held by:

✔ Cambridge ESOL to make sure teachers are fully acquainted with their exams and know how to prepare candidates to take them. You can find a country by country list at `www.cambridgeesol.org/resources/teacher/seminars.html`

✔ IATEFL (International Association of Teachers of English as a Foreign Language) also have a yearly conference and special interest groups online for teachers who want to develop in particular areas. Take a look at their homepage `www.iatefl.org` for further information.

Getting Your Hands on Real Stuff

Realia refers to real objects you take into the classroom to help you teach. By this I do not mean things like dictionaries or board pens. Realia might be a tomato, a remote control or a piece of clothing which generates interest in the topic you are discussing.

Maps

Real maps are fascinating for students abroad and in native English speaking countries alike. Take the iconic London Underground tube map. You can tell a story about a day in London while students follow the locations on the map, use it to practise directions, pronunciation of place names, colours or just create an atmosphere of full immersion in your classroom.

Maps of entire countries and cities are great too and even neighbourhood layouts give students a bit of insight into how English-speaking communities work. A map of the world is a must-have when people of different nationalities meet.

Newspapers and magazines

If you can, keep your old magazines and a small supply of newspapers in the teachers' room for back up. Even though you can find images of just about everything on the net these days, students tend to feel a greater sense of accomplishment when they are leafing through an original glossy magazine in full colour. It's what native speakers do and it allows students to get better acquainted with the culture.

Printed materials offer opportunities to select reading activities from among the articles and advertisements, pictures to describe and stimulate the imagination, and interesting comparisons regarding the students' cultures whatever the publication is about. Do not forget those interesting pages like the TV guide and the problem page which reveal a nation's lifestyle and values from an unusual angle.

Personal memorabilia

Things like theatre tickets, tacky souvenirs and photographs are wonderful aids for storytelling. Learners are often curious about the secret life of the teacher and prefer having it slowly unravelled. So, get your class to guess the relevance of an object to you. Make it a game of twenty questions and only answer yes or no. This helps to get the students talking without focussing on grammar and later in the lesson they can tell their own stories and anecdotes based on similar experiences.

Playing Board Games

Specific board games are language based but even games that aren't often provide practise of other useful vocabulary such as numbers and colours and phrases such as 'It's your turn!' or 'I have no idea!'.

It is always worth having a dice and some counters stashed in your bag anyway as many printable and downloadable resources involve this kind of turn taking. Of course you can design your own snakes and ladders or trivia games as well.

Some particularly effective games include:

- ✔ **Scrabble:** For great spelling and vocabulary practice for all levels, this is a board game which you play by distributing letters of the alphabet on small tiles. The players have to make words and place them on the board in a crossword type formation. You get extra points for using trickier letters like Q and Z.

✔ **Scategories:** For upper-intermediate level students and above. It is fun and effective for building groups of similar vocabulary. Players have a time limit and they have to think of words which are suitable for particular categories. You get extra points for originality.

✔ **Taboo:** This gets students defining words without giving away what it actually is. A player gets a card with a main word to define and describe to their partner or partners, but there are other words on the card which that player is not allowed to use and this makes the game quite challenging.

If you do not have the funds to buy board games (and they can be quite costly), arrange a class project in which students design their own.

Roping in Friends and Family

Language is all about communication and the people you communicate with most are your friends and family. Some have unusual accents, others have fascinating stories to tell and still others have jobs which raise eyebrows. Why not take someone you know into the classroom to provide your students with a little variety?

One of the disadvantages of always being around your students is that they become dependent on their familiarity with you. They may convince themselves that all English speakers have the same pronunciation, gestures and expressions as you. And of course you can only milk your personal anecdotes so much. After that they become old hat. So bribe one of your mates to come in for 30 minutes and see how your class cope with the situation. If they are particularly nervous, you can always get them to prepare interview questions to ask your pal beforehand.

People who are not used to dealing with non-native speakers have a tendency to shout or speak too slowly. Encourage your friend to be natural at all times. Students can ask for repetition if they need it.

If you cannot get anyone to come in, get yourself a tape recorder and see whether your friends and family mind you recording ten minutes of a normal dialogue. These authentic listening texts tend to be very tricky for students to understand, but short clips are usually manageable. You can use these to show students that, just like them, native speakers use poor grammar and incomplete sentences too, sometimes, but it is the overall communication which really counts.

Pointing to Charts and Posters

By charts and posters I mean both those designed for teaching English and ordinary ones from your own culture.

Everyday posters advertising films, pop groups or whatever else are useful in two ways. Firstly, they set the scene in the classroom. Students will definitely get the feeling of full immersion into an 'English' world if the images around them represent the language and culture. The vocabulary will seep in subconsciously or consciously, if you make a poster the basis of your lesson. There is a constant reminder of that teaching point on the wall which reinforces the idea.

You can ask shopkeepers for out of date posters which would otherwise end up in the rubbish, or write off to larger organisations you are interested in for freebies. Most big companies and charities love the publicity.

Posters and charts designed for EFL can be useful and can save time in class. For example, if you have a phonemic chart (a display of all the symbols which represent the 44 sounds in the English language) and a verb table on the wall, you can quickly point to the right sound or verb when a student slips up. The class can refer to these displays by themselves, too, so they can increase their independence.

Of course the question is, 'How do I get hold of them?' Well if you have not yet attended any EFL seminars, conferences and events where these things are freely available in conjunction with new book releases, write to publishers of EFL books and ask them. Oxford University press at www.oup.co.uk, Cambridge University Press at www.cambridge.org/elt , Longman at www.pearsonlongman.com and Thomson ELT at www.elt.thomson.com are very cooperative with requests like these.

Keep your posters fresh by putting up new ones every few months. Old ones don't generate interest after a while. If you are overseas, see if your friends back home can send you a few and if they are in really short supply, rotate them so you swap the posters with a teacher in another classroom.

Appendix A

Lesson Plan Templates

· ·

*T*his appendix offer templates you can use in planning and observing lessons. These should help know what to look for in a good lesson, at a glance.

PPP Lessons

The first template, Figure A-1, sets out the Presentation, Practice and Production model for lesson planning. (I cover these concepts in Chapters 5 and 6.) I also include a section on any 'warmer' activity you might want to do to relax and engage the class before getting into the meat of the lesson. You can include details of interaction, so you can say who is speaking to whom, and the table also has a time column so you can say for how long the stage lasts.

PPP Lesson

Class:
Level:
Aim and Objectives:

Materials:

Anticipated problems:

Time	Warmer
	Presentation
	Practice
	Production
	How successful was the lesson? Explain.

Figure A-1:
Template
for a
lesson with
Presentation,
Practice
and
Production
stages.

Skills Lessons

The template in Figure A-2 is for a reading and listening skills lesson. These are receptive skills so they need to include gist and detail stages. So, for example, in a reading lesson there is usually an easier task to get students skimming through the text (for the gist) and then another which requires more time and careful analysis of it.

Listening/ Reading Lesson

Class:
Level:
Aim and Objectives:

Materials:

Anticipated problems:

Time	Warmer
	Preparation task
	Gist task
	Detail task
	How successful was the lesson? Explain

Figure A-2:
Template
for Listening
or Reading
skills lesson

Needs Analysis

Before taking on a one to one course you need to find out as much as you can about the student. The template in Figure A-3 provides a basis and record for student assessment.

Needs Analysis for One to One Lessons
Student's name: Language: Background:
Level and form of assessment: Reading   Writing Listening   Speaking Pronunciation
Long term aims: Short term aims: What does the student need to do in English? Interests: Learning Preferences:
Course Length: Course Location: Proposed timetable:
Suggested Materials

Figure A-3:
Template for recording individual needs of one to one students.

Observing Lessons

Hopefully you will have opportunities to observe other teachers. The template in Figure A-4 helps you to focus on what is taking place and how teachers achieve successful lessons.

Observing Other Teachers

Teacher's name:

Class profile and level:

What were the aims and objectives of the lesson?

How well was target language presented?

Was the teacher's language well graded?

Comment on the teacher's use of the board.

How varied was the interaction?

Which activities did the class do?

Which materials did the class use?

How clear were the instructions?

To what extent did students participate?

Did the stages of the lesson flow?

How did the teacher handle correction and feedback?

Which points from the lesson would I like to apply?

Is there anything I will avoid doing?

Figure A-4:
Template for notes when observing others teach.

Appendix B

TEFL Locations around the World

In this appendix, I offer information about some popular locations for TEFL jobs.

In many places employers ask potential teachers to have a TEFL certificate. While courses vary, evidence of 100 hours of training or more is desirable. Whether this needs to include teaching practice with students or not depends on the employer.

Brazil

Brazilians are ethnically diverse but most people speak Portuguese. Football is a national obsession and most people are Christian. They are exceptionally friendly. Networking is important in Brazil. Use your contacts to get ahead (if you have any).

- **Accommodation:** Quite expensive in the larger cities.
- **Classes:** Lots of business people and other adult learners.
- **Contracts:** Generally for 10 months, though it's often easier to find work once you're there. Hours are often unsociable.
- **Cost of living:** Expenses are low. You can live well but not save much.
- **Qualifications:** You can find work without any qualifications. Schools offer training.
- **Salary:** £375 a month. The local currency is the Real.
- **Travelling:** TAM Linhas Aeras, British Airways
- **Visa:** For an official work permit you need two years of compatible experience (in TEFL or a similar educational field) and a degree.
- **Where to teach:** Sao Paolo, Brasilia and Rio de Janeiro

China

China is one of the most historic civilisations in the world. The main languages are Mandarin and Cantonese. The people respect foreigners and are generally friendly. It helps if you ride a bike.

Standards vary so much in China that you should get as much information as you possibly can before accepting a job.

- **Accommodation:** About £140 per month

- **Classes:** Ages vary from young children to older business executives but there could be up to 100 students in a class! You may find yourself submerged in homework to mark.

- **Contracts:** Jobs are available year round. Be prepared to negotiate. You can expect to get help with accommodation, and have medical insurance and airfares provided and to get ten days paid holiday plus public holidays. You work an average of 15 hours per week.

- **Cost of living:** For the average Foreign Teacher it's usually necessary to take on private lessons to allow for the standard of living you are used to.

- **Qualifications:** Degree, but TEFL certificate not always necessary. Foreign Teachers are classified differently from Foreign Experts who must have an MA in a related field and teaching experience in higher education. This distinction applies mainly to university work.

- **Salary:** Foreign Experts have half their salaries paid in a hard currency, approximately £1,000 per month and the rest in the local currency.

- **Travelling:** China Eastern Airlines, China Airlines

- **Visa:** You need a Z-visa before arriving, and this takes two months or more to obtain.

- **Where to teach:** Shanghai, Beijing, Guangzho, Shenzhen. These cities are better paid but very crowded.

Italy

The north and south vary greatly in terms of pace of life. Life in the south follows a more leisurely Mediterranean pace but the north is faster and more efficient. People are very image conscious but hospitable. This is a beautiful country and a good place to start a career.

- ✔ **Accommodation:** £400 per month.

- ✔ **Classes:** Many private schools run courses for adults but state schools ask for native speaker conversation classes. Students tend to be a bit rowdy but good natured.

- ✔ **Contracts:** Contracts run from autumn to spring.

- ✔ **Cost of living:** Slightly cheaper than the UK but eating out costs less.

- ✔ **Qualifications:** Native speakers can find work without qualifications but not at the best schools.

- ✔ **Salaries:** £900 per month or more

- ✔ **Travelling**: Cheap airlines like Ryanair fly here.

- ✔ **Visa:** EU citizens don't need one.

- ✔ **Where to teach:** Rome, Milan and tourist cities

Japan

The Japanese are still interested in old traditions. Japanese people follow rules so expect to conform. They are hospitable people but live a very high-speed lifestyle. They give more importance to body language than most English speakers and tend to be ambitious.

- ✔ **Accommodation:** About 20 per cent of net salary.

- ✔ **Classes:** Classes are varied and can include local primary schools or business people. The students' focus is often on correctness, but most lessons are conversation based.

- ✔ **Contracts:** Contracts run April to March with long teaching hours. But you get a bonus on completion of contract and seven weeks paid holiday. Apply for the best jobs in your home country.

- ✔ **Cost of living:** It's possible to save if you don't splurge on bars and entertainment.

- ✔ **Qualifications:** A degree is needed for an instructor visa but you can find work without one while in Japan.

- ✔ **Salaries:** £1,700 per month.

- ✔ **Travelling:** Japan Airlines, All Nippon Airways, United Airlines.

- ✔ **Visa:** You need a working visa and you can obtain a teaching licence through accredited schools.

- ✔ **Where to teach:** Tokyo

Poland

The people are very keen to learn as English is important to get a good job. The people can appear serious but they aren't particularly.

- **Accommodation:** Around £300 depending on the location.

- **Classes:** Some schools use team teaching with a Polish teacher. Students are of all ages and the focus is on conversation.

- **Contracts:** Contracts from September to June include 20 days paid holiday (some schools offer a free ski pass). You teach 23 hours a week on average. You get help with accommodation, Polish lessons and medical insurance.

- **Cost of living:** The cost of living is low, about a quarter of UK costs.

- **Qualifications:** Degree and TEFL certificate but no experience necessary.

- **Salaries:** About £600 per month.

- **Travelling:** British Airways, American Airlines, Polskie Linie Lotnicze (national carrier).

- **Visa:** EU nationals preferred as no visa is required.

- **Where to teach:** Warsaw, Krakow, Wroclaw, Gdansk and Poznan.

Russia

Russia is relatively safe but violent crime is on the increase. Winters are very harsh. There are still a high number of unscrupulous schools who pay late or not at all. The people are very open and there are scores of places of historical interest.

- **Accommodation:** Affordable, but power cuts are frequent.

- **Classes:** Business English is particularly in demand.

- **Contracts:** You work 25 hours a week starting in September for 9 months to a year with 3 weeks paid holiday.

- **Cost of living:** Reasonably cheap. Transport and accommodation are affordable but more so in the smaller towns.

- **Qualifications:** A degree and certificate are required in most cases.
- **Salaries:** £300 per month and free accommodation or about £25 an hour for private lessons.
- **Travelling:** Aeroflot, KLM and Russian Sibir Airines.
- **Visa:** Employers should arrange a work permit before you arrive but most foreigners work illegally and may end up paying bribes.
- **Where to teach:** Moscow and St Petersburgh.

Saudi Arabia

Male and female students and staff are segregated at universities. It is a Muslim country under Sharia law. Alcohol is banned, most jobs are for men and everything stops for prayers.The daytime temperature is very high, often, above 50 degrees.

- **Accommodation:** This is quite expensive if you are independent from a company but the standard is high.
- **Classes:** Classes have up to 30 students and classroom discipline can be quite hard. You have to follow a strict curriculum and use set materials.
- **Contracts:** You work 5 to 6 days a week, 33 contact hours plus administrative time on a one or two year contract that includes help with accommodation, airfare and medical cover. You get 4 weeks paid holidays plus national holidays and an end-of-contract bonus
- **Cost of living:** The general costs are the same as most European countries but imported food is quite expensive.
- **Qualifications:** A degree plus a diploma or MA and two years experience.
- **Salaries:** £1,500 a month tax free plus £550 housing allowance or free accommodation plus help with transport costs.
- **Travelling:** Saudi Airlines
- **Visa:** It isn't possible to get a working visa without a job offer. Individuals from certain religious faiths are not eligible and you need to be over 22.
- **Where to teach:** Jeddah and Riyadh.

South Korea

South Korea has a reputation for being quite safe. It's a good place to save money and still enjoy a high standard of living. There is basically one race and one language. Many people are religious. Buddhism, Christianity, Confucianism and Shamanism are the most common religions. Lots of students are interested in technology and pop music.

- **Accommodation:** It is usually arranged for you but deposits are very high.

- **Classes:** Most students are primary and secondary school age. On average there are ten students per class. The focus is on conversation.

- **Contracts:** On average, you work 30 hours a week on a one-year contract. You get a bonus for completing the contract, along with help with airfare and medical cover. You get two weeks paid holiday per year plus public holidays.

- **Cost of living:** Outgoings only amount to about 30 per centof your salary.

- **Qualifications:** It's best to have a degree. Some jobs are available to those without a TEFL certificate and inexperienced teachers too.

- **Salary:** Approximately £1300 per month. Local currency is South Korean Won (KRW).

- **Travelling:** Korean Air, Jeju Air.

- **Visa:** A working visa is necessary.

- **Where to teach:** Seoul and Busan.

Spain

The Spanish enjoy socialising, eating out and their old traditions.

- **Accommodation:** You need to see the property before you rent as you may not be able to pull out if you change your mind.

- **Classes:** All ages and an average of 12 per class.

- **Contracts:** Thry run September through June, about 25 hours per week and 4 weeks paid holidays plus national holidays. Help offered with accommodation and an end-of-contract bonus.

- **Cost of living:** Not as good value as it used to be but living is cheaper in the south.
- **Qualifications:** Degree plus certificate. Experienced teachers and Spanish speakers are favoured.
- **Salaries:** £1,150 per month.
- **Travelling:** There are low cost airlines like Easyjet and Ryanair.
- **Visa:** Not necessary for EU nationals.
- **Where to teach:** Big cities – Madrid and Barcelona – have the best opportunities.

Turkey

Turkey offers fascinating places to visit and a warm climate. Although a Muslim country there is a buzzing nightlife and people dress in Western clothes in the cities.

In the large cities TEFL teachers are seen as expendable because they often come and go.

- **Accommodation:** It can be expensive unless you share (for about £400 per month in Istanbul).
- **Classes:** Most students are adult professionals but children's classes are common too. Ten students per class in private schools but as many as thirty in state schools. There is demand for private lessons.
- **Contracts:** A one year includes two weeks paid holiday, help with accommodation, utility bills and medical insurance for about 25 hours per week.
- **Cost of living:** Quite low but you can't save much.
- **Qualifications:** Some jobs available for unqualified native speakers but graduate, certificate holders preferred.
- **Salary:** £11 per hour.
- **Travelling:** Turkish Airlines, Easyjet, British Airways
- **Visa:** Schools should pay for a work permit but some teachers work on a three month tourist visa.
- **Where to teach:** Ankara, Istanbul, Bursa

Vietnam

Vietnam is influenced by China, France, Russia and USA so it had a fascinating culture. It is a beautiful country and over half of the population is under 35 years old. The food is good and there are many foreign restaurants. Apparently the cities are very noisy and polluted but exciting.

- **Accommodation:** Only people in certain areas are allowed to rent to foreigners.

- **Classes:** School and university age students. They are motivated and respectful.

- **Contracts:** Most positions are part-time in private schools (many teachers work for two schools). You work 20 hours per week during a 12-month contract with 20 days paid holidays plus national holidays off. You get a bonus on completion of your contract and help with heath insurance, flights and accommodation.

- **Cost of living:** Food is cheap and there are options to suit every budget.

- **Qualifications:** Degree and certificate.

- **Salary:** $15 per hour.

- **Travelling:** British Airways, Air France, KLM.

- **Visa:** Convert a tourist visa to a working visa.

- **Where to teach:** Ho Chi Minh City (formerly Saigon), Hanoi.

Index

● **G** ●

• *M* •

• *N* •

● *Q* ●

FOR DUMMIES®

Making Everything Easier! ™

UK editions

BUSINESS

978-0-470-51806-9

978-0-470-77930-9

978-0-470-71382-2

FINANCE

978-0-470-51806-9

978-0-470-71382-2

978-0-470-69960-7

HOBBIES

978-0-470-69960-7

978-0-470-77085-6

978-0-470-75857-1

Body Language For Dummies
978-0-470-51291-3

British Sign Language
For Dummies
978-0-470-69477-0

Business NLP For Dummies
978-0-470-69757-3

Cricket For Dummies
978-0-470-03454-5

Digital Marketing For Dummies
978-0-470-05793-3

Divorce For Dummies, 2nd Edition
978-0-470-74128-3

eBay.co.uk Business All-in-One
For Dummies
978-0-470-72125-4

English Grammar For Dummies
978-0-470-05752-0

Fertility & Infertility For Dummies
978-0-470-05750-6

Flirting For Dummies
978-0-470-74259-4

Golf For Dummies
978-0-470-01811-8

Green Living For Dummies
978-0-470-06038-4

Hypnotherapy For Dummies
978-0-470-01930-6

Inventing For Dummies
978-0-470-51996-7

Lean Six Sigma For Dummies
978-0-470-75626-3

**Available wherever books are sold. For more information or to order direct go to www.wiley.com
or call +44 (0) 1243 843291**

05380_p1

FOR DUMMIES

A world of resources to help you grow

UK editions

SELF-HELP

978-0-470-01838-5

978-0-7645-7028-5

978-0-470-75876-2

Motivation For Dummies
978-0-470-76035-2

Personal Development All-In-One
For Dummies
978-0-470-51501-3

PRINCE2 For Dummies
978-0-470-51919-6

Psychometric Tests For Dummies
978-0-470-75366-8

Raising Happy Children
For Dummies
978-0-470-05978-4

Reading the Financial Pages
For Dummies
978-0-470-71432-4

Sage 50 Accounts For Dummies
978-0-470-71558-1

Study Skills For Dummies
978-0-470-74047-7

Succeeding at Assessment Centres
For Dummies
978-0-470-72101-8

Sudoku For Dummies
978-0-470-01892-7

Teaching Skills For Dummies
978-0-470-74084-2

Time Management For Dummies
978-0-470-77765-7

Understanding and Paying Less
Property Tax For Dummies
978-0-470-75872-4

Work-Life Balance For Dummies
978-0-470-71380-8

HEALTH

978-0-470-69430-5

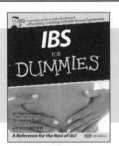
978-0-470-51737-6

978-0-470-71401-0

HISTORY

978-0-470-99468-9

978-0-470-51015-5

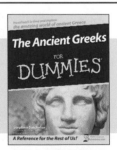
978-0-470-98787-2

**Available wherever books are sold. For more information or to order direct go to www.wiley.com
or call +44 (0) 1243 843291**

FOR DUMMIES®

The easy way to get more done and have more fun

LANGUAGES

978-0-7645-5194-9

978-0-7645-5193-2

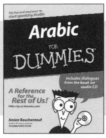

978-0-471-77270-5

MUSIC

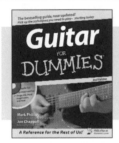

978-0-7645-9904-0

978-0-470-03275-6
UK Edition

978-0-7645-5105-5

SCIENCE & MATHS

978-0-7645-5326-4

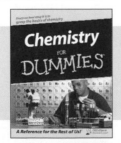

978-0-7645-5430-8

978-0-7645-5325-7

Art For Dummies
978-0-7645-5104-8

Baby & Toddler Sleep Solutions
For Dummies
978-0-470-11794-1

Bass Guitar For Dummies
978-0-7645-2487-5

Brain Games For Dummies
978-0-470-37378-1

Christianity For Dummies
978-0-7645-4482-8

Filmmaking For Dummies,
2nd Edition
978-0-470-38694-1

Forensics For Dummies
978-0-7645-5580-0

German For Dummies
978-0-7645-5195-6

Hobby Farming For Dummies
978-0-470-28172-7

Index Investing For Dummies
978-0-470-29406-2

Jewelry Making & Beading
For Dummies
978-0-7645-2571-1

Knitting For Dummies, 2nd Edition
978-0-470-28747-7

Music Composition For Dummies
978-0-470-22421-2

Physics For Dummies
978-0-7645-5433-9

Schizophrenia For Dummies
978-0-470-25927-6

Sex For Dummies, 3rd Edition
978-0-470-04523-7

Solar Power Your Home For Dummies
978-0-470-17569-9

Tennis For Dummies
978-0-7645-5087-4

The Koran For Dummies
978-0-7645-5581-7

FOR DUMMIES®

Helping you expand your horizons and achieve your potential

COMPUTER BASICS

978-0-470-27759-1

978-0-470-13728-4

978-0-471-75421-3

DIGITAL LIFESTYLE

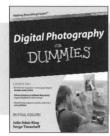

978-0-470-25074-7

978-0-470-39062-7

978-0-470-42342-4

WEB & DESIGN

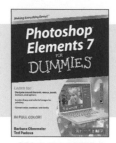

978-0-470-39700-8

978-0-470-32725-8

978-0-470-34502-3

Access 2007 For Dummies
978-0-470-04612-8

Adobe Creative Suite 3 Design
Premium All-in-One Desk Reference
For Dummies
978-0-470-11724-8

AutoCAD 2009 For Dummies
978-0-470-22977-4

C++ For Dummies, 5th Edition
978-0-7645-6852-7

Computers For Seniors For Dummies
978-0-470-24055-7

Excel 2007 All-In-One Desk Reference
For Dummies
978-0-470-03738-6

Flash CS3 For Dummies
978-0-470-12100-9

Green IT For Dummies
978-0-470-38688-0

Mac OS X Leopard For Dummies
978-0-470-05433-8

Macs For Dummies, 10th Edition
978-0-470-27817-8

Networking All-in-One Desk Reference
For Dummies, 3rd Edition
978-0-470-17915-4

Office 2007 All-in-One Desk Reference
For Dummies
978-0-471-78279-7

Search Engine Optimization
For Dummies, 3rd Edition
978-0-470-26270-2

The Internet For Dummies,
11th Edition
978-0-470-12174-0

Visual Studio 2008 All-In-One Desk
Reference For Dummies
978-0-470-19108-8

Web Analytics For Dummies
978-0-470-09824-0

Windows XP For Dummies, 2nd Edition
978-0-7645-7326-2